Ultimate Agile Administration with Jira

Solutions for Agile Project Administration
Using Dashboards, Automation
Rules, and Plugin
Integration with Jira

Yogita Chhaya

www.orangeava.com

Copyright © 2023, Orange Education Pvt Ltd, AVA™

All rights reserved. No part of this book may be reproduced, stored in a retrieval system, or transmitted in any form or by any means, without the prior written permission of the publisher, except in the case of brief quotations embedded in critical articles or reviews.

Every effort has been made in the preparation of this book to ensure the accuracy of the information presented. However, the information contained in this book is sold without warranty, either express or implied. Neither the author nor **Orange Education Pvt Ltd** or its dealers and distributors, will be held liable for any damages caused or alleged to have been caused directly or indirectly by this book.

Orange Education Pvt Ltd has endeavored to provide trademark information about all of the companies and products mentioned in this book by the appropriate use of capital. However **Orange Education Pvt Ltd** cannot guarantee the accuracy of this information. The use of general descriptive names, registered names, trademarks, service marks, etc. in this publication does not imply, even in the absence of a specific statement, that such names are exempt from the relevant protective laws and regulations and therefore free for general use.

Jira® is a proprietary product developed by Atlassian Corporation.

First published: December 2023

Published by: Orange Education Pvt Ltd, AVA™

Address: 9, Daryaganj, Delhi, 110002

ISBN: 978-81-96782-60-3

www.orangeava.com

Dedicated To

My beloved Parents,

family members
and

my mentors

About the Author

Yogita Chhaya is an engineer and educator and has extensive experience in the field. She has served as an independent Jira software educator for multinational companies and educational institutes and is a seasoned Jira Administrator. With over 20 years of experience in production, product management, process management and various roles within telecom companies, she has also been involved in the education and training sectors. Her active involvement includes working on Agile transformation, evaluating various Atlassian tools, managing server migrations and conducting training on Jira software along with add-on applications.

About the Technical Reviewer

The author, **Subramanyam Gunda**, brings over 15 years of professional experience in the IT and service industry to the table, with a rich background as an Agile Consultant (Agile Product Owner, Lead Scrum Master, Agile coach).

He takes immense pride in his writings and publications, having authored two impactful books. His journey began with the Dell-EMC organization publishing his three Data Domain technical KB articles, a game-changing moment that bolstered his confidence in both his subject matter expertise and writing skills. His first book, **"ABCs of Agile Scrum Framework: Secrets to Successful Project Management,"** served as a valuable reference for countless project managers and Agile enthusiasts. Following its success, his second book, titled **"Business Analysis Life Cycle & the IT Business Analyst's Role in Traditional, Digital, and Agile Worlds,"** garnered critical acclaim, awards, and recognition. Currently, he is crafting his third book on Agile concepts (revision of his first book) and his fourth book on Tarot readings.

In addition to his literary achievements, Subramanyam has secured **gold, silver, and bronze medals** for India in the "Atlympics - 2021 competition," a prestigious event hosted by the Atlassian Organization. Beyond his professional pursuits, he passionately volunteers his time and serves in various capacities, including as an **'Atlassian Community Leader for the Visakhapatnam chapter,'** an **'Atlassian Creator,'** and a member of the **'Atlassian Community Advisory Board.'**

Outside of his career and volunteer work, Subramanyam enjoys participating in online Sudoku and Rubik's Cube competitions, where he has earned numerous accolades as well as writing blogs on his website.

He generously dedicates time to reviewing fellow author's books, offering constructive feedback and valuable suggestions. Among the prominent titles he has reviewed are "Supercharging Productivity with Trello," "The Art of Crafting User Stories," and "Unleashing the Power of UX Analytics," all published by Packt.

You can connect with the author through the following platforms:

LinkedIn: https://linkedin.com/in/gsubashb4u
YouTube: https://www.youtube.com/@gsubashcosmopolitan
Personal website: https://www.gsubashcosmopolitan.com/
Atlassian Chapter: https://ace.atlassian.com/visakhapatnam/

Acknowledgements

I am grateful for the support I received from my parents when I started learning Atlassian products. They were always with me on the journey of learning and supported me at every step I took. It would not have been possible to write this book without their inspiration.

I am thankful to my family members for supporting and encouraging me throughout my writing journey. They encouraged me to write this book and share whatever I know through it.

I am grateful to all the organizations that provided support when I was a beginner and later as a trainer. I have worked with many organizations and individuals. Writing this book wouldn't have been possible without their support.

Above all, I thank the team that guided, supported and helped me write this book. I am thankful to the reviewer and technical reviewer of the book who guided me throughout the writing process. Their inputs have made this book insightful and invaluable for readers seeking practical understanding and real-world applications.

Preface

This book covers the fundamentals of Agile, including Agile values and principles. It also introduces the Scrum and Kanban frameworks, important terms in Jira, and how to create a Jira site. The book covers project templates in Jira and explains the importance of creating the right project. Additionally, it covers all concepts related to Jira Administration and customization with examples.

This book covers both types of projects, whether they are managed by administrators or teams. It explores all the concepts related to Agile project management, reporting, and tracking Agile metrics. The content includes backlog management, sprint operations, insights provided by Jira, and harnessing the power of Jira filters. The book highlights the importance of automation in Jira and the concept of using smart values in automation rules. It also provides use cases and step-by-step guides for administrator tasks. Additionally, it covers the Advanced Roadmap, useful for capacity planning and tracking cross-project work in large organizations. Furthermore, it explains the significance of adding plugin applications to expand the functionality of Jira software and how to purchase such software from the Atlassian Marketplace.

This book is divided into 12 chapters. They will cover Agile fundamentals, Jira Cloud basics, complete Jira Administration with examples, multiple use cases, and step-by-step processes. Learners will be able to use Jira software more efficiently and will find administration easier and more interesting. The details are as mentioned below.

Chapter 1: The book will start with an introduction to Agile, providing an overview of Agile frameworks, the difference between Agile and waterfall methodology and explaining the basics of Scrum and Kanban frameworks. It will then take you through Jira concepts, various products in the Atlassian ecosystem and Jira Terminology, and explain why it is famous.

Chapter 2: This chapter will cover the understanding of project definition and creating various projects using standard templates in Jira. It will also provide detailed information about the differences between team-managed and company-managed projects. Additionally, the chapter will offer details on customizing a template and provide an overview of the available templates.

Chapter 3: It will cover user creation, groups, and permissions from the administrator's perspective. The chapter will include use cases, adding users, project roles in company-managed projects, and details about various permissions in Jira. These permissions help create and customize permission schemes.

Chapter 4: This chapter will cover the creation of issues, creating a product backlog, sprint boards, and all related operations and customizations. It will encompass all the features of Agile boards, sprint operations, creating epics and versions. The chapter will also cover understanding Jira Insights on backlog and board.

Chapter 5: This chapter will cover how to add issue types and issue type schemes as an administrator. It will include information about issue status, resolutions, priority, and issue type hierarchy levels. The chapter will guide you on creating sub-task issue types, issue operations, associating an issue type with a project, and understanding issue type schemes.

Chapter 6: This chapter will focus on creating new custom fields, ways to customize fields on the screen, and details about the types of custom fields available in Jira. It will also explain how to add context to the fields, locked custom fields, and field configuration schemes with examples. Lastly, it will cover creating screens, screen schemes, issue-type screen schemes, and use cases, providing step-by-step explanations with examples for each topic.

Chapter 7: This chapter begins with an understanding of workflows and their components. It covers the steps to create, edit, and delete workflows, including global transitions, adding screens to set resolution, advanced workflow features, and a comparison between active and inactive workflows. Each concept in this chapter is explained with examples, highlighting common mistakes to avoid while creating workflows and providing relevant use cases.

Chapter 8: This chapter starts by explaining basic and advanced search methods and how to create and save filters. It provides insights into Jira's built-in filters, managing subscriptions, various filter operations, and JQL with examples. The chapter then covers dashboards, explaining how to add gadgets, customize dashboards according to your needs, and use the wallboards feature. It covers the types of reports available in Jira and provides detailed explanations of all Agile reports. Finally, it gives an overview of Atlassian Analytics.

Chapter 9: This chapter begins with an understanding of and accessing automation rules in Jira, including various elements of automation rules. It covers the usage of automation templates, the automation playground, and the performance insights on automation rules executed. The chapter guides you through the steps to create automation rules and provides multiple examples of rules. Finally, it discusses a few use cases of automation rules.

Chapter 10: This chapter starts with understanding team-managed projects, their features, and how to set them up. It includes information on adding people, roles, access levels, and Agile features. The chapter then covers issue types in team-managed projects, creating custom issue types, configuring workflows, and defining statuses, transitions, and transition properties. It also discusses adding/removing workflow rules, Agile board features, managing backlogs, understanding insights, and the Timeline view. Lastly, it addresses reports, migrating from team-managed to company-managed projects and vice versa, and provides use cases related to team-managed projects.

Chapter 11: This chapter begins with tips for Product Owners, Scrum Masters, and Software Developers. It covers creating projects with sample data, creating a project with multiple boards, and importing issues in Jira. Additionally, it discusses various Administrator roles in Jira, understanding Advanced Roadmap, viewing a sample plan, creating a plan, Timeline View, Dependency Report, setting up teams, creating releases, creating cross-project releases, adding filters, and configuring issue hierarchies above Epics in Advanced Roadmap. Finally, it provides an overview of JIRA Product Discovery and includes use cases.

Chapter 12: This chapter starts with an introduction to the Atlassian Marketplace, guiding readers on selecting plugins and explaining key terms of the applications listed on the marketplace. It also covers how to install plugins and provides an overview of Admin-tools plugins. Lastly, it offers an overview of popular plugins and important use cases.

Colored Images

Please follow the link to download the
Colored Images of the book:

https://rebrand.ly/418456

You can find code bundles of our books on our official Github Repository.
Go to the following link to explore further:
https://github.com/ava-orange-education.

Errata

We take immense pride in our work at **Orange Education Pvt Ltd,** and follow best practices to ensure the accuracy of our content to provide an indulging reading experience to our subscribers. Our readers are our mirrors, and we use their inputs to reflect and improve upon human errors, if any, that may have occurred during the publishing processes involved. To let us maintain the quality and help us reach out to any readers who might be having difficulties due to any unforeseen errors, please write to us at :

errata@orangeava.com

Your support, suggestions, and feedback are highly appreciated.

DID YOU KNOW

Did you know that Orange Education Pvt Ltd offers eBook versions of every book published, with PDF and ePub files available? You can upgrade to the eBook version at **www.orangeava.com** and as a print book customer, you are entitled to a discount on the eBook copy. Get in touch with us at: **info@orangeava.com** for more details.

At **www.orangeava.com**, you can also read a collection of free technical articles, sign up for a range of free newsletters, and receive exclusive discounts and offers on AVA™ Books and eBooks.

PIRACY

If you come across any illegal copies of our works in any form on the internet, we would be grateful if you would provide us with the location address or website name. Please contact us at **info@orangeava.com** with a link to the material.

ARE YOU INTERESTED IN AUTHORING WITH US?

If there is a topic that you have expertise in, and you are interested in either writing or contributing to a book, please write to us at **business@orangeava.com**. We are on a journey to help developers and tech professionals to gain insights on the present technological advancements and innovations happening across the globe and build a community that believes Knowledge is best acquired by sharing and learning with others. Please reach out to us to learn what our audience demands and how you can be part of this educational reform. We also welcome ideas from tech experts and help them build learning and development content for their domains.

REVIEWS

Please leave a review. Once you have read and used this book, why not leave a review on the site that you purchased it from? Potential readers can then see and use your unbiased opinion to make purchase decisions. We at Orange Education would love to know what you think about our products, and our authors can learn from your feedback. Thank you!

For more information about Orange Education, please visit **www.orangeava.com**.

Table of Contents

Getting Started with Agile, Jira, and Jira Terminologies

Introduction

This chapter will cover the basics of Agile methodology, including the history of Agile and how it differs from the waterfall approach. We will then understand Scrum and Kanban, two popular methodologies of software development. We will explore Jira, different Jira products, and reasons why Jira is being used by different industries. At the end of the chapter, we will cover Jira terminology commonly used in the field.

Structure

In this chapter, we will discuss the following topics:

- History of Agile
- The difference between Waterfall and Agile
- Agile Mindset
- 4 Values and 12 Principles of Agile
- Various Agile Frameworks
- Defining Scrum
- Scrum Roles, Ceremonies, and Artifacts
- Defining Kanban
- Kanban practices, principles, benefits, and disadvantages

- Creating User Stories and Product backlogs
- Estimating and prioritizing work in Agile
- Agile metrics and performance tracking
- About Jira
- Step-by-step guide to creating a Jira site
- Jira's popularity
- Jira Terminology

History of Agile

Back in the 1990s, products were not solely dominated by software applications. They were a combination of hardware and software products. It is important to note that software was becoming increasingly complex and important in its own right. This is one of the factors that led to the need for a new way of developing software. It used to take more than a few years to complete the development cycle and launch a product. By the time it was handed over to the customer, their requirements had changed due to the long lead time and the products had already entered the market. In addition to that, some of the features were of no use to the customers. In software development, there were many processes to be followed, and a lot of documentation was required to be done as a part of the process.

As the years passed, software projects were becoming more important, and it was felt that a new process or new way of developing software was required by everyone. The same thing was experienced in other industries such as automotive, aerospace, healthcare, and many others.

Many industries, beyond software development, faced challenges with long project cycles. Issues such as change in customer requirements, late feedback, increased cost, time spent on documentation, and most importantly, how to deliver continuously were challenges faced by project teams. The need for a more responsive and iterative approach became evident as businesses sought to stay competitive in rapidly evolving markets.

Toyota's introduction of the Toyota Production System (TPS), which revolutionized manufacturing, was the beginning of the foundations of Agile. It was founded between 1945 and 1975 by Japanese industrial engineers. TPS prioritized flexibility, waste minimization, and ongoing improvement. To encourage flexibility and effectiveness in software development, agile techniques drew inspiration from TPS and adopted its ideas. While Agile drew inspiration from TPS, it was not directly founded during that period; instead, it was formalized in 2001 with the Agile Manifesto.

Evolution Toward the Agile Manifesto

1980s: In the early 1980s, the seeds of Agile methodology were sown with the emergence of lightweight software development approaches. The Waterfall model, a sequential and document-heavy methodology, dominated the scene. However, cracks begin to show as projects face delays, scope changes, and poor communication.

1990s - Iterative and Incremental Practices: As the 1990s dawned, software practitioners started experimenting with iterative and incremental practices.

Late 1990s - Crystal and DSDM: Towards the late 1990s, two notable methodologies, Crystal and Dynamic Systems Development Method (DSDM), emerged.

1990s - Extreme Programming (XP): In the late 1990s, Kent Beck introduced Extreme Programming (XP).

2001- The Agile Manifesto Takes Shape: In 2001, 17 people from the software industry met at a place, and they agreed upon a way of working which is known as the Agile Manifesto. There were people from the software industry who were following Scrum, XP, FDD, and many different methodologies. They did not like the word **Lightweight** for this new methodology and agreed and decided to name it **Agile,** meaning responding to change.

Implementing an Agile way of working organization-wide is known as Business Agility. It refers to an organization's ability to adapt quickly to market changes, seize opportunities, and deliver value to customers. It enables businesses to respond quickly to changing customer needs. It is implemented by many organizations worldwide to stay ahead in today's dynamic business environment.

Difference between Waterfall and Agile

Agile and waterfall project management strategies are two separate approaches to project management. In the waterfall model, the next phase starts only after the earlier phase is completed. In waterfall methodology, requirements gathering, design, development, testing, and deployment phases are accomplished in sequence. It emphasizes extensive planning, documentation, and a fixed scope, making it suitable for projects with well-defined requirements and limited changes. It is therefore considered to be rigid and not able to manage unplanned changes.

Agile, on the other hand, is a flexible and iterative strategy that emphasizes adaptive planning and collaboration. It divides work into discrete sprints or iterations, allowing for continual feedback and adjustments. Agile values change and encourage client participation throughout the project. It encourages self-organizing teams and frequent communication, and focuses on providing incremental value. Agile teams use documentation to communicate and collaborate, but they don't produce as much documentation as waterfall teams.

Table 1.1 illustrates the difference between Waterfall and Agile Methodology:

Aspects	Waterfall Methodology	Agile Methodology
Project Phases	Distinct phases – requirements, design, development, and more	Continuous cycles - sprints
Development Approach	Sequential and linear	Iterative and incremental
Project roles	Specific roles are assigned for each phase (for example, Business Analyst, Designer, Developer, Tester, Project Manager)	Product owner, Scrum Master, Development teams
Quality Assurance	Testing at the end of the cycle	Continuous testing and quality assurance
Team Structure	Hierarchical with predefined roles	Cross-functional self-organizing teams
Communication	Less customer involvement	Close collaboration with customers
Documentation	Extensive documentation throughout	Documentation as needed
Flexibility	Limited flexibility to changes in requirements	Welcomes changes in requirements throughout the project
Feedback	Limited customer feedback during development	Regular customer involvement and feedback
Delivery time	Longer delivery time	Shorter delivery time
Change Implementation	Difficult to accommodate changes	Welcomes changes, even in later stages of development

Risk Management	Addressed in early planning, may not handle unforeseen risks well	Ongoing risk management
Project outcome	Well-defined scope and deliverables	Evolving scope and adaptable deliverables
Suitability	Projects with stable and known requirements	Projects with dynamic or evolving requirements

Table 1.1: *Waterfall vs. Agile methodology*

Agile Mindset

Being agile is more about beliefs, values, attitudes, and behaviors. For example, in a game of Rugby, the entire team works towards achieving a goal by adapting to the situation, collaborating, and with the "everyone is equal" attitude. It can be applied to any industry and any functional group, such as marketing, human resources, operations, and more. It is a way of working in which one must co-create, explore new ideas, experiment and experience, innovate, and remain adaptable.

4 Values and 12 Principles of Agile

In the 1990s, there was a period when projects were frequently delayed due to lengthy processes and sequential approaches to software development. The released products did not meet customer expectations due to the time lag, resulting in numerous order cancellations. These frustrations led to the creation of the Agile Manifesto by 17 leaders. This manifesto includes 12 principles and 4 values, which we will cover in this section.

4 Agile Values

There are multiple Agile methodologies, each of which applies the four values of the Agile Manifesto in different ways to guide teams in developing good quality software.

1. **Individuals and Interactions over Processes and Tools**

   In the waterfall model, more importance was given to rigid processes. Even after spending a lot of time following these processes, the final software products were not of the best quality and error-free. It is possible to design and develop innovative software products if more importance is given to smart and competent people who can sit together, discuss, share, and solve problems. Processes should be followed, but they need to be simplified. Tools have to be customized to follow processes easily and make the development faster.

2. **Working Software over Comprehensive Documentation**

   There was a time when very detailed documents were prepared for the features, requirements, test cases, diagrams, and releases. This was not helpful to provide value to the customer, and it used to delay the product releases. Delayed releases and obsolete features were the cause of the loss of business. More importance is given to working software, which is provided to the customer, and based on the feedback, further development is done. As per Agile Manifesto, providing value first is of more importance than creating outdated documents.

3. **Customer Collaboration over Contract Negotiation**

   In the old ways of project development, customers used to come into the picture at the beginning, once during the development cycle, and finally at the end. The products were developed based on what is written in the contract documents. In an agile way of working, customers come into the picture to provide feedback on a small piece of software, and based on the feedback and their actual needs, further development is carried out. This way it is possible to do immediate corrections if it is going in the wrong direction with the help of a customer. Continuous interaction with the customer is helpful to find out the right needs than what is written in the legal documents.

4. **Responding to Change over Following a Plan**

   Traditionally, plans were prepared well in advance. However, it was not possible to incorporate any changes in that plan. Even a small change in the requirement was considered impossible. When a plan is made with agility in mind, it provides direction initially. Based on a rough plan, product development is started and then there is a scope for change. A small change in specification is discussed by all the stakeholders and taken up as an opportunity rather than an obstacle.

Agile Principles

The 12 principles act as guiding principles for the Agile methodologies. They outline a culture that embraces change and emphasizes customer-centric product development. These principles emphasize the importance of aligning new products with business needs:

1. **Customer Satisfaction through Early and Continuous Delivery**

   By iteratively delivering working software, the customer is satisfied as he is getting some valuable features early in the cycle. At the same time, in every release cycle, he is going to receive something new which makes the customer happy.

2. **Welcome Changing Requirements, Even Late in Development**

   In this dynamic world, everything changes continuously. Similarly, by incorporating changes in the requirements during the entire software development life-cycle, one can create the right products. By doing so, the final released software application is aligned with the actual and evolving requirements of the customer. Agile allows scope for changes even late in the development process.

3. **Deliver Working Software Frequently**

   This principle recommends delivering new versions in a shorter time span, as opposed to the earlier longer time span. By doing this, the number of bugs per release is significantly reduced, leading to an overall improvement in the success of the software release. The release cycles are measured in the number of days rather than months.

4. **Collaborate Daily between Business People and Developers**

   In the Agile way of working, there are no barriers to communication between business teams and developers. Business teams must communicate about the business requirements, any changes from the customer's side, and also whether these changes can be managed or not by the developers. By collaborating with developers, any misunderstandings can be avoided. Business analysts have to convert any business language to a language that developers can understand. Even if the teams are geographically far from each other, providing feedback on a daily basis helps in getting good outcomes.

5. **Motivated Individuals**

   It is about creating a conducive work culture and keeping the workforce motivated. Every member is allowed, trusted, and encouraged to give new ideas and find better ways of designing new products. If the team members are motivated, they can eventually create innovative architectures, designs, and products.

6. **Face-to-face Conversations**

   Communication is the key to success. The same thing is emphasized in Agile. It could be physical meetings in the office or video conference meetings where people can communicate efficiently. Developers and teams must communicate daily to understand the initial and evolving requirements.

7. **Measure of Progress through Working Software**

   Customers want a working and good quality product. It is the measurement of the overall performance of the team. The software is considered to be of good quality based on the feedback from the end-user.

8. **Promote Sustainable Development**

   The teams should work at the same pace irrespective of the number of changes introduced. Any member or employee should not be burdened by the work more than his/her capacity. Otherwise, it can result in burnout of the teams and hence can affect the quality of the product.

9. **Continuous Attention to Technical Excellence**

   Agile emphasizes on the good design of the product. This is a must-have for each and every team. It ensures that the software application is adaptable, maintainable, and scalable for future enhancements.

10. **Simplicity**

    This principle suggests keeping the processes simple. Simplicity does not mean skipping important processes but it means avoiding complexity in design and coding. A working software product with less number of features is better than a problematic product having multiple features.

11. **Self-organizing Teams**

    If the teams are empowered and autonomous, they can get better results. The agile teams consider themselves accountable and are ready to take responsibility for their work. Teamwork, Commitment collaboration, and Competency are the core skills to become more agile. The teams require a coach or a mentor but not a manager.

12. **Regularly Reflect on Continuous Improvement**

During the meeting, teams reflect on how they can improve the processes, productivity, and performance by making small changes. It is a continuous process to create a culture of continuous learning and working on improvement areas.

Various Agile Frameworks

We have covered Agile Scrum and Kanban in this chapter, among the many Agile frameworks listed as follows:

- **Kanban**: We have covered the details of this framework in the next section.

- **Scrum**: We have covered the details of this framework in the next section.

- **Feature-Driven Development (FDD)**: FDD is a software development methodology that follows an iterative and incremental approach. In FDD, the development process is broken down into manageable pieces −features− and then it is built incrementally. In this process, an overall model is developed, followed by creating a feature list, feature-wise planning, features-based design, and features development.

  In FDD, the development process is structured around feature teams. Each of these teams is assigned the responsibility of delivering specific features. This way, the development effort is divided into smaller, more manageable tasks, making it easier to track progress and ensure that each feature is developed effectively. It maintains the iterative approach.

  One of the important characteristics of FDD is its emphasis on collaboration. It promotes close interaction among team members, stakeholders, and clients. It helps to understand the project requirements correctly.

  It also emphasizes well-defined processes. To summarize, it is a structured and flexible approach to software development.

- **Extreme Programming**: Extreme Programming (XP) is an Agile software development methodology that promotes collaboration, adaptability, and high-quality code. It emphasizes practices like continuous testing, pair programming, and frequent releases. With a focus on customer involvement and iterative development, XP makes sure that software remains responsive to changing requirements. By fostering teamwork, automation, and streamlined processes, XP enables developers to deliver reliable software efficiently while maintaining a sustainable work pace.

Extreme Programming is suitable for teams working on dynamic projects with evolving requirements.

- **Adaptive Software Development (ASD)**: ASD is a software development approach that embraces change as an inherent part of the process. ASD involves three distinct phases: speculation, collaboration, and learning. Speculation includes creating a preliminary plan based on what's known, while collaboration encourages open communication and active participation from both the development team and stakeholders. The learning phase emphasizes adapting the plan based on new information and insights gained throughout the process. ASD recognizes that software projects often encounter unexpected shifts and encourages a flexible and iterative approach to development, ensuring that the end result aligns closely with evolving needs and requirements.

- **Dynamic Systems Development Method (DSDM)**: It is an Agile methodology that focuses on delivering functional solutions within a fixed timeframe and budget. DSDM divides development into specific time-bound phases, promoting regular user involvement and feedback. It encourages collaboration between developers, users, and business representatives to ensure that the software aligns with business needs. DSDM emphasizes the importance of delivering the most valuable features first, and it provides a set of principles and practices to guide teams in building high-quality solutions while accommodating changes. Overall, DSDM provides a structured framework for Agile software development, aiming to strike a balance between fixed constraints and adaptability.

- **Scrumban**: Scrumban is a hybrid approach that combines the practices of both Scrum and Kanban methodologies. In Scrumban, teams use Scrum's structured framework but add elements from Kanban to enhance flexibility and continuous improvement. This allows teams to transition smoothly between planned iterations (sprints) and a more flow-based approach. Scrumban is especially useful for teams that are already familiar with Scrum and want to introduce Kanban's focus on optimizing workflow and minimizing bottlenecks. Scrumban can be implemented when a company wants to allow more flexibility to the teams or for a team facing problems implementing scrum.

Defining Scrum

Scrum is an Agile project management framework to create solutions for complex problems. It can be compared to the game of Rugby in which the goal is set and achieved by working on the principles of collaboration, teamwork, transparency, and agility. In scrum, work is divided into small time intervals called sprints, which can last for 1–4 weeks. The work items are also divided into small chunks called stories, tasks, and more. Each sprint begins with a planning meeting where the priority of the tasks to be taken is decided. The team meets daily to discuss the tasks done, tasks to be taken up, and to report any obstacles in completing the tasks planned to achieve the sprint goal. The teams are empowered, motivated, and work collaboratively to adapt to changing requirements at the same pace.

Scrum Roles, Ceremonies, and Artifacts

This section explains scrum roles, ceremonies, and artifacts.

In scrum methodology, there are three defined roles: scrum master, product owner, and the development team, which collaborate with each other:

- **Scrum Master**

  Scrum Master is a facilitator and a scrum expert. He makes sure that everybody in the team understands how the team has to collaborate, set the sprint goal, and achieve the same. He helps the team to remove any impediments and leads the scrum meetings.

- **Scrum Team**

  The scrum team is a team of developers and testers working together, collaborating, and working towards achieving the sprint goal. Team members can communicate with the product owner to understand the product specifications and task priorities. The team follows the guidance provided by the scrum master in case of any obstacles such as resources, server availability, or any other problems faced during the sprint.

- **Product Owner**

  Product owner is the single point of contact between the customer/end user and the scrum team. He manages the product backlog, helps in sprint planning, and participates in scrum meetings. He is also responsible for product backlog grooming and deciding the priorities of the user stories.

Scrum ceremonies provide opportunities for planning, tracking, and feedback. During these ceremonies, scrum teams interact with each other to understand the requirements, plan sprints, communicate about the obstacles, demonstrate the working software, and move forward with the lessons learned and action plan.

- **Sprint planning**

  It is a collaborative planning done by the product owner, scrum master, and development team. They discuss the priorities and decide which tasks to be included in the sprint backlog. During this ceremony, the team decides the sprint goal, which means deciding what they will deliver/develop in this sprint. The team estimates the effort required for each task and creates a plan to achieve the sprint goal.

- **Daily Stand-up**

  It is conducted daily in which team members and the scrum master discuss the progress done.

  Points to discuss in Daily Scrum are as follows:
  - What did I do yesterday as per the current sprint plan?
  - What will I do today to meet the Sprint goal?
  - Share about any impediment that prevents me/team towards completing the ongoing task in the sprint.

  The members discuss the work done on the tasks, which task they will be taking up next, and share any impediments with the scrum master. It builds a culture of transparency, collaboration, and accountability among the team.

- **Sprint Review**

  It is done at the end of the sprint. In this ceremony, team members demonstrate the features and functionality developed to the stakeholders. Based on the feedback from the stakeholders, improvements can be made in the next sprint.

- **Sprint Retrospective**

  This ceremony is held to reflect on the completed sprint. In this ceremony, what went well, what could be improved, and actions to be taken are discussed. The team and developers identify the areas for improvement. A culture of continuous improvement and learning is created by conducting this ceremony.

There are three main artifacts in Scrum: Product backlog, Sprint backlog, and Increment.

- **Product Backlog**

  Product backlog is a list of features, bugs, and any other type of requirements to develop a product and is managed by the product owner.
  - It is a complete list of items to design and develop the product.
  - It is an ordered list and evolves continuously.

- o The product owner is fully responsible for this artifact.
- o It includes features, functionalities, fixes, and any other details required.

- **Sprint Backlog**

  Sprint Backlog is a complete list of tasks to be taken up in the next sprints and is managed collectively by everyone on the team.

  - o It is a complete list of work items to be taken up in a sprint.
  - o It is a detailed list that includes estimation and who will work on what details.
  - o It is updated or maintained by the developers.

- **Increment**

  In scrum methodology, increment is the combination of the software developed earlier plus the software developed in the recent sprint, which is integrated, tested, and ready to be released.

  - o It is work that is complete and meets the definition of done.
  - o It must be a working feature/functionality that can be used by the customer.
  - o An increment does not necessarily equal a release.

Agile scrum artifacts are the details used by the team and stakeholders. It is generated during the planning, breaking the tasks, working on the sprints, and at the end of the sprint. There are also other artifacts such as the definition of done and the Burndown chart.

Creating User Stories and Product Backlogs

User stories are a way of writing customer requirements in a simple language that anyone can understand. The number of such user stories, along with other tasks and features, are added to create the product backlog. The product backlog can be visualized and prioritized in a project management tool and is regularly updated by product owners to meet new business needs.

User Stories

- It is a document that contains information about the product requirements of the end-user in an understandable format.
- It contains information such as a description of the user, what exactly

the user wants from that feature/functionality, and how the user will benefit from that feature.

- For example: As a user, I can find important items on the board by using the customizable "Quick Filters" so that I don't have to search for those issues every time and work efficiently.

- For each and every user story, there is an acceptance criteria written, which makes sure the specific conditions are met. Based on the criteria, it is accepted as a working functionality or else it gets rejected.

- User stories can be divided into sub-tasks to simplify the work by the developers.

- It is user-centric and a new way of writing requirements in Agile methodology.

- User stories will evolve based on received feedback, providing clear specifications for both technical and non-technical team members.

Product Backlog

- A product backlog is a prioritized list of features, functionalities, improvements, suggestions, and bugs in detail.

- It is a bucket of tasks from which one can take up tasks and create a sprint backlog based on the priority decided by the scrum team.

- It is continuously refined during the development cycle and tasks can be added and modified based on the change in the requirements and other conditions.

- Priority of the work items is decided based on the value it provides to the customer.

- It is created and maintained by the product owner and is updated to meet the final objective of the product to be developed.

- The team and product owner estimate the tasks in the product backlog and break them down based on the complexity of the tasks.

- In a project management tool, it can be viewed on boards and then moved to the sprint backlog based on priority.

Defining Kanban

Kanban, derived from the Japanese word for **signboard**, was originally implemented by Toyota in Japan as part of their manufacturing processes. This innovative system served as a signaling mechanism, effectively enhancing the efficiency of their manufacturing units by visualizing bottlenecks within the system.

Kanban is a **Pull system**. In this method, work is done when there is a demand. Known as Just In Time (JIT), Kanban methodology employs a board where tasks or work items progress from left to right as the work unfolds. This concept has been embraced not only by manufacturing but also by software development teams. On a Kanban board, tasks are categorized into three main statuses: **To do**, where prioritization occurs before moving on to design, coding, testing, and release tasks in progress; and finally, tasks are moved to the **Done** status, signifying completion.

Here are some of the Kanban practices, principles, benefits, and disadvantages:

- **Core Practices**
  - Visualize the workflow
  - Limit WIP (Work In Progress)
  - Manage flow
  - Make process policies explicit
  - Take feedback
  - Improve collaboratively, evolve experimentally
- **Principles**
  - Start with what you know
  - Agree to pursue incremental, evolutionary change
  - Respect the current process, roles, responsibilities, titles
  - Encourage acts of leadership at all levels in your organization
- **Benefits**
  - Identifying issues
  - Flexibility
  - It can save time
  - It empowers teams
  - Balance productivity
  - Increased customer satisfaction
- **Disadvantages**
  - Cannot be used independently
  - May be difficult where dependencies are involved
  - Inability for an iteration
  - Too simple board
  - Lack of time representation

Approaching Kanban

The Kanban approach should be selected in the following situations:

- When the teams are new to the Agile way of working and the team is very small.
- When the nature of work varies continuously, such as changing priorities, task durations, and inflow of new requirements.
- Optimizing flow is more important than fixed timeframes.
- When work items cannot be easily broken down into sprints.
- When there is a need to be flexible and adapt to changes in requirements, market conditions, and customer feedback.
- When there is a need for managing work in progress to identify bottlenecks and manage capacity.
- When there is a need for continuous improvement in processes and more visibility of task status and progress through Kanban boards.

Comparison of Scrum and Kanban Frameworks

Scrum and Kanban frameworks are similar; however, there are some distinctions, as mentioned in *Table 1.2*:

Factors	Scrum	Kanban
Planning	Done at the beginning of the sprint/iteration	JIT Planning means - no planning is done
Sprint	It can be of 1-4 weeks time	There are no sprints/iterations
Roles	PO, SM, and team	No Roles defined: There might be an Agile Coach
Boards	Indicates the workflow steps	Indicates the workflow steps and WIP limits
Commitment	Team commits for each sprint: Sprint may fail if capacity is not measured	Commitment is based on Capacity: WIP limits help team members working on multiple tasks
Workload	Workload: Limits WIP per iteration	Workload: Limits WIP per status

Modifica-tions	Once the sprint begins, not allowed to add tasks in the iteration...scope creep	You can add tasks in the backlog and take up based on the priorities
Industries	Software Development, Construction, Data Analytics, Advertising, Pharmaceuticals	Marketing, Content creation, Manufacturing, Healthcare, Fashion

Table 1.2: Comparison of Scrum and Kanban frameworks

Estimating and prioritizing work in Agile

Estimating and deciding the priority of tasks is an important aspect of Agile planning. The task estimation is done with the help of techniques such as story points, t-shirt sizing, Fibonacci sequence, and many more. In these techniques, estimation is done based on the complexity of the tasks and not on the time taken. Tasks are moved to the sprint after deciding the priority. Priority may change throughout the cycle and the decision is taken by the team based on the value it provides to the customer. The most important features are delivered first to the customer. This way, it is a value-driven approach that takes into account the feedback provided by the customer.

Agile metrics and performance tracking

Agile metrics are a quantitative measurement of the agile project life cycle used to track and improve performance. We have defined some must-learn Agile metrics as follows:

- Agile metrics are used to track the project and improve the performance of the team and develop better products.
- Burndown charts and burn-up charts measure the amount of work remaining and completed, respectively. It helps to understand the progress towards the sprint -goal.
- Cycle-time is a measurement of the time it takes from start to finish the project. It helps to understand the speed and efficiency of the teams.
- Lead-time is a measurement of the time it takes a feature to enter the backlog, then design-coding-release, and finally reach the customer.
- Velocity is a measurement of how much work a team can complete in a given time frame. It is measured in story points or number of stories completed.

- Epic and release burndown charts track the progress over an epic or release, which is the larger body of the work.
- There are many other metrics and charts such as Control chart, Cumulative flow diagram, No. of defects, Customer support requests, Customer retention rates, and many more. These are used to measure the performance of the Agile project life cycle.

About Jira

Jira is a robust project management tool used by Agile teams worldwide. It was designed by an Australian software company - Atlassian in 2002. It has evolved as a unique tool, which has many variants and can be customized for all types of projects and teams. Jira offers features to plan, track, and release software and collaborative platforms for teams. It is used for issue management, bug tracking, agile project management, and IT service management with the help of customizable workflows and integration with other add-ons. Jira is a popular tool for many other tasks, such as requirements gathering, test case management, and documentation.

A step-by-step guide to creating a Jira site

We will learn how to set up Jira Software, Jira Service Management, and Confluence on Cloud.

These are the steps to create a Jira site free for 10 users:

1. Go to :https://www.atlassian.com/software/jira/pricing

Figure 1.1: *Step 1 to create Jira site*

2. Click Get it free:

Figure 1.2: *Step 2 to create Jira site*

3. Optionally, select **Confluence** OR `Jira Service Management` as the second product. If not needed, you can continue without selecting any option:

Figure 1.3: *Step 3 to create Jira site*

4. Enter your email address and the name of your desired site.

5. Click **Agree**.

6. Jira will create your site and guide you through the process of creating projects. You can skip these steps if you want.

7. Your site is ready.

Different Jira products

Let's explain some Jira products as follows:

- **Jira Software**: A tool used worldwide to manage projects for software teams, featuring agile development, time tracking, issue management, and customizable templates.

- **Jira Work Management**: Solution designed for business teams, such as Marketing, Sales, HR, Finance, and their projects. It is a friendly tool built for cross-team collaboration and coordination.

- **Jira Service Management**: Service desk and ITSM solution with ticketing, incident management, problem management, and self-service features

- **Jira Align**: It is an Enterprise Agile Planning platform that helps improve visibility, strategic alignment, and enterprise adaptability to accelerate your digital transformation.

- **Jira Product Discovery**: A tool for product teams to organize and prioritize ideas, share product roadmaps, and connect business and tech teams, all in Jira.

Additionally, there are other Products that are used for version control repository, code review, team collaboration, and incident management:

- **Bitbucket**: A source-code management and version control repository with code collaboration and CI/CD capabilities.

- **Opsgenie**: Incident management and alerting tool for prompt response and resolution of critical issues.

- **Statuspage**: Communication tool for real-time status updates, incident notifications, and customizable incident response pages.

- **Trello**: Visual project management tool using boards, lists, and cards for organizing tasks and projects.

- **Sourcetree**: Sourcetree is a free Git client for Windows and Mac, which simplifies how you interact with your Git repositories.

- **Bamboo**: Bamboo is a continuous delivery pipeline that offers resilience, reliability, and scalability for teams of any size.

- **Fisheye**: Fisheye makes it easy to search, track, and compare code changes.

- **Crucible**: Crucible is a collaborative code review platform that helps you find bugs and improve code quality.

- **Confluence**: Team collaboration software for creating, organizing, sharing documents, project plans, and knowledge bases.

Jira's Popularity

Jira is a very famous and customizable tool that has been used by Agile teams and other teams for 20 years. Here are some features and functionalities of Jira as follows.

- **Designed for All types of teams**

It is a unique tool that is the right fit for software development and various other teams, such as HR, marketing, sales, service, and more. It was originally designed for bug tracking in software development, but it has evolved for all types, sizes, and industries.

- **Pricing and Plan**

  Jira products are available in a free plan for 10 users and three different variants. There are three variants available based on the pricing, number of users, features, and other criteria.

- **Customizable Project Templates**

  Jira provides built-in project templates for various purposes, such as:

  o   Scrum

  o   Kanban

  o   Bug Management

  Each project can be of two types:

  o   Company-managed Project

  o   Team-managed Project

  In addition to this, there are many other templates to manage various processes and projects. We will understand the same in *Chapter 2, "Working with Project Templates"*.

- **Time tracking**

  Jira has a time tracking feature that shows the time estimated, time spent, and time left for a task.

- **Bug Management**

  In Jira, a template for bug management is readily available. It can be customized easily to manage the bugs for agile software development teams. One can add fields available to customize the process in more detail.

- **Issue Management**

  One can create issue types/task types as per the requirements of the projects. Issues can be created, edited, and managed based on permissions and roles.

- **Search Filters**

  The searching feature in Jira is helpful to find out any issues by setting criteria to filter issues. There is a basic search and an advanced search.

Basic search helps filter issues based on task types, projects, assignees, status, and more, while advanced search uses Jira Query Language (JQL), which consists of a set of keywords, functions, operators, and values.

- **Timeline**

  Jira has a feature called Timeline View that has been used for planning, tracking, and creating tasks and map dependencies. In this view, one can create parent and child issues and schedule the same. The linking is done automatically between the tasks created in the timeline view. So, all the tasks created are child issues under an epic, which is the parent task.

- **Advanced Roadmap**

  Advanced Roadmap is a feature of planning across multiple teams and projects. It is an inbuilt feature in Premium and Enterprise versions. You can plan based on capacity, priorities, set dependencies, and explore different scenarios in the Advanced roadmap.

- **Automation in Jira**

  Jira has rich templates for automation rules. Automation rules help teams automate the repetitive tasks and simplify the processes. There is an automation library for beginners to learn and implement the rules. The rules are of two types: Project-specific and Global rules.

- **Community Support**

  Atlassian community is a group of users of Atlassian products and Community leaders. It is a very big community where one can ask questions and clear doubts. Beginners can get help from community leaders and other people in the group as and when it is required. By collaborating with experienced people, one can learn everything about Atlassian products.

- **Boards**

  Jira boards are powerful tools used for visualizing, updating, and tracking purposes. There are two types of boards: Scrum and Kanban boards. Jira boards can be customized for sorting the issues based on priority and other criteria. One can also match the statuses in Jira workflow and Jira boards. It also provides insights about the epics, sprints, and issues to be worked on. One can move tasks between statuses as per the customized workflow.

- **Dashboards and Reporting**

  Jira is a rich project management tool with customizable dashboards and reporting features. One can add gadgets and create their own dashboards, making it easy to present critical information to management during meetings. Jira's reporting functionality provides Agile metrics, such as burndown charts and cumulative flow diagrams, allowing teams to track project progress and identify bottlenecks. Jira offers reports for time tracking, workload, and resolution time, enabling teams to make data-driven decisions and optimize their processes.

Conclusion

We are now familiar with the Agile manifesto and concepts of Scrum and Kanban methodologies in Agile software development. We also learned about the various Jira products and other product solutions offered by Atlassian. We know the reasons behind Jira's popularity and its terminologies.

In the next chapter, we will learn how to create the first project in Jira, configure different projects, and explore a few examples of project templates in Jira.

Terminologies

- **Attachment**: A file attached to a Jira issue.
- **Backlog**: A list of user stories, bugs, and features for a sprint or a product to be worked upon.
- **Board**: It is the place from where information about the work items can be read and updated. It provides status-based information, and the tasks can be moved from one status to another on the board.
- **Burndown Chart**: It shows the amount of total work estimated and remaining in a sprint.
- **Component**: It is a subcategory of the project; for example, Modules of a project.
- **Custom Field**: It is a field used by the users to capture additional information about the issue.
- **Control Chart**: It provides information about the lead-time and cycle-time for a project or sprint.
- **Dashboard**: Using this feature, one can present information about the key metrics of a project.
- **Dependency**: A relationship between two or more issues when they rely on each other to get completed.
- **Epic:** A large task that has to be broken down into smaller tasks or stories.
- **Fix Version**: A version of a software application in which a bug is fixed.

- **Group**: A collection of users/Administrators in Jira who have common permissions and responsibilities.
- **Issue**: It is a unit of work, which is also named as a task. It can be based on the work one is supposed to do. For example, tasks, bugs, epic, story, and more, which can be tracked through workflow.
- **Impediment**: An obstacle that can prevent work on an issue.
- **JQL (Jira Query Language)**: It is Jira's own language used to search and display an issue.
- **JSM**: It stands for Jira Service Management.
- **JWM**: It stands for Jira Work Management.
- **Key**: A unique identifier for each and every issue in Jira.
- **Label**: A tag that can be used to search and sort the issues in Jira.
- **Notification**: An email sent from Jira to notify events like create, edit, delete issues, and many other events.
- **Project**: A combination of issues, components, workflow steps, and other resources in Jira to work towards achieving a goal.
- **Priority**: It defines the level of importance assigned to the issues used to decide its order in the backlog.
- **Parent issue**: An issue in Jira, which is related to one or multiple child issues.
- **Release**: A version of a software application that is delivered to the customer.
- **Resolution**: The way of fixing an issue in Jira and sending it to the resolved status.
- **Screen**: It is the combination of fields that creates a form to accept information about an issue.
- **Story**: It is the task type in Agile project management, which is used to describe the end user's needs.
- **Sprint**: It is the time span during which the software development teams design, develop, and implement the small working piece of software. It is also called an iteration and can be 1-4 weeks.
- **Story point**: It is a unit of estimation used by Agile teams. It is the measurement of the relative complexity of a story.
- **Swimlane**: It is the way to categorize the issues. Based on the categorization, teams can see which issues to work on.
- **Sub-task**: It is the child issue of task, story, and more, which is smaller than the parent task.

- **Task**: A piece of work in Jira that needs to be done to complete a process.
- **Time-tracking**: The way of logging and tracking the time spent on different tasks in Jira.
- **Transition**: When a task moves from one status to another in Jira, it is called transition.
- **User**: Any person who works to manage and track issues in Jira.
- **Version**: A release of a software application, which is a set of number of issues and bug-fixes.
- **Velocity**: It is the measure of how much work a team can take up in a sprint. It could be based on story points, issue counts, value, and more.
- **Work-flow**: It is the process-steps to complete a task from the start to resolution.
- **Work-log**: A record of the time spent while working on an issue in Jira.

CHAPTER 2

Working with Project Templates

Introduction

In this chapter, we will learn about project templates in Jira. We will cover the types of projects, types of project templates, and how to configure the projects for your specific business needs. Additionally, we will discuss the distinctions between team-managed and Company-managed projects along with tips on when to select the appropriate project type based on your requirements.

Structure

In this chapter, we will discuss the following topics:

- Defining a project in Jira Software
- Definition and purpose of project templates
- Benefits of using project templates in Jira
- A step-by-step guide to creating a project
- Choosing the right project type: Team-managed vs Company-managed projects
  - The difference between Company-managed and Team-managed Projects
- Exploring different project template types and their purposes
- Examples of successful project template implementation
  - Agile scrum software development project template
  - IT Service Management project template
- Important Use-cases

Defining a Project in Jira Software

A project comprises tasks that a team works on to achieve a specific goal. In Jira, a project can be seen as a container for organizing, tracking, and accessing these tasks as required. The team collaborates on these tasks to accomplish a predetermined objective.

Definition and Purpose of Project Templates

Project templates are a combination of standardized process flows, task types, and individuals involved in the project, among other elements. They serve as a tool for standardization that can be applied to multiple projects. A proper template selection is crucial for Jira administrators or project administrators as it saves time during project execution. The settings and configurations can be shared across multiple projects, allowing team members to consistently focus on the actual work. It is also essential for all members of the organization to be aware of which project template to use.

Benefits of Using Project Templates in Jira

We will cover the following five benefits of using project templates in Jira:

- **Time Saving**: The project manager doesn't need to create projects from scratch every time, resulting in significant time saving.

- **Error Reduction**: Standardized templates minimize the risk of overlooking crucial steps, leading to fewer errors.

- **Improved Efficiency**: Streamlining project management processes and reducing manual work enhances overall efficiency.

- **Standardization:** Project managers can easily apply standardized workflows, issue types, and custom fields using project templates, eliminating the need to create them repeatedly for new projects.

- **Scalability:** Project structures and settings can be replicated effortlessly, reducing the workload for project management.

Step-by-Step Guide to Creating a Project

To create a project, you can follow these step-by-step instructions as mentioned below:

1. Login to your Jira account: Open the browser and navigate to the Jira login page and enter your credentials to login to your Jira account.

2. Select **Create project.**

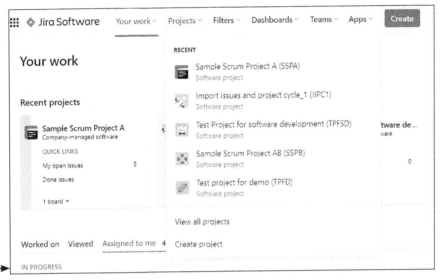

Figure 2.1: How to create Project in Jira Step-2

3. Select `Software development` from the sidebar.

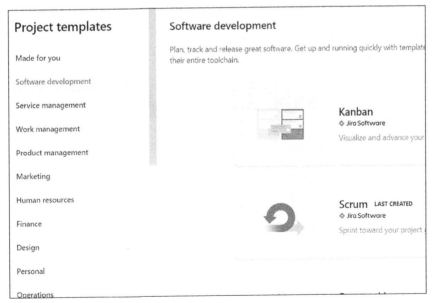

Figure 2.2: How to create Project in Jira Step-3

4. Select `Scrum, Kanban`, or `Bug tracking` software project.

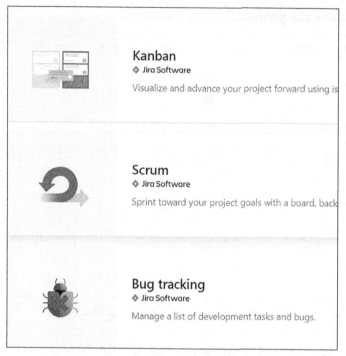

Figure 2.3: *How to create Project in Jira Step-4*

5. Select `Use template`.

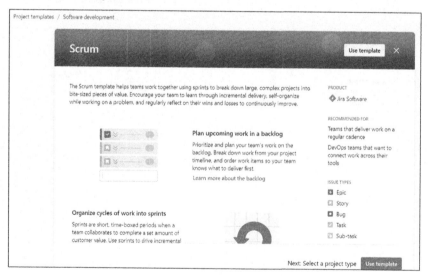

Figure 2.4: *How to create Project in Jira Step-5*

6. Now select `company-managed project` or `team-managed project` as per your requirement.

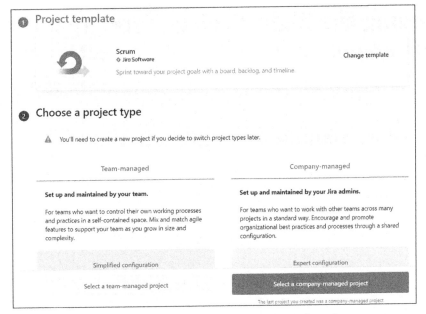

Figure 2.5: *How to create Project in Jira Step-6*

6. Add the name of the project and it will generate the key of the project. You can also connect with other development tools at this stage.

7. Now click **Create project.**

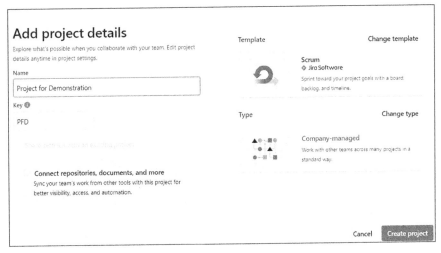

Figure 2.6: *How to create Project in Jira Step-8*

9. You have successfully created a new project in Jira.

Once the project is created, you can start to customize and work on the same.

Choosing the Right Project Type: Team-managed vs Company-managed Projects

While selecting the project type, you must select either a team-managed project or company-managed project in Jira. The project type can be decided as per your business requirements and the current process you follow. We will guide you to select the right type of project in this section.

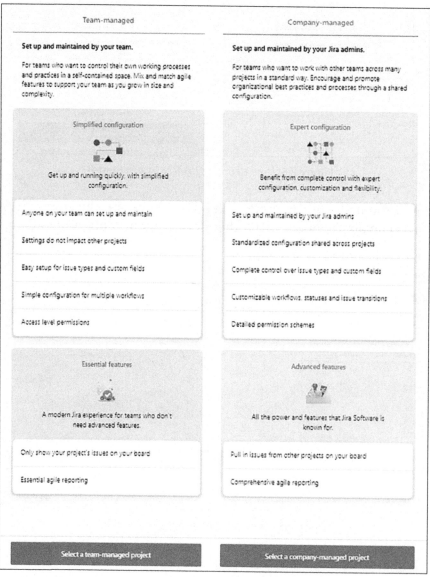

Figure 2.7: *Choosing the right project template: Team- vs Company-managed project*

The Difference between Company-managed and Team-managed Projects

There are some factors which differentiate the two types of projects in Jira. It will help in choosing the right type of project template.

	Team-managed Project	Company-managed Project
Who can manage	Team members	Administrators
Set-up and Customization	Can set up easily and faster. Project administrator or anyone can do it without getting help from the Administrators	Its customization requires an experienced Administrator
Add/remove issue types, priority, Custom fields	Can be added and applicable to a specific project without affecting others	Can be added and applicable and used by all the projects with the same configuration
Workflows and Screens	It can be set-up by anyone in the team and is applicable to that project only	It can be customized by Jira Administrators and applies to all the projects with the same schemes
Permission schemes	Simplified (Access-level) permissions	Advanced permissions
Roadmaps	Basic Timeline and Advanced Roadmap (Not for all versions)	Basic Timeline and Advanced Roadmap (Not for all versions)
Project Boards	Cannot show the other project's issues on a single board	Can combine the tasks from multiple projects on a single board

Table 2.1: Company-managed vs Team-managed Project in Jira

Factors to Consider While Choosing Team-managed Projects

As a Jira Administrator/project administrator, one must consider the factors as listed below while selecting the team-managed projects:

- The team is small and prefers not to customize everything.
- The team aims for a quick and straightforward setup to start promptly.

- Basic Timeline features and/or Advanced Roadmaps with few limitations are acceptable for planning
- You want to work at your own pace and in your own space without collaborating with other teams.
- The organization is too small.

If your team size and customization requirements are as mentioned in this section, then you should go for a Team-managed Project.

Factors to consider while choosing Company-managed Projects

As a Jira Administrator/project administrator, one has to consider the factors as listed below while selecting the company-managed projects:

- You have a dedicated Jira Administrator and want to customize across projects.
- A large organization wants to streamline processes through complex configuration of workflows and screens.
- Advanced roadmaps are necessary for planning.
- Detailed permissions are required.
- An advanced workflow editor is needed, providing access to conditions, validators, and post-functions.
- You want to customize different screens for creating, viewing, and editing issues based on the issue type.
- Different issue types require separate workflows.
- Customized schemes shared across projects for
  - Issue type
  - Workflow
  - Screen
  - Fields
  - Permission
  - Notification
  - Issue security

If your team size and customization requirements are as mentioned in this section, then you should go for Company-managed Project.

Exploring different Project Template Types and their Purpose

There are primarily three different categories of project templates available in Jira: Jira Software, Jira Service Management, and Jira Work Management. Additionally, there is a separate category called Jira Product Management. Each of these categories offers various templates tailored to specific processes and products within Jira.

When selecting project templates, you can choose based on the Jira software products you are using and the specific processes you wish to follow. It's important to note that different versions of Jira may have their own unique project templates. In this chapter, we have focused on project templates available in Jira Cloud.

For more comprehensive information and the latest details, it is recommended to refer to the Atlassian documentation.

There are different project templates to manage various processes, teams, and projects. A detailed list of the templates with their purpose is mentioned in Table 2.2.

Product Name	Project Template	Purpose of the Template
Jira Software-Software Development	Kanban	Use this template to reduce bottleneck, planning flexibility, and recommended for teams that control work volume from backlog
	Scrum	Prioritize and plan your team's work on the backlog. Break down work from your project timeline, work in sprints, and order work items so your team knows what to deliver first
	Bug Tracking	Manage a list of development tasks and bugs

Jira Service Management	General Service Management for IT teams	This template offers IT teams a centralized platform to capture, assess, and handle requests effectively. It streamlines the process for employees to submit their requests, ensuring prompt responses and enabling them to find the information they need quickly. Additionally, it empowers employees to self-serve by providing access to relevant articles linked to the request forms
	General Service Management for Business teams	This template helps business teams with a central place to collect, prioritize, and manage requests. It simplifies the process for employees to submit their requests while enabling your team to respond to them using workflows that support their processes
	HR Service Management	This template helps HR teams manage service demands by consolidating requests from multiple channels (email, chat tools, request portal), providing full visibility of payroll, onboarding, change requests, and general HR inquiries
Jira Work Management	Project Management	From simple to complex projects, this template provides a simple way of coordinating multiple deadlines, teams and stakeholders involved. Rally all involved parties within a single source of truth and see projects from start to execution

	Performance Review	Simplify and alleviate the stress of performance reviews for both employees and managers. Prepare your employees by providing clear expectations and involving them in ongoing conversations throughout the process. Emphasize outcomes and effectively measure job performance to ensure readiness for the next review cycle
	Sales Pipeline	This template is ideal for sales teams to manage their leads. Track opportunities throughout the sales cycle, forecast revenue, and nurture relationships from lead to customer, all in one convenient place
Jira Product Discovery	Product Management	The product discovery template provides your product team with a special place to understand customer problems and create effective solutions. It helps your team work together by collecting and prioritizing ideas, aligning everyone on product plans, and improving communication between business and tech teams, all within Jira

Table 2.2: *Important Project Templates and their Purpose*

In addition to the above-mentioned templates, there are other templates in Jira cloud such as process control, web design, personal task planner, budget creation, procurement, etc.

Configuring Projects

Once you have created the project, you can configure it as per the requirements of your team. One can use it to track the tasks, for managing bugs, or as a helpdesk for the HR department.

Examples of Successful Project Template Implementation and Configuration

We will learn about two important project template implementations in Jira as follows:

- Scrum template in software development and
- IT Service Management project template in Jira service Management

Agile Scrum Software Development Template

In this section, we will learn all the customization features for an agile scrum software development template. We will cover topics such as workflows, add people, screens, custom fields, Agile scrum boards, and metrics.

Important Permissions

In order to create the project and perform all the configurations, one should login as a Jira Administrator and have Administer Jira Global permission.

Managing Projects

Select ⚙ >**Projects**. You can create projects, add project categories, and move the project to trash from this as shown in *Figure 2.8*.

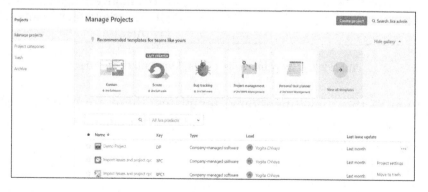

Figure 2.8: *Manage Projects from Administration*

Select a project and go to **project settings**. We will understand various configurations in Jira to customize everything in a **Company-managed** project.

People

Add people to your projects as users and assign the roles for a project as shown in *Figure 2.9*. For example, people who are assigned the role of **Scrum Masters** will have all the permissions given to the Scrum Master role. These roles are defined in the general system administration, which are applicable to all the projects in Jira.

Figure 2.9: *Adding people in a Project*

Permissions

Project permissions define who can access a project and what they can do (create and comment on issues, for example).

- One can define project permissions based on users/groups/role. These are customized permissions, and it is called a **permission scheme**.
- The other type of permissions is set from system administration, which are known as **Global permissions**.
- The permissions can be edited and/or a different scheme can be assigned to a project.

Figure 2.10: *Project-based Permissions*

Notifications

Jira has the capability to inform the relevant individuals about specific events that occur within your project, such as when an issue is commented on. You have the flexibility to choose the specific people, groups, or roles who should receive these notifications. The way these notifications are set up for your project is determined by the notification scheme. If you wish to alter the notifications, you can either select a different notification scheme or make modifications to the currently selected scheme.

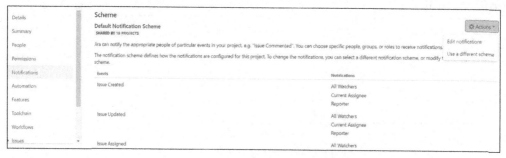

Figure 2.11: *Notification Scheme*

Automation

One can create Automation rules, which can be applied to a specific project only. For example: `When all stories are completed-> then close epic`. We will explore more about automation rules in *Chapter 9: Jira Automation Rules*.

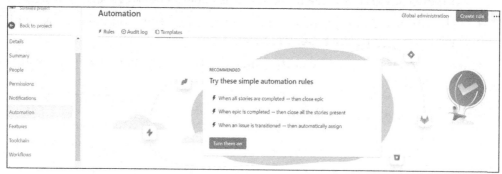

Figure 2.12: *Create Project specific Automation rules*

Features

In the features section, various features can be enabled or disabled. For instance, timeline, tool integration, product backlog, fold reports, and components are some examples. Jira offers a set of default features that are already enabled based on the type of project team or company management.

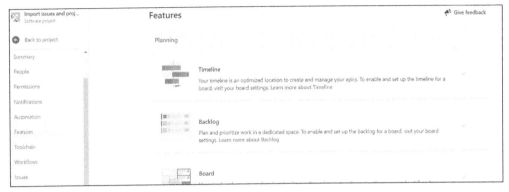

Figure 2.13: Enabling features in Scrum project

Workflows

In the workflows section, Jira administrators have the ability to perform several actions. They can add an existing workflow and associate it with a specific issue type, add workflows from the marketplace, or switch workflow schemes. *Chapter 7: Configuring Workflows in Jira for Agile Projects* will provide further insights and details on this topic.

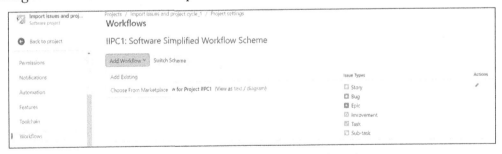

Figure 2.14: Associating workflow with Project

Screens

There are three types of screens in Jira: **Create, Edit,** and **View**. All three types of screens can be customized using fields. These screens can be customized on a per-issue basis. **Screen schemes** are combinations of screens designed for various issues. Finally, screen schemes can be assigned to a project.

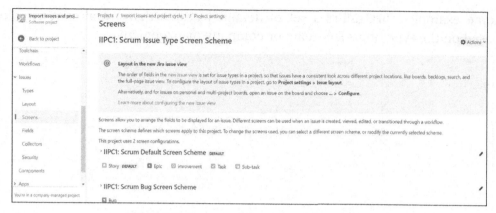

Figure 2.15: *Screens and screen-schemes in Jira*

Fields

Jira provides two types of fields: system (standard) fields, which are predefined and should not be modified, and custom fields, which can be added by users. Custom fields can include options such as text fields, multi-select fields, and many more. By adding custom fields to screens, users can create screens that meet their specific process requirements.

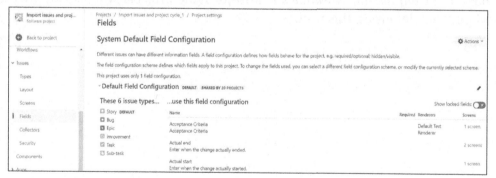

Figure 2.16: *Field Configuration*

Components

`Components` are subsections of a project. They are used to group issues within a project into smaller sets. For example, group issues that describe work on specific data objects, services, plug-ins, or APIs within their project.

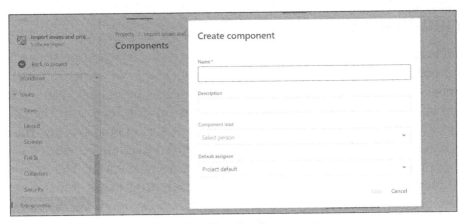

Figure 2.17: *Creating Components*

Development Tools

In a Scrum project template, Jira is connected with different development tools to make collaboration and work more efficient. Some common tools that are used with Jira are as follows:

- **Version control systems (VCS)** like Git or SVN, which help track code changes and connect with Jira.

- **Continuous Integration (CI)** tools such as Jenkins or Bamboo, which automate the building and testing of code triggered by Jira events.

- Code review tools like `Crucible` or `Bitbucket`, which allow team members to review each other's code and work together with Jira.

- Agile project management tools like **Confluence**, which are linked with Jira to create project documentation and make it easy to share knowledge.

Figure 2.18: *Development Tools*

Scrum Boards

Scrum boards in Jira provide a simple way to track tasks and progress. Scrum boards consist of columns representing different stages of work, such as **To Do, In Progress** and **Done.** Jira provides three statuses by default. The workflows can be customized as per the process followed by the team and the columns can be added on the board as per the workflow. Scrum boards show the tasks, bugs, and user stories that the team has committed to complete during a sprint. The board usually reflects the work planned for a single sprint. The tasks on the board can be easily moved across the columns as it progresses. It makes it easier to plan, prioritize and track work, ensuring that everyone is on the same page and the project stays organized. One can customize the boards by categorizing the issues for viewing them in a better way.

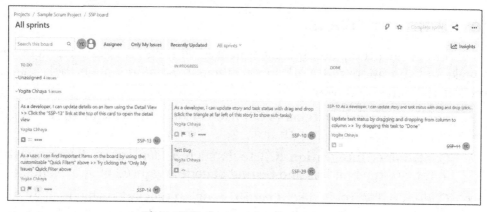

Figure 2.19: *Customizing Scrum Board*

Agile Metrics

The Scrum project template in Jira provides a way to measure Agile metrics, which help teams understand their progress and performance. Some of the key metrics that can be measured using Jira are as follows:

- **Velocity:** Jira calculates the velocity metric automatically based on the amount of work completed in each sprint. It shows how much work the team can accomplish on average, allowing them to plan future sprints more effectively.

- **Burndown Chart:** Jira generates a burndown chart that visually represents the progress of work throughout the sprint. It helps the team track if they are on track to complete all the planned work by the end of the sprint.

- **Lead Time:** Jira captures the time it takes for a user story or a task to move from the backlog to completion. This metric helps identify bottlenecks and optimize the flow of work within the team.
- **Cycle Time:** Jira also tracks the time it takes for an item to move through the different stages of the workflow. By analyzing cycle time, teams can identify areas where improvements can be made to increase efficiency.

By using the Scrum project template in Jira, teams can easily access these Agile metrics, enabling them to evaluate their performance, make data-driven decisions, and continuously improve their processes.

IT Service Management (ITSM) Project Template

Implementing an **IT Service Management (ITSM)** project template in Jira helps organizations to efficiently manage their IT services and support operations. By following the steps below, you can successfully implement an ITSM project template in Jira.

Creating an ITSM Project

Create a new project by selecting the `ITSM` project template in Jira. Provide a project name and key to uniquely identify the project within the Jira instance. Assign a project lead who will manage the project's implementation.

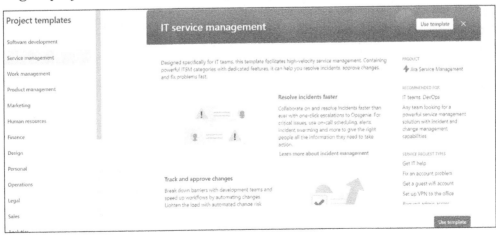

Figure 2.20: *IT Service Management Project Template*

Configuring Project Settings

Decide the project settings according to the organization's requirements. Customize the project description, lead, and permissions to ensure proper access control. Set up the notification scheme, ensuring that the relevant stakeholders receive timely updates and notifications.

Defining Request Types and Forms

Service requests are specific tasks or actions that users or customers request from a service desk or IT department. These requests can vary widely depending on the organization's services, such as software installation, access requests, hardware repairs, password resets, or general inquiries.

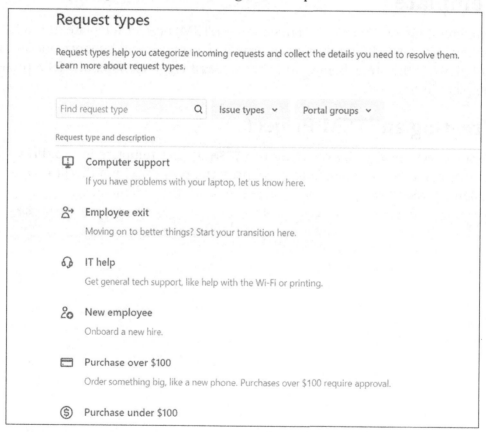

Figure 2.21: *Request Types in Jira Service Management*

Request types are predefined categories or templates that represent different types of service requests. They help categorize and streamline the process of handling different types of customer inquiries or tasks. For example, you might have request types like password reset, software installation, or hardware issue.

- Customize the request types to align with the organization's ITSM processes.
- Define the various types of IT service requests, such as incidents, service requests, or changes.
- Modify the request forms to capture essential information from users, such as category, impact, urgency, and detailed descriptions.

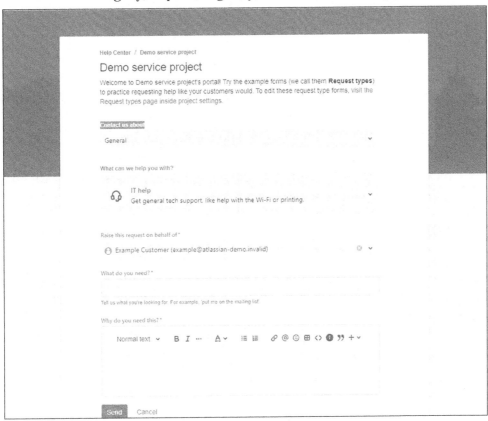

Figure 2.22: Service Project Portal

Establishing Service Level Agreements (SLAs)

SLA is an agreement or commitment between a service provider and a customer that defines the expected level of service regarding response and resolution times for service requests. SLAs help set performance expectations, prioritize work, and ensure timely delivery of services. Jira Service Management allows you to define SLAs based on different parameters like request type, priority, or customer segment.

Figure 2.23: *Service Level Agreements in ITSM project*

- Establish SLAs to ensure timely response and resolution of IT service requests.

- Define SLA metrics, including response time and resolution time, based on organizational goals and customer expectations.

- Associate the SLAs with the corresponding request types to enable automatic monitoring and tracking.

Creating Custom Queues and Workflows

Queues in Jira Service Management are lists or collections of service requests that share a common characteristic or need attention. They help service agents or teams organize and prioritize their work by grouping requests based on different criteria, such as request type, SLA breach, assignee, or priority. Agents can easily view and manage the requests in their assigned queues to ensure timely response and resolution.

- Create the queues and workflows to match the organization's ITSM processes and stages.

- Configure the stages and statuses that represent the lifecycle of IT service requests.

- Customize the workflow transitions, conditions, and validators to streamline the request handling process.

Assigning and Managing Tickets

Agents in Jira Service Management are the individuals or teams responsible for handling and resolving service requests from customers or users. They play a crucial role in delivering great customer service and ensuring efficient service delivery. Agents are assigned to specific queues or groups based on their expertise and workload. They review incoming requests, categorize them accurately, and prioritize them based on urgency. Agents work closely with customers/users, gathering necessary information, troubleshooting issues, and providing regular updates on request progress. They utilize Jira Service Management's tools to track, assign, and manage requests, ensuring that service level agreements are met and customers are satisfied. Agents in Jira Service Management are the front-line representatives who work diligently to provide high-quality support.

- Assign incoming IT service requests to the appropriate team members or support agents.
- Leverage Jira's built-in features to track the progress of each ticket.
- Utilize internal collaboration tools within Jira to facilitate communication and collaboration among team members for efficient issue resolution.

Monitoring and Report Generation

Jira Service Management Cloud offers default reports and custom reports. Default reports can be utilized to measure essential functions within service projects. While these reports cannot be modified, they offer valuable insights into assessing your team's compliance with SLAs. It also offers custom reports such as Time to resolution, SLA success rate, created vs resolved, etc.

- Utilize Jira's reporting and monitoring capabilities to gain valuable insights into IT service performance.
- Generate reports and metrics on request volume, response times, SLA compliance, and overall performance.
- Set up personalized dashboards to monitor key performance indicators and identify areas for improvement.

By following these steps, organizations can successfully implement an ITSM project template in Jira, enabling them to streamline their IT service management processes, deliver prompt customer support, and achieve higher efficiency and customer satisfaction levels.

Important Use-cases

In this section we will learn about different use cases of Jira projects in which we will include How to create a project with sample data, how to change the project, how to move issues from team manage to company manage projects, how to migrate issues from team manage to company managed and vice versa.

1. **Create projects in Jira with Sample data**: Jira allows you to create a Scrum and Kanban project with some sample data. It is helpful to evaluate and understand features in Jira.

This feature is extremely helpful for those who are new to Jira and want to explore the features and functionality. We will learn the step-by- step process to create projects.

    a. Login to Jira as Jira Administrator.

    b. Go to the Board section in any project and select `Create board.`

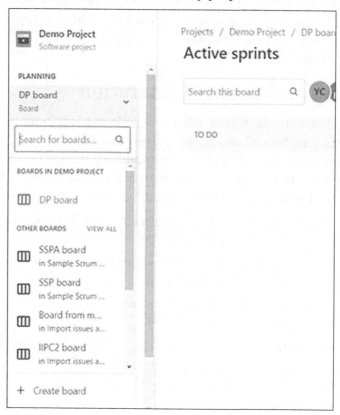

Figure 2.24: *Adding a board from Create board*

    c. Jira provides you two options to create a `Scrum` or `Kanban board with sample data`. Select to create a board with sample data. Enter all the required details and it will create a project with a board.

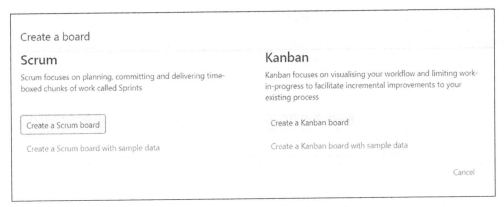

Figure 2.25: *Creating a Board with sample data*

4. The Scrum board looks like this in the *Figure* 2.26. Similarly, you can create a Kanban board.

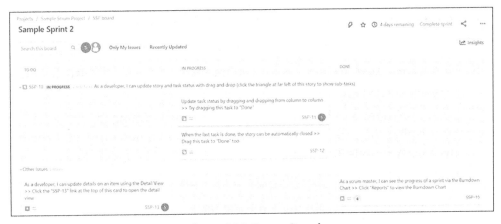

Figure 2.26: *Scrum Board*

Important link for reference:

https://community.atlassian.com/t5/Jira-Software-questions/Sample-projects-to-practice-and-develop-skills/qaq-p/1747661

2. **Change Project-type in Jira or Migrate between projects (Team-managed to Company-managed and Vice-versa)** : A team currently works in one type of Jira project or a specific template like Jira Software's company-managed Scrum project and you want to migrate to a different project type or template like Jira Software's team-managed Kanban project or Scrum project.

You can follow these steps to Bulk-change issues.

"Only Users with Global permission Make Bulk Changes and the relevant project permissions can do this"

a. Go to **Projects** > `Create project`

b. Create a new project in which you want to migrate all the issues from the old project

c. Select the `team-managed` or `company-managed` project and create a new project after confirming the type of project. Enter all the required details such as `Project-name`, `Project-key`, etc.

d. You have created a new project to migrate all the issues.

e. Select the filter for a project which you want to migrate to another project

f. In the top-right corner, select `More` > `Bulk change all`.

g. Navigate to **Projects** > `Create Project`.

h. Generate a new project where you intend to transfer all issues from the previous project.

i. Select either a `team-managed` or `company-managed` project. After confirming the project type, proceed to create a new project. Provide all necessary details, including `Project Name` and `Project Key`.

You have successfully established a new project for issue migration.

j. Choose the appropriate filter for the project that you wish to migrate to another location.

k. In the upper-right corner, click on `More` > `Bulk change all.`

Figure 2.27: *Selecting Buk-change all issues*

l.   Choose **Bulk change all issues**. Select all issues and hit **Next**.

m.   Select **Move Issues to new projects**.

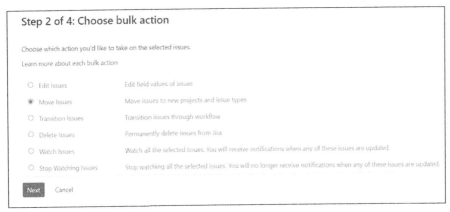

Figure 2.28: *Selecting Move Issues*

n.   Select the right project to move to and map all issue-types.

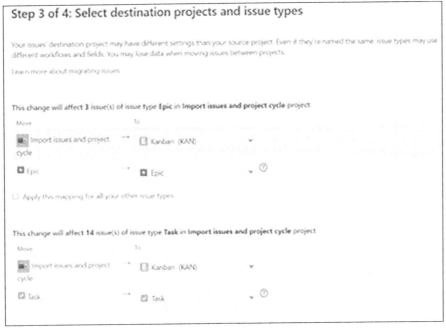

Figure 2.29: *Selecting projects and Mapping of Issues*

o.   Select **Next** in the final step.

p.   On the final screen, click **Confirm.**

Figure 2.30: *Confirming Move/Migrate Issues*

q. All the issues will be migrated to the new project. However, you need to check for mapping statuses and workflow schemes in both the projects.

Important links for reference:

1. https://support.atlassian.com/jira-cloud-administration/docs/convert-a-project-to-a-different-template-or-type/

2. https://support.atlassian.com/jira-software-cloud/docs/migrate-between-team-managed-and-company-managed-projects/

3. https://support.atlassian.com/migration/docs/perform-a-cloud-to-cloud-migration-for-jira/

Conclusion

We are now familiar with how to create a project and select the right type of project template as per the size of the team/organization and the business process. We also understood important project template implementation and how to configure Jira for the same.

In the next chapter, we will learn about how to add users, creating groups, project roles, and permissions.

CHAPTER 3

Creating Users, Groups, Roles, and Understanding Permissions

Introduction

When working with Jira, creating users, groups, project roles, and permission schemes is essential for efficient project management and collaboration. Users can be added and assigned specific roles, granting them appropriate access and responsibilities within the system. Groups allow for easy management and assignment of permissions to multiple users simultaneously. Project roles help define different levels of involvement and responsibilities for team members. Lastly, permission schemes determine what actions and operations each user or group can perform within Jira. Together, these elements form the foundation for organizing and controlling access to project resources, ensuring smooth teamwork and effective project execution.

Structure

In this chapter, we will discuss the following topics:

- Creating Users
  - Invitation statuses in Jira
- Creating Groups

- Creating Project Roles
  - Example of Creating a Project Role
- Groups vs Project Roles
- Understanding Permissions and Access Control
  - Global Permissions and its Examples
  - Project Permissions and its Examples
  - Jira admin helper to troubleshoot permissions
  - Issue Security Permissions
- Understanding Permission Scheme
  - Associating a permission scheme with Project
- Points to Remember
- Conclusion

Creating Users

Whenever a person joins the organization, it is required to add/invite users to the Jira software. To do this, log in to your Jira instance as an administrator. You need administrative privileges to create new users.

1. Log in to your Jira instance with administrative privileges.

2. Navigate to the User management section by selecting the gear icon and clicking on **User Management**. This will redirect you to the admin. atlassian.com page, where new users can be added.

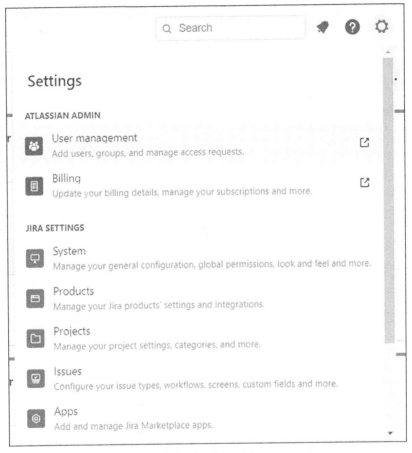

Figure 3.1: *Selecting User Management*

3. From the top right corner, click on `Invite users.` Start by adding the email addresses of the users.

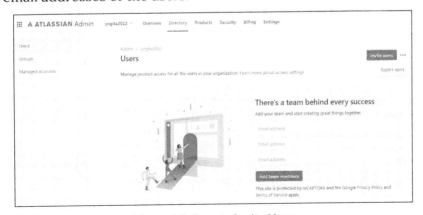

Figure 3.2: *Page to Invite Users*

4. For Jira Cloud, enter the email address of the user to add them as a new user.

5. If you need to add multiple users, simply enter their email addresses separated by commas.

6. Once the email address is entered, you can choose the user's role from the dropdown menu.

Figure 3.3: *Inviting Users and Adding to Groups*

7. After entering the email address, you can proceed to select the **product access** and **role** for that specific user. The user's role determines what permissions they have in Jira.

8. Beneath the **product access** list, you will find the option to assign groups to the user. Choose the relevant group for each user.

9. The groups that the user is a member of determines which permissions they have in addition to their role permissions

10. If you wish to send a personalized message to the user, you can do so. If not, deselect the personalized message option.

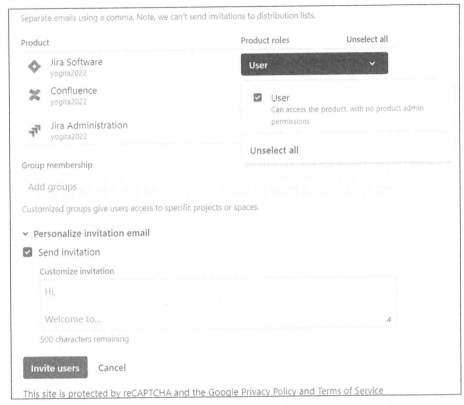

Figure 3.4: *Inviting Users, Adding Product Role, and Sending Personal Invitation*

11. Below the personalized message section, click `Invite users.` This completes the user invitation process successfully.

Invite Statuses in Jira

We have listed the following examples of the different invite statuses you'll see in your User Management screen:

- **Invited (invitation not sent)**: This status indicates that the user has been created by the administrator, but no Email has been sent to invite them.

- **Invited**: This status indicates that the user has been created and an Email invitation has been sent to them. Their status will change to active if they access one of the products.

- **Active**: The user is actively using at least one of the products they have access to within your organization.

- **Suspended:** This user's product access has been temporarily revoked within your organization. However, their access can be reactivated at any time. It's possible that they still have access to other products in different organizations.

- **Deactivated:** This user has been deactivated by the organization administrator and they cannot log in to any Atlassian products.

From the users' list page, select **Show Details**. From this page, administrators can perform the following operations as listed and as shown in *Figure 3.5*:

- **Assign organization role**: This allows the administrator to assign an organization role to the user. Organization roles define the user's permissions across all products in the organization.

- **Can prompt to reset passwords**: This allows the administrator to prompt the user to reset their password. This can be useful if the user has forgotten their password or if the administrator suspects that their password has been compromised.

- **Suspend access**: This allows the administrator to temporarily revoke the user's access to all products in the organization. This can be useful if the user is violating the organization's policies or if they are suspected of malicious activity.

- **Remove user**: This allows the administrator to permanently delete the user from the organization. This should only be done as a last resort, as it will delete all of the user's data in the organization.

- **Grant access to a product**: This allows the administrator to grant the user access to a specific product in the organization. This can be useful if the user needs to access a product that they do not currently have access to.

- **Add the member to a group**: This allows the administrator to add the user to a group in the organization. Groups can be used to assign permissions to users more easily.

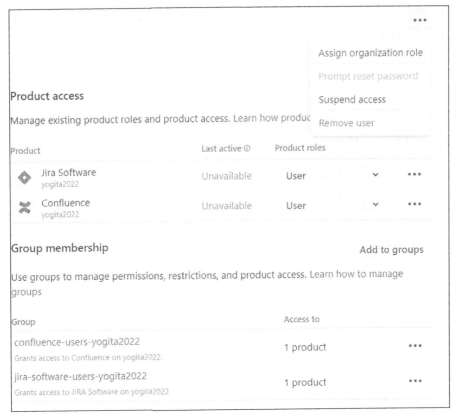

Figure 3.5: *Options for Administrator to add a User to groups and products access role*

We are now confident about how to add/invite users, add the users to a group, and many other operations. We will learn to create groups in the next section.

Creating Groups

When you have multiple users in your organization who need to be grouped based on criteria other than roles but require the same permissions or restrictions, you can create a group of users. Follow the outlined steps to create groups:

1.   Log in as a Jira administrator.

2.   Go to `admin.atlassian.com` to create groups.

3.   Select **Groups** from the left navigation bar.

4.   Select the **Create group** from the right-hand side.

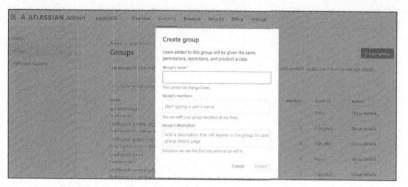

Figure 3.6: *Creating Group and Adding Details*

5. Enter all the details such as group name, members name, and description of the group.

Jira creates some default groups, which are listed as follows:

*   Jira Administrators
*   Jira software users
*   Site-admins

In addition to these, one can create and add groups such as Hardware group, Developers, Design group, Marketing group, etc.

On the Groups page, select show details for one of the groups. One can perform the following actions from this page:

1. Add group members

2. Edit group name

3. Edit group description

4. Grant product access

Figure 3.7: *Adding/Editing Group detail*

We have created a group and now we will learn to create project roles in Jira. Groups are for global and project roles are specific to a project.

Creating Project Roles

Project roles in Jira are specific to a project and are created to customize permissions based on a role in an organization. For example, permissions for creating sprints, managing scrum boards, access to reports and dashboards, etc. These may be different for each and every project, organization, and they can be customized with the help of permission schemes.

Now we will understand the following step-by-step process to add a project role:

1. Select ⚙ >**System**.

2. Select **Project roles** under security on the left navigation bar.

3. On this page, it displays a list of all project roles.

4. Under **Add Project Role** at the bottom of the page, enter your new role's **Name** and a **Description.**

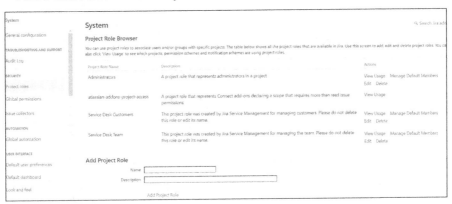

Figure 3.8: Project Role Browser

5. Select the **Add Project Role** button.

6. Project administrators can assign members once a new project role is created.

Example of Creating a Project Role

If you want to create a scrum master role so that all the sprint and board operations can be managed by him, follow the provided steps to create the role and associate the same with the permission scheme and project:

1. Create a project role called `Scrum Master.`

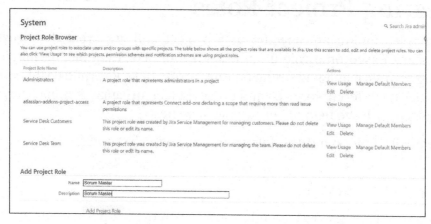

Figure 3.9: *Adding Scrum Master Project Role*

2. Create a permission scheme called the `Agile scrum permission scheme`. In this scheme, you assign the `Manage sprints` permission to the `Scrum Master` project role.

3. For a Scrum Master role, permissions required are `Manage sprints, Schedule Issues, Create Issues, Edit Issues, Browse Projects.`

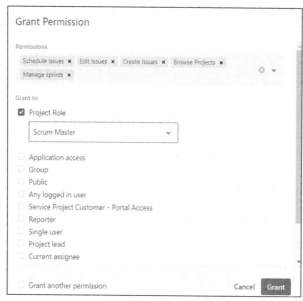

Figure 3.10: *Granting permissions to a project role Scrum Master in Agile permission scheme*

4. Associate the Agile scrum permission scheme with all scrum software development projects. To change the permission scheme, Select `Projects` > `Project settings` > `Permissions` > `Actions` >`Use a different scheme.`

Figure 3.11*: Associating a permission scheme with a project*

5. For each scrum software development project, add the appropriate Scrum Master to the `Scrum Master` project role.

Figure 3.12*: Adding people to Scrum Master project role*

Adding Default Members: On the project role browser, select default members. On that page, one can add default users/groups for that project role. Those users or groups are added to each project by default whenever a new project is created.

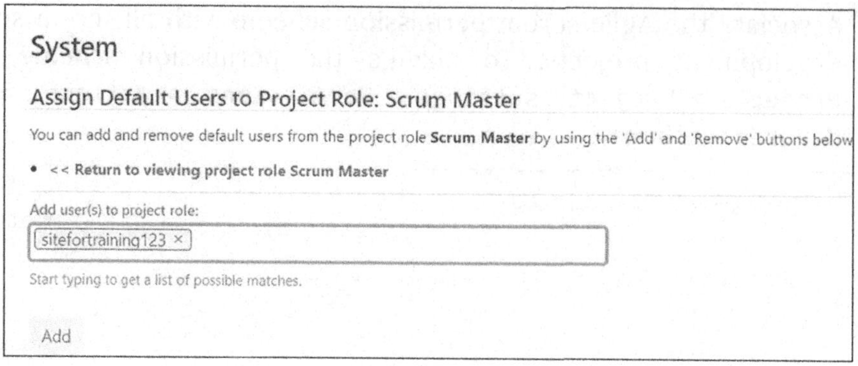

Figure 3.13: *Assigning Default users to project Role*

View Usage: Select `View Usage` on the project role browser. This page shows which workflows, permission schemes, notification schemes, and issue security schemes are currently using that particular project role. This page also shows which projects are associated with each scheme.

Project roles can be used in:

- Permission schemes
- Comment visibility
- Workflow conditions
- Email notification schemes
- Issue security levels
- Project roles can also be given access to:
- Dashboards
- Issue filters

Jira creates the following default project roles:

- Administrators
- Atlassian-add-ons-project-access

Groups vs Project Roles

In Jira, there are two distinct concepts related to user and access management: groups and project roles. Here's the difference between these two concepts.

Groups

- Groups in Jira are collections of users who share common access permissions and can be assigned to projects and issues.

- They are primarily used for simplifying user management and applying consistent permissions to multiple users at once.
- Groups can be created and managed within Jira's User Management section by administrators.
- Users can be added or removed from groups, and permissions can be granted to or revoked from groups, affecting all users within that group.
- Groups can be assigned specific permissions to control access to Jira projects, boards, and issues.

Project Roles

- Project roles in Jira are predefined sets of permissions that can be assigned to users or groups within a specific project.
- They provide a flexible way to control and manage access to project-related functions and actions.
- Jira offers default project roles such as `Administrators`, `Atlassian-addons-project-access`. Administrators can also create custom roles such as `scrum master`, `product owner` to fit their specific needs.
- Project roles can be assigned to individuals or groups at the project level, allowing for fine-grained control over who can perform certain actions within a project.
- For example, the Developers role may have permissions to create and work on issues, while the Administrators role may have full control over the project configuration.

In summary, groups simplify user management and permission assignment, and project roles provide granular access control within specific projects. These concepts can be used together to effectively manage users and permissions in Jira.

Understanding Permissions and Access Control

Permissions are settings in Jira applications, which control the users to create, view, and delete. It can allow users to create projects, create issues, view issues, delete projects/issues, create sprints, etc. There are three types of permissions in Jira. In this section, we will learn about all three types of permissions.

Global Permissions

These are the permissions applied globally, which means they are common for all projects. For example, one can set permissions to browse users and groups, share dashboards and filters, etc. To set the Global permissions, one has to log in as Jira Administrator and go to System settings. Follow the provided steps:

1. Log in as a Jira Administrator.

2. Navigate to the System settings by clicking on the **Settings** icon.

3. Choose **System** from the dropdown menu.

4. Select **Global Permissions** in the left side panel.

5. Set the desired permissions based on your requirements.

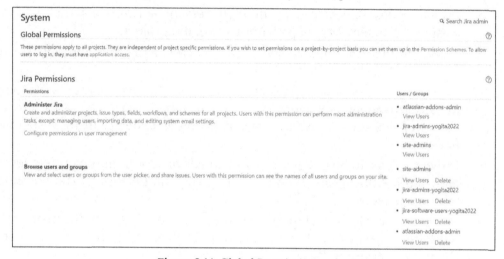

Figure 3.14: *Global Permissions page*

Examples of Global Permissions

In this section, we have covered a few global permissions, which can be used for system administration. Global permissions in Jira provide various capabilities and access levels to users.

- **Administer Jira**: Create and administer projects, issue types, fields, workflows, and schemes for all projects. Users with this permission can perform most administration tasks, except managing users, importing data, and editing system Email settings.

- **Share Dashboards and Filters**: Users with this permission can share their customized dashboards and filters with other users, enabling collaboration and information sharing across the organization.

- **Manage group filter subscriptions**: Create and delete group filter subscriptions.

- **Make Bulk Changes**: This permission allows users to perform bulk updates and modifications to multiple issues simultaneously, which helps improve efficiency.
- **Browse Users and Groups**: View and select users or groups from the user picker and share issues. Users with this permission can see the names of all users and groups on your site.
- **Create Team-managed projects**: Create projects separate from shared configurations and schemes. Team-managed projects don't affect existing projects or shared configuration like workflows, fields or permissions. Only licensed users can create team-managed projects.

We have covered all the global permissions in this section. .These global permissions play a crucial role in ensuring effective administration, collaboration, and customization within Jira, empowering users to effectively utilize the platform's capabilities.

Project Permissions

Permission schemes in Jira are used to organize and control access to projects. They determine who can view, create, edit, and assign issues within a project. These permissions are related to issues, time-tracking, attachments, etc. Project administrators can assign users to a project, but they cannot customize the permission schemes specific to that project. There are some project-level permissions available that allow you to fine-tune and manage what actions users can perform within a project.

Examples of Project Permissions

In this section, we have covered a few project permissions, which can be used from the system administration section and can be applied to `company-managed projects.`

- **Administer Projects**: Permission to administer a project which covers the ability to edit project details, components, project role membership, and project versions. Any logged-in user on your Jira site can be granted this permission.
- **Browse Projects**: Permission to browse projects and view issues in Jira projects, except issues with issue-level security.
- **Manage Sprints**: This permission is to grant people to create, start, and complete sprints in a project. One can adjust the sprint duration and goal. If a board contains sprints from multiple projects, then a user should have to manage sprints permission for all the projects.

- **View Aggregated Data**: This permission helps view insights on the backlog, boards and deployments view. It allows users to view other aggregated data like results of JQL filter queries, reports, etc. It includes average estimations, issue-count, team' cycle time. Disabling it will prevent users from viewing all types of aggregated data.

- **View Development Tools**: This is the permission to view the development tool in which the status of the issue's build data can be viewed.

- **View(Read-only) work-flow**: It provides a link to view the workflow. You can grant this permission to any logged in user.

Issue Permissions

These permissions are effective only if the users, groups, and roles are granted to browse projects.

- **Assign Issues:** It allows people to assign issues to users in Jira. This permission is different from an assignable user. In software projects, one should have project access to apply for this permission.

- **Assignable user:** This permission grants individuals the capability to be assigned issues, enabling their usernames to populate the Assignee field across any issues within your project. However, it doesn't confer the authority to assign issues to other users on your site.

  By possessing this permission, users gain the capacity to actively engage with issues. When an individual is assigned to an issue, we promptly notify them to review the associated details. This permission plays a pivotal role for core team members involved in any project.

- **Close Issues**: It allows the user to set the resolutions field to a closed state, which is based on the workflow conditions of the issue. One should have Transition issues and resolve issue permission to close issues. One must have product access to close issues in Jira.

- **Create Issues**: This permission allows users to create tasks and sub-tasks. Having this permission allows users to see the projects while creating issues. If this permission is granted to any logged-in user, it is helpful to create suggestions, bugs, etc. However, for security reasons, a few teams may not grant this permission to everyone.

- **Delete Issues**: This permission allows users to delete issues and related items like comments, field data, work log entries, etc. In Jira Software, this permission is dependent on product access permission. To maintain the cleanliness of the Jira instance, it is recommended to transition the issue to done status. Deleting issues should not be a common practice to delete issues unless it is necessary.

- **Edit Issues**: This permission allows people to modify fields like Summary, description, and other editable fields. This permission also grants the ability to convert tasks to subtasks and vice versa. In Jira Software, this permission is dependent on product access permission. Organizations with strict compliance measures restrict this permission for team members.

- **Link Issues**: This permission enables people to link issues within the same or different projects. They need the same permission in other projects to view the link. It functions when issue-linking has been enabled. In software projects, people must have product access to use this permission.

- **Modify Reporter**: This permission allows users to modify the default reporter field on any of the issues. By default, the reporter field is pre-set to the creator of the issue. In software projects, people must have product access to use this permission.

- **Move Issues**: This permission allows people to move issues to another project or change the issue-type. This permission requires the create issue permission in the target project.

- **Resolve Issues**: This permission allows the users to set or clear the resolution field and see the Fix version field. It doesn't include the ability to close the issue. In Jira Software, this permission is dependent on product access permission. It is required to have transition issue permission to be useful.

- **Schedule Issues**: This permission allows people to set or modify the Due date of the issues. It also allows ro rank(reorder) the issues on the backlog or board. They must have product access to Jira software to use this permission.

- **Set Issue Security**: It allows users to set the security levels of the issues. It allows or restricts who can view the issues. The users must have product access to Jira software to use this permission.

- **Transition Issues**: This permission allows users to view the workflow of the project and update the status. The users can move any issue through the workflow triggering post functions. It doesn't allow the users to close the issue or set the resolution field. The users must have product access to Jira software to use this permission.

Voters and Watchers Permissions

These permissions are effective only if the users, groups, and roles are granted to browse projects. First, allow users, groups, and roles to Browse those projects and then only these permissions can work.

- **Manage Watcher list**: This permission is for adding or removing people from an issue's watch list. It works on the basis of product access permission. In software projects and service projects, people must have product access to Jira Software and Jira Service Management, respectively, to use this permission.

- **View Voters and Watchers**: This allows people to see who is watching an issue. It doesn't depend on specific product access permissions to be useful.

Comments Permissions

These permissions are only applicable to those who can view the project. To make comments permissions applicable, grant users to browse the project first.

- **Add comments**: This permission allows people to comment on any issue in your software and business projects or add internal notes to requests in your service projects. In software projects, it is necessary to have product access to Jira software to use this permission.

- **Delete all Comments**: This permission allows people to delete any comments added by anyone in any project. In software projects, users must have product access to Jira software. It is recommended to preserve all the comments to ensure a comprehensive understanding of the project.

- **Delete own Comments**: This permission allows people to delete their own comments in any project. It is not dependent on product access permissions. It is helpful to modify any erroneous comments.

- **Edit all Comments**: This permission allows people to edit all the comments done by anyone. Organizations with strict compliance policies do not encourage editing comments. Whereas open organizations encourage teams to make corrections.

- **Edit own Comments**: This permission allows people to edit their own comments. This permission can be granted to any logged-in user. Organizations with strict policies restrict the editing of comments.

Time Tracking Permissions

These permissions are effective only if the users, groups, and roles are granted to browse projects. First, allow users, groups, and roles to Browse those projects and then only these permissions can work.

- **Work on issues:** It allows people to utilize the features related to the time tracking field on any of the projects' issues. One can enter a work log, which includes time spent and time remaining and a description of the work dated on that issue.

- **Delete all work logs:** This permission is to remove any work log added by anyone in projects' issues. This permission is specifically for team leaders, management roles, or other senior people.

- **Delete own worklogs**: This permission allows people to delete the work logged, description, and estimated time entered by themselves. This permission is required to delete their own worklog in case of data entry errors.

- **Edit all worklogs**: This permission allows people to edit the time logged, description of the work, estimated time, etc. This is helpful to team leaders or management roles who can modify the entries.

- **Edit own worklogs**: This permission allows users to alter the time logged, estimated time, description of the work log or any data entry errors due to changes of the scope of the work.

Attachments permissions

These permissions are effective only if the users, groups, and roles are granted to browse projects. First, allow users, groups, and roles to Browse those projects and then only these permissions can work.

- **Create Attachments**: This permission does not require project access. Any logged-in user can be granted to add files as attachments. It helps people working on projects to add some information related to the work they are doing.

- **Delete all Attachments**: This permission allows any user to remove attachments, which are attached with any of your project's issues. To delete attachments in Jira Software and Jira Service Management, it is essential to have project access.

- **Delete own Attachments**: This permission allows people to remove their own attachments. It is not dependent on product access permissions. Organizations with strict compliance policies may restrict team members from deleting their own attachments.

We have covered all the project permissions which can be customized to create a new permission scheme as per the requirement of an organization.

Jira Admin Helper to Troubleshoot Permissions

Whenever a user can or cannot see a certain issue or facing some problems to take action on issues, Jira admin helper can help. Follow the provided steps:

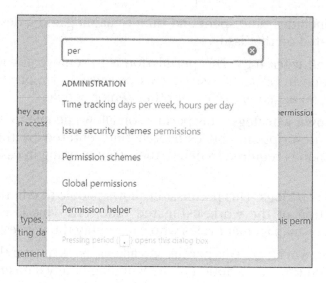

Figure 3.15: *Selecting Permission Helper*

You must be a Jira admin to use the permission helper. The steps are as follows:

1. Choose search `Jira Admin` on any page in the right upper corner.

2. Under `Admin helper`, select `Permission helper.`

3. Enter a username or leave it blank.

4. Add an issue key (for example, issue key of the user can or can't see) and the permission to check.

5. Click `Submit.`

Issue Security Permissions

Security schemes in Jira provide a way to adjust the visibility of individual issues within the constraints of the project's permissions. They allow you to control who can see certain types of issues based on issue security permissions. For instance, you can configure issue security to limit visibility to project administrators or users belonging to specific groups. This helps you to create different levels of access and confidentiality for different types of issues within your project.

Permission Schemes

Jira Administrators can assign specific permissions for different issue operations, sprint operations, commenting, time tracking, etc. Whenever a project is created, a default permission scheme is associated with it. Ideally, an administrator should create a copy of the default permission scheme and then can update the new permission scheme as per the roles and requirements of an organization. An administrator can customize the permission scheme by doing this and associate it with all the similar projects in an organization. Updating and removing permissions to customize the scheme can be done as shown in *Figure* 3.11.

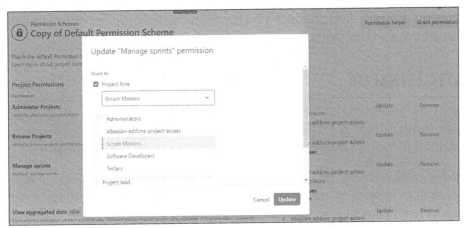

Figure 3.16: *Copying a permission scheme and Updating*

We have listed below the steps to copy a permission scheme and associate it with the project.

Associating a Permission Scheme with a Project

After deciding the project permissions for your organization/project, you can implement the scheme by linking it to the projects.

To associate a permission scheme with a company-managed project, follow these steps:

1. Choose **Projects** from the navigation bar.

2. Select the specific project.

3. From the sidebar, select **Project settings**.

4. Choose **Permissions** from the sidebar. It displays the current permissions scheme.

5. Select the **Actions** dropdown menu and choose **Use a different scheme**.

6. On the **Associate Permission Scheme** to **Project page**, select the permission scheme you want to associate with the project.

7. Click the **Associate** button to associate the project with the permission scheme.

Your project's permissions are now updated and the project now follows your permission scheme. Any changes you make in the scheme apply immediately to the project associated with the scheme.

Conclusion

We are now familiar with how to invite users, create groups, and project roles. We also understood the Global and Project-specific permissions and how to customize the permission schemes and associate them with a project.

Creating well-structured user management, groups, project roles, and permission schemes in Jira contribute to efficient collaboration, data security, and successful project outcomes.

In the next chapter, we will learn about how to manage backlog, sprints, and Agile boards.

Points to Remember

When creating users, groups, project roles, and permission schemes in Jira, here are a few points to keep in mind:

- **User management**: Make sure that each user has a unique Email ID and appropriate access privileges based on their role and responsibilities within the project.

- **Group classification**: Group users based on common characteristics, such as department, team, or project, to easily manage permissions and streamline collaboration.

- **Project roles**: Define specific roles for users, such as administrators, developers, or stakeholders, to assign different levels of access and responsibilities within the project.

- **Role-based permissions**: Assign appropriate permissions to each project role, allowing them to perform specific actions and access relevant project resources.

- **Permission granularity**: Determine the level of access required for each user or group, balancing security and collaboration needs to prevent unauthorized actions or information exposure.

- **Consider project requirements**: Understand the specific needs of the project and align user roles and permissions accordingly to ensure smooth workflows and information flow.

- **Regular review**: Periodically review user access rights and roles to maintain data security, accommodate organizational changes, and remove unnecessary permissions.

- **Too many Administrators**: Never give Jira Administrator permissions to too many people. Check it regularly and if not required by the person, revoke it.

- **Not customizing permission scheme**: Default permissions scheme may have few permissions, which are not required by your organization. Make sure to delete and update permissions and customize them for your specific requirement.

- **Communication and training**: Clearly communicate the roles and permissions assigned to each user or group, providing proper training to ensure understanding and adherence to Jira usage guidelines.

- **Documentation**: Maintain comprehensive documentation of user roles, groups, and permission schemes for future reference and easy troubleshooting.

- **Testing and validation**: Before deploying the permission schemes, thoroughly test them to validate that users and groups have the expected access and perform necessary adjustments if needed.

Important links for reference:

These links are from the Jira knowledge base or the Atlassian community. It will be helpful to understand some use cases.

1. How to change the permission scheme on a project: https://community.atlassian.com/t5/Jira-questions/how-to-change-the-permission-scheme-on-a-project/qaq-p/1955536

2. Understanding how project permissions affect project visibility in Jira cloud: https://confluence.atlassian.com/jirakb/understanding-how-project-permissions-affect-project-visibility-in-jira-cloud-1267074303.html

3. How to restrict the creation of an issue based on issue-type: https://confluence.atlassian.com/jirakb/how-to-restrict-the-creation-of-an-issue-based-on-issuetype-1267761379.html

CHAPTER 4

Managing Backlog, Sprints, and Boards

Introduction

It's important to handle the backlog, sprints, and boards well for a successful Agile project. Backlog management means arranging and deciding which tasks to do first, so we work on the most important stuff. Sprints are like short periods where we plan and finish tasks quickly. Boards show our work visually, helping the team work together better. By mastering these things, we can develop smoothly, deliver faster, and meet our customers' needs better.

Structure

In this chapter, we will discuss the following topics

- Steps to create an issue
- Different ways to create issues and product backlog
- Creating and grooming scrum product backlog
- Creating and grooming the Kanban product backlog
- Creating epic and version
- Sprint operations
- Product backlog vs. sprint backlog
- Creating and customizing scrum and Kanban boards
- Scrum board vs. Kanban board
- Use cases with References

Steps to create an issue

Issue-types in Jira: In software development projects, you can create the issue-types as mentioned below.

- Epic
- Story
- Task
- Bug
- Sub-task

In this section, we will learn about how to create an issue in Jira from any page. This process will also help you to create an issue while creating a backlog or adding issues to the backlog.

1. Select the **Create** button as shown in the following figure.

Figure 4.1: Step-1 to Create an issue

2. Enter the details of the **project**, **issue-type** and **Summary** field.

Figure 4.2: Step-2 to create an issue

3. Enter all the details about the required fields and other details. Select **Create** button. An issue has been created.

Figure 4.3: *Step-3 to create an issue*

Different ways to create issues and product backlog

One can create issues in three different ways as follows. The created issue goes to the product backlog in Scrum/Kanban projects.

1. **Creating an Issue from the Navigation bar-** Click on the **Create** tab in the navigation bar and start creating an issue.

Figure 4.4: *Creating an issue from the Navigation bar*

2. **Creating an issue from Timeline view:** The other way to create an issue is from the timeline view as shown in the *Figure* 4.5. One can create an epic, story and task from a timeline view.

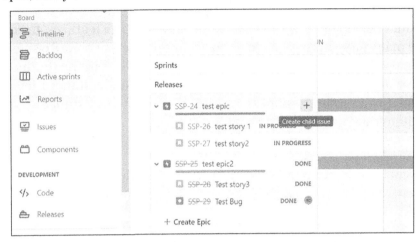

Figure 4.5: Creating an issue from the Timeline view

3. **Creating an issue from backlog:** One can also create an issue from the backlog view page. Select **+** sign and create issues such as **Bug, Task** and **Story**.

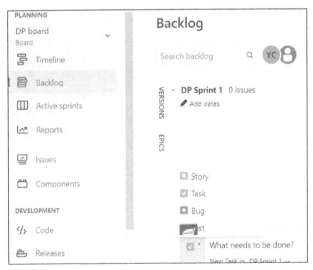

Figure 4.6: Creating an issue from the backlog

We learned about how to create stories, bugs and tasks. This way we have created a list of work items which makes a product backlog. Now we will learn important things about scrum product backlog and Kanban product backlog.

Creating and grooming scrum product backlog

The product backlog is a prioritized list of tasks such as features, tasks, stories, bugs and many more. As explained in this chapter, one can create issues from the backlog page. This way there are many stories, tasks etc. in the product backlog to achieve a product goal. In this section, we will understand a few must-be conditions for an issue to appear on the board, how to estimate the product backlog items and grooming the backlog.

Important things about scrum product backlog are:

- Subtasks cannot be viewed in the scrum product backlog.
- If the issue matches the board's filter, then only it will appear on the board.
- Issue status maps to one of the statuses of the board's status.
- If the issue status doesn't match with the board's statuses, then it should be mapped to the right status- for example in review, status can be mapped to in progress.

The following example shows a scrum product backlog and issue-details on the right side.

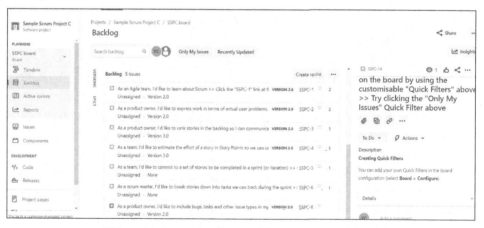

Figure 4.7: Scrum product Backlog with issue details

Important features on the product backlog page are:

- You can add issues to the product backlog.
- One can prioritize the work items. Go to the issue, right click and select send to **Top of Backlog.** You can also drag and drop the issue to the top of the backlog.

- Click three dots under the sprint name to view the sprint workload for assignees.

- Enter the details of Estimates on the issues. Enter the Estimate either in the field **Original Estimate** and/or **Story Points**.

- Click on the issue. The issue will open on the right-hand side. Now you can edit the issue details.

- One can transition the issue to the sprint. For transitioning the issue, one should have the transition issue permission. One can also transition multiple issues with the help of the *Shift* or *Ctrl* keys.

- Split an issue is a functionality used when the issue is very big.
  - When an issue is split, you can enter the estimates for both issues.
  - When you split an issue, all the fields are not inherited. However, fields such as priority, and component remain the same. You can enter a summary for the new issue created by splitting the issue.
  - Now there are two parts to the issue. The other issue will go to the backlog.

- To Flag an issue, right-click and flag an issue. Flagging means that an issue is of importance and can be taken on priority. To find the flagged issues, use the query **Flagged = Impediment**. Priority is replaced by the Flag symbol.

- One can see issues in the backlog by setting the no. of issues. If the issues are more than 100, you can set it from [icon] on the right-hand side. Select how many issues you want to display. You can select to see **"100, 500 or All" issues.**

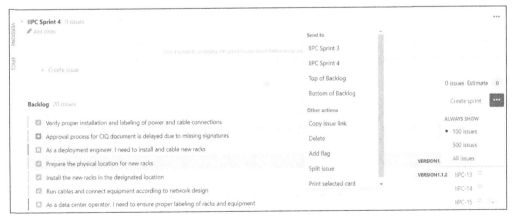

Figure 4.8: *Features on the Scrum product backlog page*

Creating and grooming the Kanban product backlog

It can be utilized only if it has been enabled by Jira Administrator or board administrator.

When you have only a few issues in your backlog, it's relatively simple to manage them in the first column of your Kanban board. However, as your backlog expands, it can become challenging to navigate and scroll through all these issues.

The Kanban backlog presents a solution to streamline your team's work planning process. It offers an improved list view that enhances the prioritization and organization of issues. With this view, you gain access to a larger backlog, enabling you to create and rank tasks with greater efficiency. This helps team members to actively work on a Kanban project to focus on their work-in-progress on the Kanban board, without being overwhelmed by the presence of planning items.

The following example shows a scrum product backlog selected for development issues. It also shows the provision to select the no. of issues on the backlog.

Important things about the Kanban product backlog are:

- If the issue matches the board's filter, then only it will appear on the board.

- Issue status maps to one of the statuses of the board's status- Kanban backlog column or any other next column.

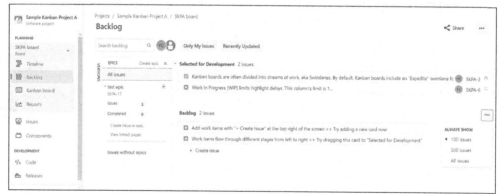

Figure 4.9: *Kanban Product Backlog page*

Important features on the product backlog page:

- You can add issues to the product backlog.

- You can prioritize the work items. Go to the issue, right click and select send to **Top of Backlog**. You can also drag and drop the issue to the top of the backlog.

- Enter the details of **Estimates** on the issues. Enter the Estimate either in the field **Original Estimate** and/or **Story Points**.

- Click on the issue. The issue will open on the right-hand side. Now you can edit the issue details.

- You can transition the issue to the sprint. For transitioning the issue, one should have the transition issue permission. You can also transition multiple issues with the help of *Shift* or *Ctrl* keys.

- Split an issue is a functionality used when the issue is very big.

  o When an issue is split, one can enter the estimates for both issues.

  o When you split an issue, all the fields are not inherited. However, fields such as priority and component remain the same. One can enter a summary for the new issue.

  o Now there are two parts to the issue. The other issue will go to the backlog

- To Flag an issue: Right-click on the issue and flag an issue. Flagging means that an issue is of importance and can be taken on priority. To find the flagged issues, use the query **Flagged = Impediment**. Priority is replaced by the Flag symbol.

- One can see issues in the backlog by setting the no. of issues. If the issues are more than 100, you can set it from ▦ on the right side. Select how many issues you want to display. You can select to see **100**, **500,** or **All issues.**

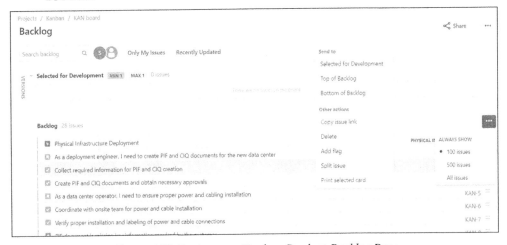

Figure 4.10: *Features on Kanban Product Backlog Page*

Creating epic and version

Epic can be created from three different places:

- From timeline view
- From create button
- From the backlog view page (as shown in *Figure 4.11*)

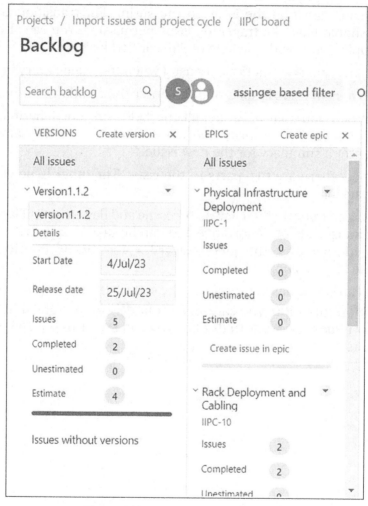

Figure 4.11: *Creating Epic and Version*

Versions can be created from two sections on the left panel:

1. Under the **Planning** section, you can create versions from **Backlog.**

2. Under the **Development** section, you can create versions from **Releases.**

***Figure 4.12**: Creating version window*

Product backlog vs. sprint backlog

Product Backlog	Sprint Backlog
A product backlog is a prioritized list of features, functionalities, improvements, suggestions and bugs in detail	It is a complete list of work items to be taken up in a sprint
It evolves continuously and is maintained by the product owner.	It is a detailed list which includes estimation and who will work on what details.
It provides a big picture of the product	It focuses on the small activity related to the sprint

***Table 4.1**: Product backlog vs. sprint backlog*

Sprint operations

In this section, we will learn about how to create a sprint, edit a sprint, reopen a sprint and delete a sprint.

Creating sprint

Sprint: It is a predefined time interval during which a scrum team does the development work. It can last from 1 week to 4-week time.

Go to the **Product Backlog** page and create a sprint as shown in the *Figure* 4.13:

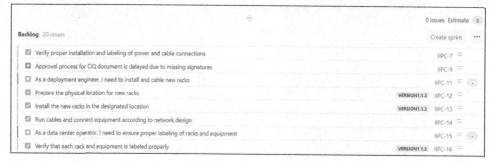

Figure 4.13: *Creating sprint from the Backlog page*

Edit sprint: Using this option, you can enter the details of the sprint.

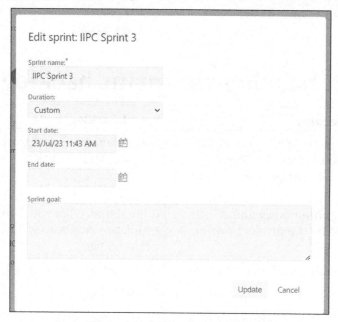

Figure 4.14: *Edit sprint window*

One can start the sprint once all the details are entered.

Figure 4.15: *Starting a sprint from the Product Backlog page*

The following figure shows the **Delete sprint**, **Edit sprint** and **Move sprint up** options. One can move up and down when there are two parallel sprints.

Figure 4.16: Various Sprint Operations

Creating and customizing scrum and Kanban boards

Boards in Jira are to track the status of tasks/issues, sprint. It is a simple and detailed representation of the status whether it is in Open, InProgress or Done status. There are two types of boards - scrum board and Kanban board. These boards can also be customized so that one can sort/group issues based on set criteria. In the next section, we will learn about how to customize the board in Jira for a company-managed project.

Customizing scrum board

In Jira, by configuring the boards one can do general settings, set swim lanes, set card colors, set filters, set the option for timeline view and map the workflow status with board columns.

To configure the boards, one must be either a project administrator or a board administrator.

The board offers the following customization options:

- General Settings and Filter
- Column Management
- Swim lanes
- Quick filters
- Card colors
- Card layout

- Estimation
- Working days
- Issue detail view
- Timeline
- Insights

Go to the board. Go to 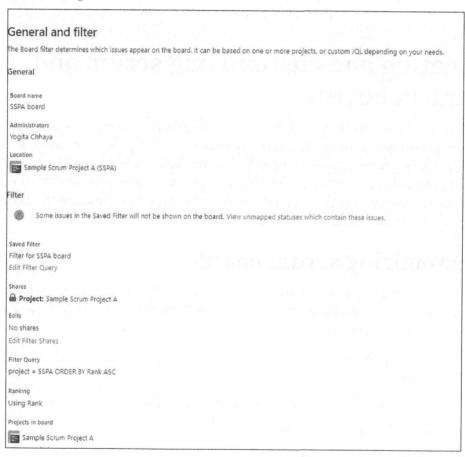 and right-click and select the appropriate settings to customize the board.

General Settings and Filter

Figure 4.17: *General Board Settings*

To create a board that shows only the issues based on criteria, you can create a board issue filter based on a JQL query. For example, you may create a board that includes issues from multiple projects, one project, or a particular component of a project.

Columns

Columns are mapped to the statuses of the workflow and they can be added, removed and reordered. Minimum and maximum constraints based on issue count can be set for each column.

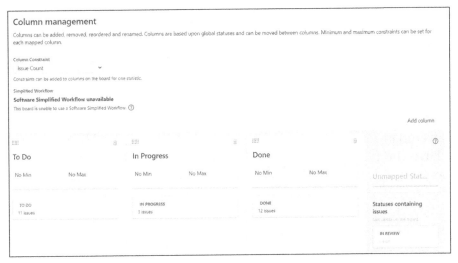

Figure 4.18: *Column Management on Board*

As shown in *Figure 4.18*, the columns display issue counts aligned with the constraints defined in the board settings. Users have the flexibility to incorporate columns onto the board according to the defined process workflow. In this example, the `IN REVIEW` status is not currently mapped. To address this, one can include an `In Review` column, as shown.

Figure 4.19: *Adding ColumnIn Review on Board*

Swim lanes: It is a row on the board to group the issues. The criteria to sort could be **Assignees**, **Epics**, **Stories**, **Projects** or **Queries**.

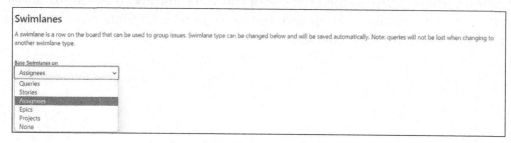

Figure 4.20: *Options for Swimlanes*

As illustrated in *Figure* 4.20, swim lanes have been configured based on assignee. Users have the flexibility to switch between issues assigned to different team members.

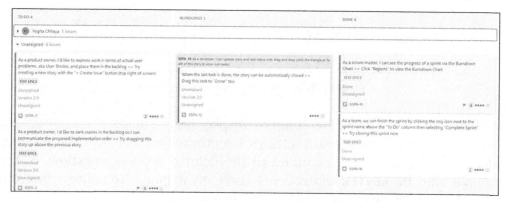

Figure 4.21: *Swimlanes Example*

Quick Filters: It can be used to filter the issues further based on added JQL query.

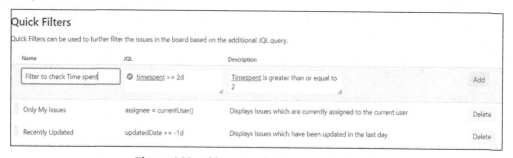

Figure 4.22: *Adding Quick Filters on the Board*

Card Colors: Card colors can be selected based on `Issue types`, `Priority`, `Assignees`, and `Queries`. You can also set it as **None**. The card colors will change based on the methods selected.

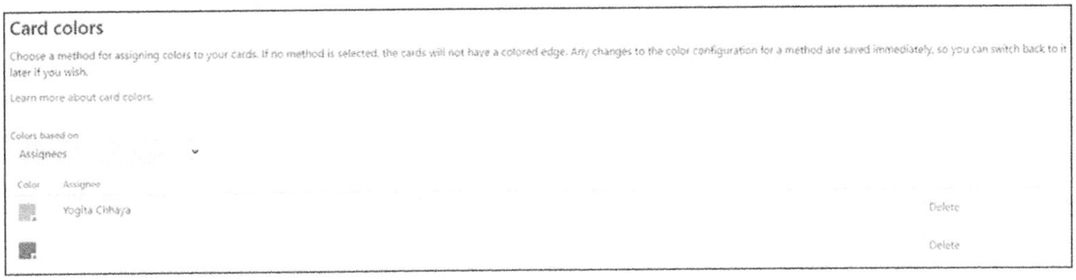

Figure 4.23: *Methods of Adding Card colors*

As shown in **Figure 4.24**, when configuring card colors based on **Assignee**, only two distinct colors are evident, representing the two distinct assignee types.

Figure 4.24: *Card colors based on Assignee*

Card Layout: Cards can be configured to show additional fields on the backlog and active sprints pages. For example, if you want to see the version of the issue you can select it for **Backlog** and **Active sprints** pages. You can also identify slow-moving issues based on the no. of days spent in the column which can be enabled as shown in *Figure 4.25*.

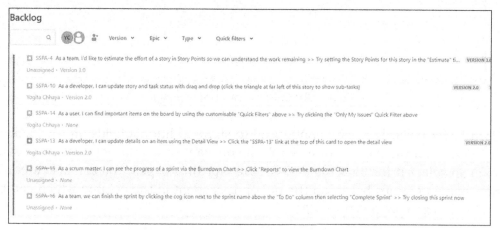

Figure 4.25: *Configuring Card Layout on the Board*

In this example, we've configured the `Issue color`, `Assignee`, and `Fix Versions` fields for the backlog view. This setup is visible in *Figure 4.26*, showcasing how **issue colors** are presented, and both the **Assignee and Fix Version fields** are prominently displayed on each individual issue.

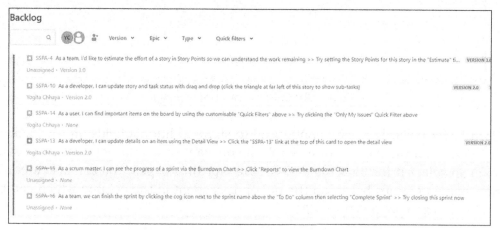

Figure 4.26: *Backlog page using Card Layout on the Board*

We've selected the **Resolution, Assignee,** and **Fix Version** fields for the active sprints view. This can be viewed in *Figure* 4.27 as well, illustrating how the chosen fields–**Resolution,** `Assignee`, and **Fix Version**–are shown on each issue, aligned with the selections made in the board settings.

Figure 4.27: Scrum board using Card Layout on the Board

Estimation: One can set the estimation criteria based on story points, original time estimate, and issue count. The velocity will be calculated based on these criteria.

Figure 4.28: Setting the Estimation Technique

Working days: You can set the `Region`, `Time zone`, `working days`, and `non-working dates` from this setting.

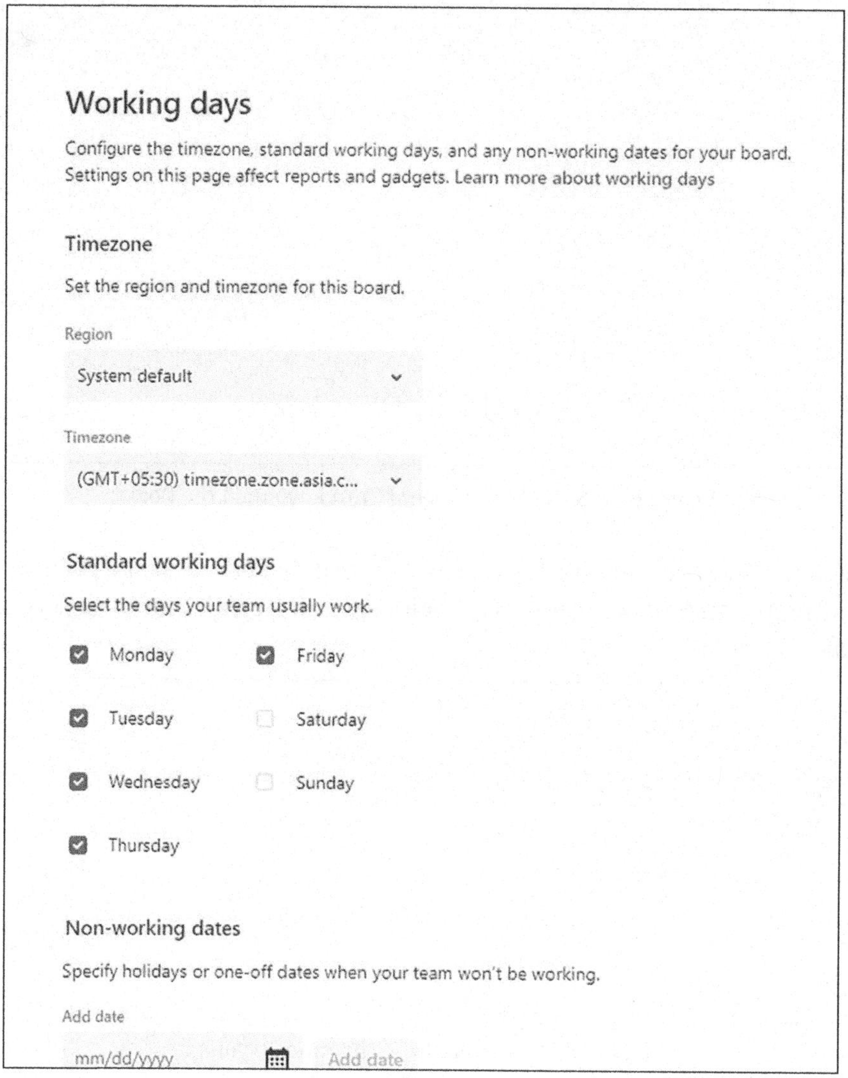

Figure 4.29: *Setting working/non-working days on the board*

Issue Detail View : You can **Add/Delete** the general fields, date fields, people, and links on the issue detail view.

Issue Detail View

⊙ **Layout in the new Jira issue view**

The order of fields in the new issue view is set for issue types in a project, so that issues have a consistent look across different project locations, like boards, backlogs, search, and the full-page issue view. To configure the layout of issue types in a project, go to **Project settings > Issue layout**.

Alternatively, and for issues on personal and multi-project boards, open an issue on the board and choose **... > Configure**.

Learn more about configuring the new issue view

Add, delete or reorder fields on the Issue Detail View.

Some fields may be hidden, depending on the field configuration scheme used for the project's issue types. Some fields may also be uneditable; to make a field editable, it must be added to the Edit Issue screen for the project of an issue.

General fields

Field name		
Category	⌄	Add
Story point estimate		Delete
Status		Delete
Priority		Delete

Figure 4.30: Configuring issue detail view

Timeline: You can enable the `Timeline` and set "child level issue". scheduling from this setting. From the timeline page, one can create, manage and visualize the epics, track the team's progress and map dependencies.

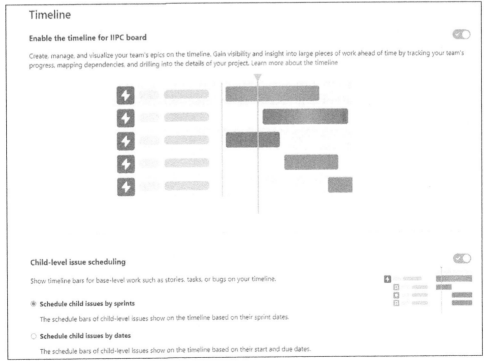

Figure 4.31: Enabling timeline settings from Board Configuration

Through the activation of the timeline feature in Jira, teams can plan their tasks using the timeline view, establish both parent and child issues, and define interdependencies. Enabling issue-linking is a prerequisite for utilizing the dependencies feature.

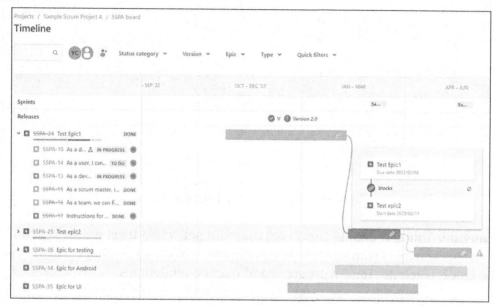

Figure 4.32: Enabling timeline settings from Board Configuration

Insights: One can manage settings such as `Sprint progress`, `Sprint burndown` and Epic `Progress` from insights. One can also do the backlog insights settings such as Sprint commitment, and issue type background from this setting.

Figure 4.33: *Setting insights features*

Users can access various parameters, such as issues requiring attention, **Sprint progress**, and **Epic progress**, as shown in *Figure 4.34* This capability helps the Scrum Master and the team in making informed decisions guided by data-driven insights on the board.

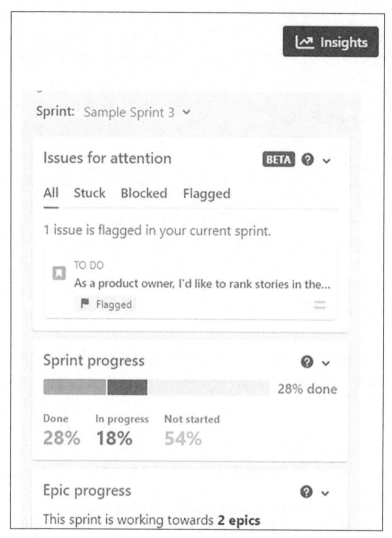

Figure 4.34: *Insights feature on the Board*

In a similar manner, Jira also provides insights within the backlog view. Users can observe parameters like sprint commitments and issue-type breakdowns. These insights prove invaluable for sprint planning, based on historical data to determine both commitment and where to allocate more attention across issue types.

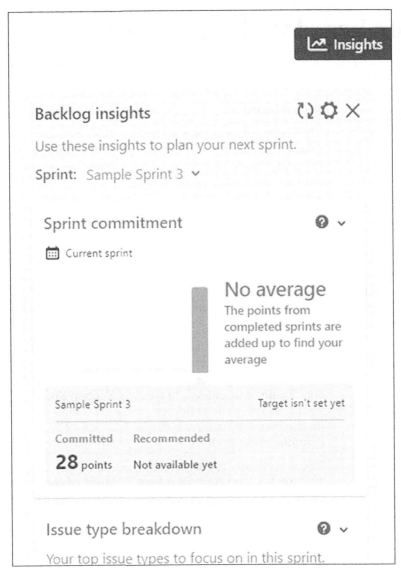

Figure 4.35: *Insights feature on the Backlog view*

Customizing Kanban board

From the customization perspective, Scrum and Kanban boards have similar features. All the features which are discussed in customizing the scrum board are applicable to the Kanban board. We will discuss the difference between scrum and Kanban boards in the next section.

Scrum board vs. Kanban board

The differences between Scrum and Kanban boards in Jira are listed in the following table.

	Scrum board	Kanban board
Planning	The issue created goes to the product backlog. Then after entering the details about estimation, priority, and so on, it goes to the 1st. sprint.	Each and every issue entered goes to the backlog column.
Sprints	The board view is for sprints and the issues in the active sprints appear on the board.	In Kanban, there are no sprints and all the issues entered appear on the board.
Commitment and priority	The team commits to completing a set of user stories within the sprint.	No commitment to specific items; priorities can change at any time.
Columns	Columns represent stages like "To Do," "In Progress," "Testing," and "Done." Any change in the workflow has to be reflected on the board by mapping the columns appropriately.	It is simpler to map the columns on Kanban Board.
Reports	There are many reports such as Burndown reports, Burn-up reports, Velocity reports and many more.	It also has similar kinds of reports. One of the important reports in Kanban is the Control chart.
Maintaining and updating Boards	It is a little demanding to maintain as there are time estimates involved.	Kanban boards are easier to maintain comparatively

Table 4.2: Scrum board vs. Kanban board

Both Scrum and Kanban boards in Jira serve different purposes and cater to different team preferences and project management approaches. The choice between them depends on the team's requirements and the nature of the project.

Conclusion

We are now familiar with how to create an issue, various ways to create issues and product backlog, Product backlog refining, and creating Epics, versions, stories, tasks, sprints and sprint operations. We also understood about creating scrum/Kanban boards and customizing boards.

In the next chapter, we will learn about Issue-types and Issue-type schemes.

Points to remember

Backlog management

- Writing correct user stories and including all the details is crucial.
- If necessary, user stories can be split into multiple tasks.
- Ensure that all issues are planned, estimated, and completed according to the plan.
- Estimation is done considering time, complexity, risk, and required effort.
- Prioritize the stories that offer the highest business value to the customer and then only take it for development.
- If you are uncertain about the details of user stories, ask the product owners for clarification.
- Group the stories in an epic to organize and track them.
- You can add new tasks, user stories, bugs, and features to the backlog based on changes in requirements and feedback received. This way, the backlog is a continuously evolving artifact.

Sprint Operations

- Once all the tasks are estimated and included in the sprint, plan the sprint for a duration of 2-4 weeks.
- Conduct daily stand-up meetings to plan daily work and address impediments with the help of the Scrum Master.
- Hold sprint planning and sprint review meetings to plan and review the work.
- At the end of each sprint, conduct a review meeting to demonstrate the completed work to stakeholders. Follow it up with a retrospective to identify areas for improvement in the next sprint.

Boards in Jira

- Use Kanban boards if you want to keep work flowing continuously. With the Kanban way of working, new tasks are taken up as soon as there's space for them.

- Use Scrum boards if your team works in fixed-length sprints. Scrum boards show the progress of each sprint on the board.

- Make sure to customize the boards to match your team's workflow. You can have stages like "To Do," "In Progress," "Review," and "Done."

- To organize and see the backlog items better, use filters and swim lanes. You can sort tasks based on who's working on them, their importance, or other criteria.

- Keep the boards always up-to-date. Team members should regularly update the status of their tasks. This way, everyone can see how things are going and if there are any issues.

Use cases with References

1. **Use case 1 – How to hide sub-tasks on Kanban Board:** To hide the sub-tasks on Kanban board, you can formulate a JQL (Jira Query Language) query that encompasses all issue types except for the 'sub-task' issue type within your project.

Link for reference:

https://community.atlassian.com/t5/Jira-Software-questions/Subtasks-on-kanban-board/qaq-p/2323195

2. **Use case 2 - Can I use both kinds of boards (Kanban, Scrum)** : Users have the capability to create both Scrum and Kanban boards within a single project. With a Scrum board, the option to generate sprints is available, whereas a Kanban board does not offer the ability to create sprints for work planning.

Link for reference:

https://community.atlassian.com/t5/Jira-questions/Can-I-use-both-kinds-of-boards-Kanban-Scrum/qaq-p/2019485

3. **Use case 3 – Can I convert the created Kanban board to Scrum board:** The kanban board cannot be directly converted into a scrum board. You have to create a new scrum board.

Link for reference:

https://community.atlassian.com/t5/Jira-Software-questions/Kanban-board
-to-scrum-Board/qaq-p/2187868

4. **Use case 4 - When the story moves to the next sprint, the story presents two sprints:** When a story moves to the next sprint, it can be searched by using a function called opensprints().

Link for reference:

https://community.atlassian.com/t5/Jira-Software-questions/When-the
-story-move-to-next-sprint-the-story-present-two-sprints/qaq-p/2450047

5. **Use case 5 - Spillover user story to next sprint:** When closing a sprint, Jira will prompt you to either transfer all incomplete stories to the next sprint or reassign them to the backlog. If chosen to move to the next sprint, the stories will retain their respective rankings.

Link for reference:

https://community.atlassian.com/t5/Jira-Software-questions/Spill-over
-user-story-to-next-sprint/qaq-p/1539800

6. **Use case 6 - How to enable sprints in Jira:** Sprint can be created when you create a   scrum project.

Link for reference:

https://community.atlassian.com/t5/Jira-Software-questions/how-to
-enable-sprints-in-our-project/qaq-p/2452632

7. **Use case 7 – Creating boards spread across projects** : There is an option in Jira to create a board from multiple projects.

https://community.atlassian.com/t5/Jira-Software-questions/Multiple
-projects-sharing-sprints/qaq-p/2141167

CHAPTER 5

Understanding Issue types and Issue type Schemes

Introduction

In Jira, issues are like the building blocks of project management. Issues represent different tasks, bugs, or things you want to work on. Each issue has a specific type, such as bug, task, or story, which tells you what it is about. The good thing is that you can customize these types as per your project requirements. Jira's issue-type schemes are helpful to organize and manage these issue types in a way that makes sense for your team. You can customize a list of tasks/issues for a particular project or multiple projects. You can perform move issues, link issues, clone issues, and log work on issues. Furthermore, you can set up workflows, control what information to fill in, and decide who can do what with each type of issue. It's like having the ability to keep your projects organized and running smoothly. So, with Jira's simple and flexible system, you can manage your work easily and get things done faster.

Structure

In this chapter, we will discuss the following topics:

- Understanding issues
- Issue Status, Priorities and Resolutions
- Understanding Parent and Child issues and issue-type hierarchy
- Creating issue-type hierarchy levels

- Examples of Jira Products Issue types
- Understanding issue types with an Example
- Configuring Issue types
- Creating sub-task issue type
- Understanding Issue-type schemes
- Associating an issue-type scheme with a project
- Understanding issue operations
- Components
- Issue Management Best Practices
- Points to Remember
- Use cases with Reference Links
- Conclusion

Understanding issues

Issues are work items on which the teams have to work. For example, an issue could be a task, bug, or Story. Issues can be created, edited, deleted, and linked to other issues in Jira. Issues can be used to track progress, manage dependencies, and communicate about work. An issue key is a number to identify an issue within a project. All issues in the same project will have the same issue-key with different nos. For example, an issue in the Sample Scrum Project has an issue-key SSP-1, SSP-2, SSP-3, and so on. Issue keys are unique and cannot be reused. This way, we can consider issues as building blocks of the project.

Issue-Status, Priority and Resolutions

You can manage issue Statuses, Priorities and Resolutions as a Jira Administrator. In this section we have covered how to add or modify issue-status, priority and resolutions in Jira.

Issue-Status: Statuses represent the various steps within a workflow, each of which can be mapped to one of the workflow steps. A workflow has multiple statuses. Jira provides default statuses when you create a project from a project template. As a Jira Administrator, you can create, edit and delete statuses within the workflow to align with your defined processes. Jira software has statuses such as **Open, In Progress, Reopened, Resolved, Closed**, and so on, depending on the type of projects you have created. *Figure* 5.1 Shows some of the statuses along with their descriptions.

Steps to add, edit and delete Statuses in Jira:

1. Log in to your Jira instance with administrative privileges.

2. Navigate to the issue section by selecting gear icon and click on **ISSUE ATTRIBUTES.**

3. Select Statuses and click on **Add Status/Edit**.

4. Add the **Name**, **Description**, **Category** and icon **URL** of the image.

5. Select **Add**.

Issues				
Statuses		Add status	Translate statuses	
Name	Category	Workflows	Order	Actions
Open The issue is open and ready for the assignee to start work on it.	To Do	14 associated workflows	↓	Edit
In Progress This issue is being actively worked on at the moment by the assignee.	In Progress	41 associated workflows	↑ ↓	Edit
Reopened This issue was once resolved, but the resolution was deemed incorrect. From here issues are either marked assigned or resolved.	To Do	3 associated workflows	↑ ↓	Edit
Resolved A resolution has been taken, and it is awaiting verification by reporter. From here issues are either reopened, or are closed.	Done	6 associated workflows	↑ ↓	Edit
Closed The issue is considered finished, the resolution is correct. Issues which are closed can be reopened.	Done	3 associated workflows	↑ ↓	Edit
Building Source code has been committed, and JIRA is waiting for the code to be built before moving to the next status.	In Progress	1 associated workflow	↑ ↓	Edit
Build Broken The source code committed for this issue has possibly broken the build.	In Progress	1 associated workflow	↑ ↓	Edit
To Do	To Do	19 associated workflows	↑ ↓	Edit
Done	Done	38 associated workflows	↑ ↓	Edit
Backlog	To Do	9 associated workflows	↑ ↓	Edit

Figure 5.1: *Issue Statuses in Jira*

Issue-Priority: An issue's priority reflects how important it is. Organizations can define and describe priority levels according to their needs. Jira has default priority levels: **Lowest**, **Low**, **Medium**, **High** and **Highest.**

Steps to add priorities in Jira:

1. Log in to your Jira instance with administrative privileges.

2. Navigate to the issue section by selecting gear icon and click on **ISSUE ATTRIBUTES**.

3. Select **Priorities**.

4. Add the **Name**, **Description** of the priority, **URL** of the image and priority color.

5. Select **Add**.

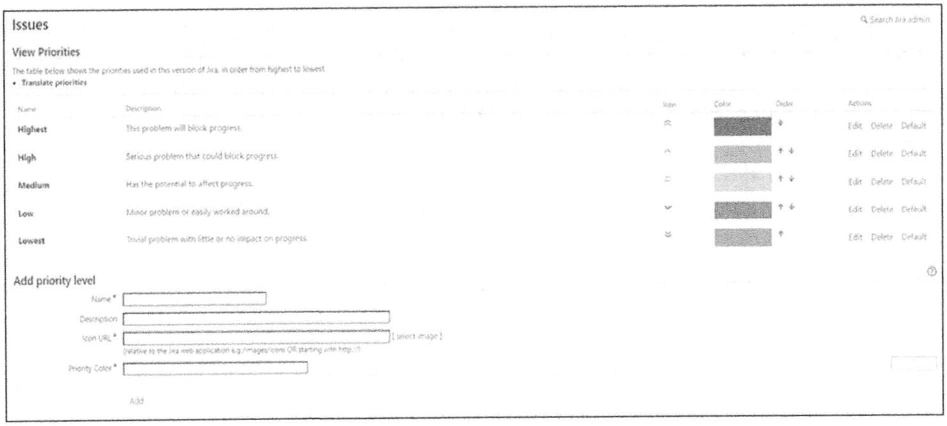

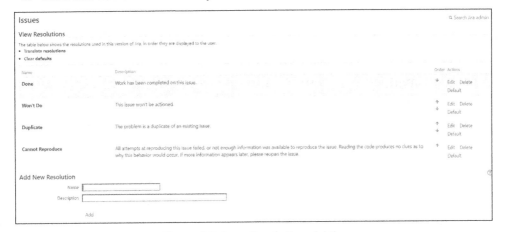

Figure 5.2: Issue Priorities in Jira

Issue-Resolutions: An issue can be considered resolved or closed in various ways. Resolutions are the available methods in which an issue can be marked as closed.

These methods include options such as **Done**, **Won't fix**, **Duplicate** and more.

Steps to add resolutions in Jira:

1. Log in to your Jira instance with administrative privileges.

2. Navigate to the issue section by selecting gear icon and click on **ISSUE ATTRIBUTES**.

3. Select **Resolutions**.

4. Add the **Name** and **Description** of the resolutions and then select **Add**.

Figure 5.3: Issue Resolutions in Jira

Understanding Parent and Child issues and issue-type hierarchy

Parent and child issues are used to relate bigger issues with smaller ones. For example, a story is a parent issue with some sub-tasks created under it. The sub-tasks are called child issues. Parent issues are larger or more complex issues, while child issues are smaller or less complex issues that are related to the parent issue. All issues can be a parent issue as well as a child issue. Sub-tasks cannot be created as a parent issue.

Let us understand the issue-type hierarchy with an example.

If the issue-type hierarchy is

- Epic
- Story
- Task
- Sub-task
- Bug

Then,

- Sub-tasks can be created as child issues under any of the higher-level issues: **Epic**, **Story**, **Bug**, or **Task**.
- Story, Bug, task, and Sub-task can be created under Epic.
- Sub-task can't be created as a parent issue, because sub-tasks are always related to a parent issue.

Creating issue-type hierarchy levels

Select ✿ > **Issues**. Select **Issue-type** hierarchy. By default, the **Epic** issue type will be associated with the Epic hierarchy level (level 1). You can create new levels by selecting create levels, as shown in *Figure* 5.4. Change the level names of the issue-type hierarchy and save the changes. It is only possible to change and add hierarchy levels as part of Jira Software Cloud Premium and Enterprise.

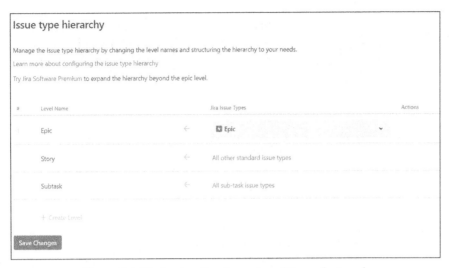

Figure 5.4: *Understanding Issue-type Hierarchy Levels*

Examples of Jira Products Issue types

In this section, we will learn about important issue types in Jira Software and Jira Service Management. Similarly, Jira work management also has various types of issues.

Jira Software-Software Projects	Issue type	
	Epic	It represents a big amount of work, such as a feature. It is required to break it down into smaller issue types such as story, Bug, task, and so on
	Bug	It is a problem in software products, which prevents its working
	Story	A user story is the unit of work that is worked upon and completed in the same sprint
	Task	It is a piece of work that needs to be done

	Sub-task	It is a child issue type that can be created under standard issue types like bug, story, and task
Jira Service Management	IT help	It is a task to create a request for IT-related help
	Incident	Reporting an incident or IT service outage
	Service Request	Request to get help from the internal or external customer service team
	Service Request with Approval	Request to get help from customer service with approval from the Manager

Table 5.1: Examples of Jira products Issue types

Understanding issue types with an Example

Epic: It represents a large amount of work. It is required to break it down into smaller issue types such as story, Bug, task, etc.

In this example, we have created a scrum project in Jira to develop an app for Banking Application. We have created an Epic-User Interface for Banking Application Development, which involves a large amount of work. *Figure 5.5* shows various child issues, such as **Stories**, **Tasks**, and **Bugs**, created under the Epic. By default, an Epic in Jira has the fields like **Assignee**, **reporter**, **story points**, **priority**, and so on, and it is possible to customize the fields on the Epic screen.

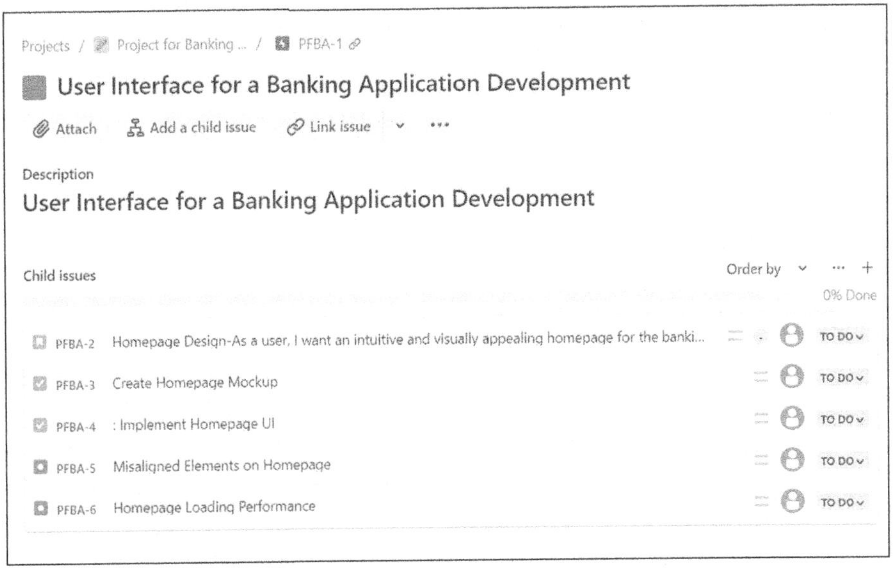

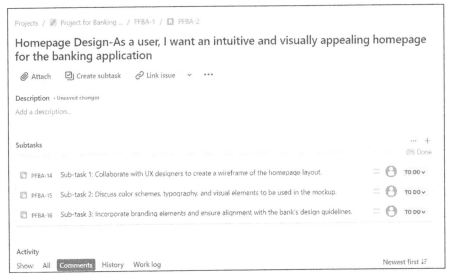

Figure 5.5: *Example of an Issue-type Epic with Child issues*

Story: A story is a smaller task that can be completed in a single sprint. It is written in non-technical language to describe the customer's requirements. You can create a sub-task under a story. The story has been written in a standard format and mentions the requirement as a user in the bank application. *Figure 5.6* illustrates the creation of three sub-tasks under a story. By default, a story in Jira has fields like `Assignee`, `reporter`, `story points`, `sprint`, `priority`, etc., and it is possible to customize the fields on the Story.

Figure 5.6: Example of an Issue-type Story with Sub-tasks

Bug: It is a problem within a software product that prevents its working.

In this example, we have created a bug `Misaligned Elements on Homepage`. If necessary, you can also divide the bug into sub-tasks, as shown in *Figure* 5.7.

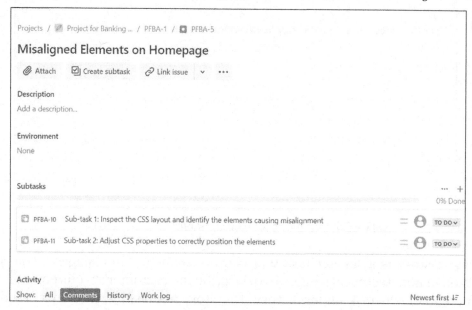

Figure 5.7: *Example of an Issue-type Bug with Sub-tasks*

Task: It is a piece of work that needs to be done. It can be a technical or non-technical task. However, it has to be completed in the same sprint.

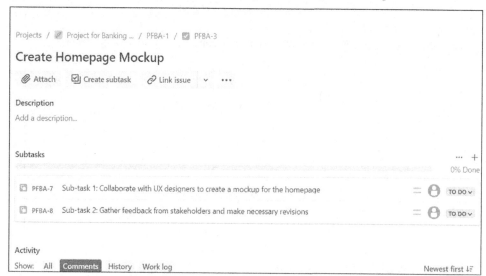

Figure 5.8: *Example of an Issue-type Task with Sub-tasks*

Configuring issue types

To add and Configure issue types, you must be a Jira Administrator with Administer Jira permission.

Each Jira product has a predefined set of issues as per the need of your team and project requirements. In software development projects, examples of issue types include **Bug**, **Story**, and **Tasks**. Similarly, in IT service projects in Jira service Management, examples of issue types include IT Help, task, and service request. Upon creating an issue, you can view various options for issue types.

Figure 5.9: *Creating issues in JSM*

In *Figure* 5.10, you can view the issue types: **Bug**, **Story**, **Epic**, and **Task**. These are the issue types in Jira software.

Figure 5.10: *Creating issues in Jira Software*

Steps to add an issue type in Jira:

1. Select ⚙ >`Issues`. Select `Add issue type`.

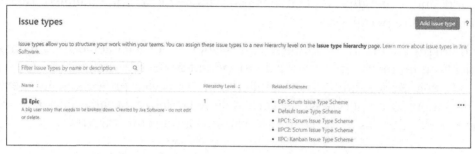

Figure 5.11: Step-1 of Adding new issue types in Jira

2. Now you can add issue types as per your project requirement. For example, you can add an issue type like **Suggestion**. Issue types can be either `Standard Issue Type` or `Sub-task Issue Types`. Select the standard issue type and then click on `Add`.

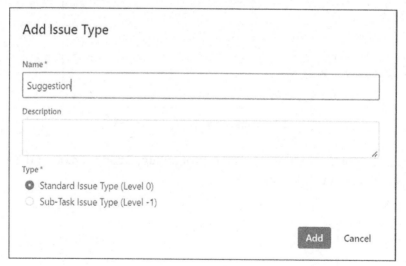

Figure 5.12: Step-2 of Adding new issue types in Jira

You can edit, delete, and translate issue types as follows:

- **Editing:** By editing the issue types, you can change the name of the issue type, description, and avatar.

- **Deleting:** By deleting an issue type, it is permanently deleted. So, make sure to change all the existing issues to other issue types. Then you can delete an issue type.

- **Translating**: Using this page, you can add issue-type translations for the installed languages. It is possible to add a name and description for the other languages.

Creating Sub-task Issue type

Jira has a feature to create generic sub-tasks, which are usually created as a child issue. In addition, you can also customize subtask issues in Jira.

For example, a software team has to create Design, Coding, Testing, and Release tasks for each software development task. You can add all these subtasks as a sub-task issue type as follows:

1. Select ✿ >Issues.

2. Select **Sub-task** from the left navigation bar.

3. Select **Add sub-task issue type**.

In this manner, you can create multiple sub-tasks under a main task, such as story or task.

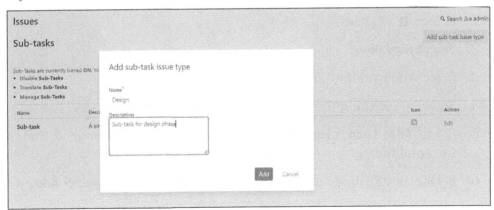

Figure 5.13: *Adding new sub-task issue types in Jira*

Enabling/Disabling Sub-task

By default, sub-tasks are enabled. You can Enable or Disable subtasks as explained in the following steps. You cannot disable subtasks if there are a few sub-tasks already created.

- Select ✿ >Issues.
- Select **Sub-tasks**.
- **Enable/Disable Sub-tasks**.

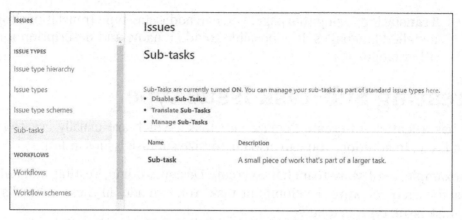

Figure 5.14: *Enable/Disable/Manage sub-task issue types in Jira*

Adding conditions on workflow based on a sub-task status

You can create a workflow with a condition based on the status of the sub-task. This condition can be added to the issue transition. It will not allow the parent task to be resolved until all the sub-tasks are resolved. The steps to implement this condition are as follows:

1. Select ✿ >`Issues`.

2. Select `Workflows`.

3. Select the workflow and go to `Edit`.

4. Select a transition to resolve and click `Conditions`.

5. Select `Add Condition`, `Sub-task Blocking Condition`, and then `Add` the condition.

6. Select the sub-task statuses (`Resolved`, `Done`) and then select `Add`.

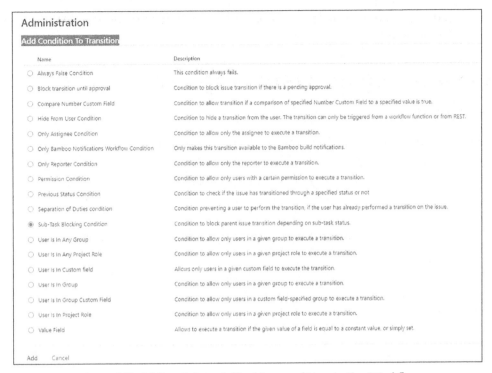

Figure 5.15: *Adding Sub-task Blocking condition in Jira Workflow*

We will understand the workflows in detail in *Chapter 7, Configuring work-flows in Jira*.

Understanding Issue-type schemes

Issue-type schemes allow you to create a list of issue types that are applicable to a project. This list of issue types will be available while creating an issue and is referred to as an issue-type scheme.

The advantages are as follows:

- Select the right type of issues in a project.
- Select the default issue types and set a sequence of issue types while creating an issue.
- Share the same list of issue types across the same type of projects.
- Helpful to Administrators to maintain the issue types with respect to projects.

You can set up an issue-type scheme having a standard set of issue types and then associate it with a project. Subsequently, you can also add some issue types and then use the same scheme. This provides flexibility to add issue types as and when it is required.

Associating an issue-type scheme with a project

A Jira administrator can associate an issue-type scheme with a project. It can also be selected by a project administrator. In the following steps, we will learn how to associate an issue-type scheme with a project:

1. Select ✿ > `Issues`.

2. Select `Issue-type scheme`. And select `Add Issue-type Scheme`.

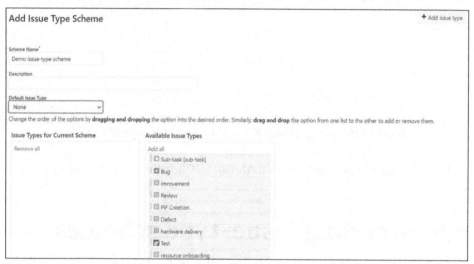

Figure 5.16: *Creating a new issue-type scheme*

3. You can drag and drop the available issue type into the list of issue types for the current scheme.

4. Select **Save**.

5. Now you are ready with the new issue-type scheme.

6. You can also select the default issue type on this page.

7. The default issue type can be seen while creating a new issue.

Add Issue Type Scheme

Scheme Name
Demo issue-type scheme

Description

Default Issue Type

None	⌄

None
Bug
Review
resource onboarding

...ging and dropping the option into the desired order. Similarly, **drag and**

Available Issue Types

Remove all   Add all

- Review   Sub-task (sub-task)
- Bug   imrovement
- resource onboarding   PIF Creation
                                  Defect
                                  hardware delivery

Figure 5.17: Setting default issue types and adding new issue types in a scheme

Once an issue-type scheme is created, Jira Administrator can associate it with a project.

Steps to associate an issue-type scheme with a project:

1. Select ⚙ > `issues`.

2. Select `issue-type scheme`.

3. Select `Associate` from the ••• on the right-hand side.

4. Select the project from the list, as shown in *Figure 5.18*, and associate it.

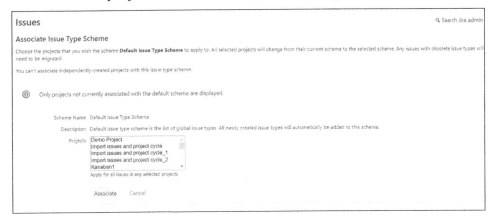

Issues   🔍 Search Jira admin

Associate Issue Type Scheme

Choose the projects that you wish the scheme **Default Issue Type Scheme** to apply to. All selected projects will change from their current scheme to the selected scheme. Any issues with obsolete issue types will need to be migrated.

You can't associate independently-created projects with this issue type scheme.

ⓘ   Only projects not currently associated with the default scheme are displayed.

Scheme Name   Default Issue Type Scheme

Description   Default issue type scheme is the list of global issue types. All newly created issue types will automatically be added to this scheme.

Projects   Demo Project
            Import issues and project cycle
            Import issues and project cycle_1
            Import issues and project cycle_2
            Kanaban1
            Apply for all issues in any selected projects

            Associate   Cancel

Figure 5.18: Associating an issue-type scheme with a project

Associating an issue-type scheme from Project-settings:

The issue-type scheme can also be associated with a project from the project settings, as mentioned in the following steps:

1. Select a project.

2. Select **Project Settings**.

3. Select **Issues** and select **Actions** on the right-hand side.

4. Select use a different scheme.

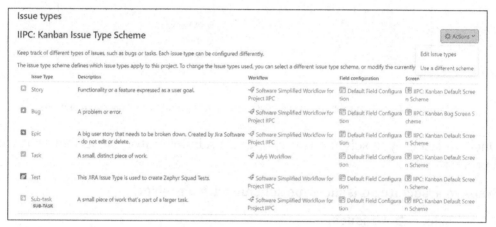

Figure 5.19: *Associating an issue-type scheme with a project from project settings*

Understanding Issue Operations

In this section, we will learn about some basic issue operations such as issue-linking, cloning an issue, logging work on an issue, and moving an issue.

- **Issue-linking:** When creating an issue, you can define relationships between issues, such as is blocked by, is cloned by, duplicate issues, and so on.

Figure 5.20: *Understanding Issue-linking*

- **Moving issues:** It is featured in Jira to move issues from one project to another project. Moving issues should be done only if it is required in some situations, such as issues created in the wrong project. It is better to give **move issue permission** to specific individuals, as moving issues randomly can create problems for everyone.

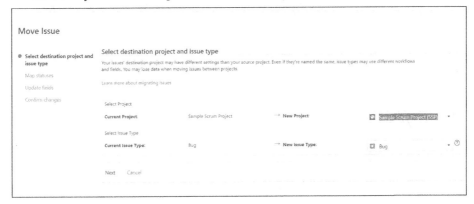

Figure 5.21: *Understanding Moving Issues*

- **Cloning issues:** Cloning helps you to duplicate an issue within the same project, copying most information from an issue, like the **Summary** and **Description** fields and more. Cloned issues are created as separate issues from the original issue.

Figure 5.22: *Understanding cloning issues*

- **Logging work on issues**: As shown in *Figures* 5.23 and 5.24 you can select Log work from the ⋯ icon on the right-hand side. And then enter the time in a standard format (2w4d3h40m).

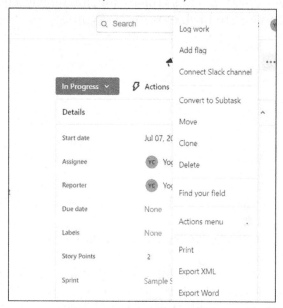

Figure 5.23: *Selecting Log work*

After selecting **Log work**, as shown in *Figure* 5.22, you can enter the details.

Figure 5.24: *Logging work on Jira Issue*

You can comment on an issue, enter an estimation, label an issue, and assign an issue to the assignee.

Components

Components are used to define sub-modules in a project. For example, for a Banking application, User Authentication, Reporting and Analytics, Mobile Banking are sub-modules. You can create components as a Jira Administrator.

To create components,

1. Navigate to project sidebar, select **Project Settings** > **Components**

2. Click on **Create Component**.

3. Enter the details such as **Name, Description, Component Lead** and **Default Assignee.**

Figure 5.25: *Components in Jira*

To Edit or Delete components,

1. Navigate to the ⬛ icon on the right side.

2. Click on ⬛ and select **Edit** or **Delete**.

Issue Management Best Practices

Jira has been used by many organizations for many years. Here are the best practices for issue management in Jira:

1. Choose the appropriate issue type (**Story**, **Bug**, **Task**, and so on) that accurately represents the work item.

2. Provide a clear description of the task to ensure a common understanding among team members. Include details like estimation and due date.

3. Assign tasks to the relevant team members and fill in the reporter field.

4. Set the priority field based on the task's urgency and importance.

5. Avoid adding excessive details in Jira that might confuse teams. Provide concise and relevant information about the task.

6. Utilize labels to categorize issues and components to assign issues to specific parts of the project.

7. Develop a habit of commenting on issues to share progress updates, challenges, and solutions. Comments also enhance collaboration

8. Enter all necessary details such as Story Points, issue-links, Fix versions wherever applicable.

9. Enable time tracking and ensure regular work log entries. This helps in generating reports and metrics analysis.

10. Utilize the attachment feature in Jira but avoid attaching excessively large files. Attach important files that provide essential issue details.

11. Integrate Jira with third party add-ons to access advanced features for project management, source code management and documentation.

12. Utilize bulk-editing whenever necessary to manage multiple issues efficiently.

Conclusion

We are now familiar with how to create an issue type, examples of issue types in Jira Software and Jira Service Management, child and parent issues, important issue operations, creating a new issue-type scheme, and associating an issue-type scheme with a project.

In the next chapter, we will learn about customizing screens and screen-schemes.

Points to Remember

- Issue types are the work items in Jira such as Task, Bug, Story, and so on.
- There are two types of issues in Jira: Standard issue types and Sub-task issue types.
- While customizing issue types, do not add too many issue types to avoid confusion.
- There are some custom issue types provided in Jira. Utilize these as per the requirement of your team or project.
- If you want to create new issue types, analyze the workflow and process of the organization and then create new issue types.
- Sub-tasks are for very small pieces of work. Use sub-tasks to divide the bigger tasks into very small tasks. Sub-tasks are child issues and do not create them as individual tasks.
- Issue-type schemes are a combination of multiple issues and are used to associate a group of issue types with a project.
- Review the issue-type schemes regularly and update the same.
- Communicate with everyone in the team about the right usage of the tasks and sub-tasks.
- To add and Configure issue types and issue-type schemes and to associate it with a project, you must be a Jira Administrator with "Administer Jira" permission.

Use cases with Reference Links

1. What are the issue type schemes best practices while associating a new issue type scheme with a project- Refer the link to understand in detail.

https://community.atlassian.com/t5/Jira-Software-questions/issue-type-schemes-best-practices/qaq-p/2283656

2. If I remove an issue type from a Workflow Scheme, will the past issues be deleted? -Read all the details on the link provided

https://community.atlassian.com/t5/Jira-Software-questions/If-I-remove-an-issue-type-from-a-Workflow-Scheme-will-the-past/qaq-p/2324428

3. Is there any effect if we remove the "Issue type Schemes" that are not associated with any project in Jira cloud. – You can delete Issue type Schemes" that are not associated with any project in Jira cloud.

https://community.atlassian.com/t5/Jira-Software-questions/Issue-Type-scheme-deletion/qaq-p/1599984

4. Default issue types - bug issue type missing.- If bug issue-type is missing, it has to be created once again.

https://community.atlassian.com/t5/Jira-Software-questions/Default-issue-types-bug-issue-type-missing/qaq-p/2425067

5. How to separate an issue type scheme and field scheme which are shared between projects?- Refer the link to understand in detail.

https://community.atlassian.com/t5/Jira-questions/How-to-separate-an-issue-types-scheme-and-field-scheme-which-are/qaq-p/2203767

6. Can we set up an issue type "xyz" above issue type "Epic"?- Refer the link to read detailed answer.

https://community.atlassian.com/t5/Jira-Software-questions/Can-you-please-advise-how-we-can-set-up-an-issue-type-quot-xyz/qaq-p/2283828

7. When I have selected an Epic, I can create one or many sub issues (Task or Stories) but when I have a Feature (the new issue type) I can add one or many sub issues but only of issue type task, can I change that so that I can add one or many sub issues (Task or Epics) – It is only possible to change and add hierarchy levels as part of Jira Software Cloud Premium and Enterprise. It is possible to add the issue level above Epic in Jira Advanced Roadmap. - Refer to the link to read a detailed answer.

https://community.atlassian.com/t5/Jira-Software-questions/Issue-types/qaq-p/1939411

8. Why are Issue Types missing from Backlog `+ Create issue` mini -dropdown- Refer the link to read detailed answer.

https://community.atlassian.com/t5/Jira-Software-questions/Why-are
-Issue-Types-missing-from-Backlog-Create-issue-mini/qaq-p/2253730

9. Associating an Issue Type Screen scheme to a project- Refer the link to read a detailed answer.

https://community.atlassian.com/t5/Jira-questions/Associating-an-Issue
-Type-Screen-scheme-to-a-project/qaq-p/2431392

10. Unable to comment on Jira Issues

https://community.atlassian.com/t5/Jira-questions/Unable-to-comment-on
-Jira-Issues/qaq-p/1922904

CHAPTER 6

Customizing Fields, Field Configuration schemes, Screens, and Screen schemes

Introduction

Jira is a project management tool in which you can add fields, customize screens, and create custom screen schemes as per your project's requirements. In this chapter, we will learn about how to add a custom field to create different screens. It can be of different types, such as Text fields, Numeric Fields, and many more. A screen is made up of system fields and custom fields. It is used to enter data from the users. A combination of screens to create, edit, and view issues are known as Screen schemes. These screen schemes can be associated with an issue and with a project.

Structure

In this chapter, we will cover the following topics:

- Understanding fields and creating custom fields
- Types of custom fields in Jira with Examples
- Adding context to a custom field
- Locked custom fields

- Understanding Field Configuration
- Field Configuration Scheme with an Example
- Understanding Screens
- Creating Screen Schemes, Issue-type screen schemes, and associating them with a Project
- Use-cases of Screens and Screen schemes
- Conclusion
- Points to Remember
- References

Understanding Fields and Creating Custom Fields

Fields are an important part of Jira, as it allows users to enter information and generate reports based on it. Let us understand how you can create new custom fields and associate the same with screens.

Note: To customize all the fields and screen schemes, you have to log in as a Jira Administrator with Administer Jira Global Permission

Creating custom fields in Jira:

1. Select ⚙ > **Issues**.

2. Under **FIELDS**, select **Custom Fields**.

3. Select **Custom Fields** and click on **Create Custom field**.

4. In this **example**, we will create a custom field named severity. **Severity** has 4 levels: **Blocker**, **Critical**, **Major**, and **Minor**.

5. Select a field type such as **Select List** - single choice, as shown in *Figure 6.1*.

Figure 6.1: Creating Custom-field Select-list (Single-choice)

6. Enter the levels as **Blocker**, **Critical**, **Major**, and **Minor**, and then select **Create**.

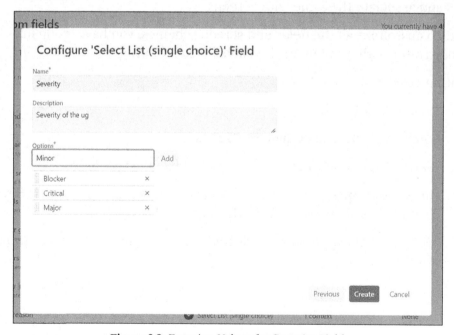

Figure 6.2: Entering Values for Severity Field

7. You can associate it with Bug Screens, as shown in *Figure 6.3*. Now the severity field will appear on the screens, which are associated with the field.

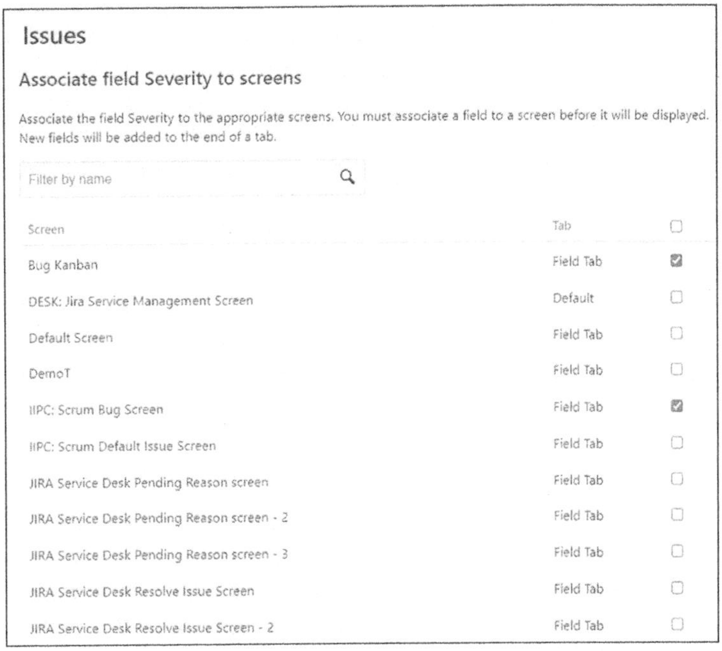

Figure 6.3: *Associating Severity field to Screens*

Types of Custom Fields in Jira with Examples

There are mainly two types of Custom fields in Jira as follows:

- Standard Custom Field
- Advanced Custom Field

Table 6.1 lists both the types of Custom fields and how they can be used.

	Types of Custom Field	How it is used
Standard Custom Field	Checkboxes	Choose multiple values using checkboxes. Checkboxes allow people to select multiple options for a list to complete the field. Checkbox fields help with data entry by reducing entry errors that could appear in free-form text fields, for example. They also increase correct completions by limiting the options a person has to complete the field.

	Date Picker	A custom field that stores dates and uses a date picker to view them. Date picker fields allow people to provide date information using a calendar selection to complete the field. People can also complete the field by typing dates into the field.
	Date Time Picker	A custom field that stores dates with a time component. Like date picker fields, date time picker fields allow people to provide time of day information using a calendar and dropdown time selector to complete the field. Time fields have two input areas: one to specify the date, and one to specify the time.
	Labels	Add labels to issues.Label fields allow people to tag issues with reusable text snippets entered as free form text. Jira suggests existing labels to help reduce entry errors. People can also create new labels by typing into the label field.
	Numeric Field	A field that stores and validates numeric input. Number fields allow people to provide numerical information as free-form text. A single line text box allows people to complete the field with a number. People can safely enter numbers between -1 trillion and 1 trillion (100,000,000,000,000). Note: Jira rounds decimals to the nearest 1000th place. For example, 5.555555 will be rounded to 5.556. People can enter large numbers using scientific notation. For example, the number 5,000 can be entered as 5e3.

	Radio Buttons	A list of radio buttons. Radio buttons allow people to select a single option from a list to complete the field. Radio buttons help with data entry by reducing entry errors that could appear in free-form text fields, for example. They also increase correct completions by limiting the options a person must complete the field.
	Select list (Cascading)	Choose multiple values using two select lists. Cascading select fields allow people to narrow their selection list by branching select fields into parents and children options. People select an option from the parent dropdown list and are presented with that options sub-list to select from. Cascading select fields help categorize options in a select list and reduce the number of choices needed to complete the field correctly.
	Select list (multiple choice)	Choose multiple values in a select list
	Select list (single choice)	A single select list with a configurable list of options
	Short text (plain text only)	The short text(up to 255 characters) field is commonly used to add context, organize the issues, or to provide information to the team. For more complex formatting, use the paragraph custom field.
	URL Field	People use this field to input a single URL.
	User Picker (Single User)	Choose a user from the user base via a pop-up picker window
	Paragraph ()	This field is used for longer text. It is a multiline text field which supports rich text format, such as URLs, bold, underlined, etc.

Advanced Custom Field		
	Date of first response	The date of the first comment on an issue by anyone other than the reporter
	Days since last comment	Date/time since last comment (restricted comments are considered on a per user basis). This field is not searchable or sortable.
	Domain of Assignee	The Assignee' 's domain name
	Domain of Reporter	The Reporter' 's domain name
	Global Rank	Global rank field for Jira Software use only
	Global picker (multiple groups)	Select multiple user groups using a popup picker window
	Global picker (Single group)	Select a user group using a popup picker window
	Last commented by a User Flag	Shows "true" if the latest commenter is not a member of the Jira developer group (jira-developers).
	Last public comment date	Date and time of the most recent public comment (excluding restricted comments). This field *is* searchable and sortable.
	Message Custom Field (for edit)	A custom field whose default value will be displayed as HTML or as rendered wiki markup in OnDemand on an 'Edit' screen.
	Message Custom Field (for view)	A custom field whose default value will be displayed as HTML or as rendered wiki markup in OnDemand on the 'View' screen.
	Number of attachments	A specialized field that stores the count of attachments linked to an issue.
	Number of comments	A custom field designed to hold the count of comments associated with an issue.

	Participants of an issue	Shows the reporter, current assignee, and everyone who has commented on the issue.
	Project picker (single project)	Select from projects accessible to the user within the system.
	Team	Link issues with a particular team.
	A read-only text label	A text label that is view-only, allowing values to be generated programmatically (Used internally for imports from Mantis). Maximum of 255 characters.
	Time in status	Store statistics about the number of time/times an issue has spent/been in its statuses. This field generates the Average Number of Times Spent in Status and Average Time Spent in Status charts.
	User Picker (multiple users)	Select multiple users from the user base using a popup picker window.
	User Property Field (<255 characters)	A read-only custom-field that displays a user property.
	Name of last updater or commenter	Show the name of the most recent updater or commenter depending on the latest activity.
	Version Picker (multiple version)	Select a version from the options accessible within the project.
	Version Picker (single version)	Select one version from the options provided within the project.

Table 6.1: Types of Custom fields (source: https://support.atlassian.com/jira-cloud-administration/docs/custom-fields-types-in-company-managed-projects/)

Examples of adding Custom fields

In this section, we will learn about how to add custom fields in Jira and how they can be helpful.

1. **Adding Date-time picker field:**

   • Select ⚙ > **Issues.**

   • Select **Custom fields** and click on **Create Custom field.**

- Select the standard option: **Date Time Picker.**
- Add the Custom field and associate it with screens as per the project's requirement.

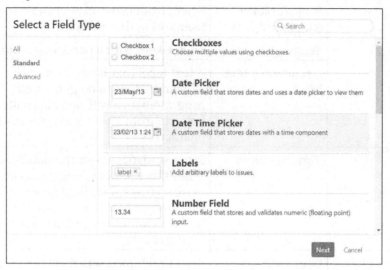

Figure 6.4: *Adding Date Time Picker Field*

After adding the field, check for the functionality of the custom field. This field is used to select both date and time.

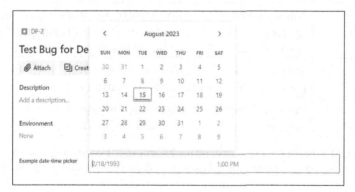

Figure 6.5: *Example of Date and Time Picker field View*

2. **Adding Username of last Updater/Commenter field**

- Select ⚙ > **Issues**.
- Select **Custom fields** and click on **Create Custom field.**
- Go to the **Advanced** option on the left-hand side and select **Date Time Picker**.

- Add a Custom field and associate it with screens as per your requirement.

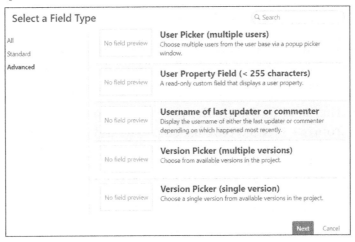

Figure 6.6: *Adding Advanced Custom Field*

After adding the field, check for the functionality of the custom field. This field is used to check the username who updated or commented on an issue.

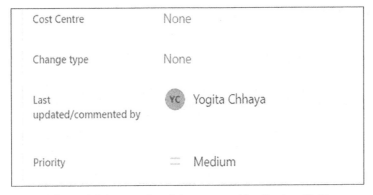

Figure 6.7: *Last updated/commented by Custom Field*

Adding Context to a Custom Field

In Jira, custom fields allow you to capture and store additional information beyond the default fields provided by the system. Adding context to Jira custom fields means providing extra information or specifying the purpose of the field, which helps users understand how to use and interpret the field's values. Contextual information can include descriptions, examples, guidelines, and explanations that help users in filling out the field correctly.

Let us understand the concept of adding context to a Jira custom field using the example of a **Change Type** field.

Example: Custom Field–Change Type

Context: The **Change Type** field is used to classify the nature and significance of changes being made to a project or system. It helps in understanding the purpose and impact of the change.

Description: This field indicates the type of change being introduced. Please select the appropriate change type based on the definitions provided.

You can create a new custom field context if it is required to associate different default values and options with different projects or issue types.

The step-by-step process to add context is as follows:

1. Select ✿ > **Issues**.

2. Select **Custom fields** under **Fields**.

3. Select the custom field to which you want to add a new context. On the same page, go to ▪▪▪ on the right side and select **Contexts** and default value > **Add new context**.

4. Enter a label and description for the new context. These are not for the end- users but it is for administrator's reference only.

5. When selecting the applicable issue types, choose the issue types that you want this custom field to appear in.

6. In the section for applicable contexts, choose either a global context or specific projects that you want this custom field to appear in. The custom field will only appear on issues types you have selected.

7. Select **Add.**

After configuring a custom field, you'll have to specify on which screens it should be displayed.

In *Figure* 6.8, we have added a new context for the **Change Type** custom field.

Figure 6.8: *Adding context to Custom Field Change Type*

In this example, the custom field **Change Type** is provided with context to help users understand its purpose and how to select the appropriate value.

The change type can be viewed on the create screen as per the issues and projects selected while setting the contexts. If it is set for **Global Context**, it is applied to all issues in Jira.

Figure 6.9: *Change Type Custom field on Create Screen*

Locked Custom Fields

Some specific custom fields are created when Jira products are installed. These fields are also created while Jira add-ons are installed. For example, a Sprint field is created when Jira software is installed. These specific custom fields are locked. It cannot be configured, but you can add these fields to screens and view the field details.

To view field information or associate them with screens:

1. Select ⚙ > `Issues`.

2. Select `Custom Fields` under `Fields`.

3. Go to ▦ on the right side and select the right option.

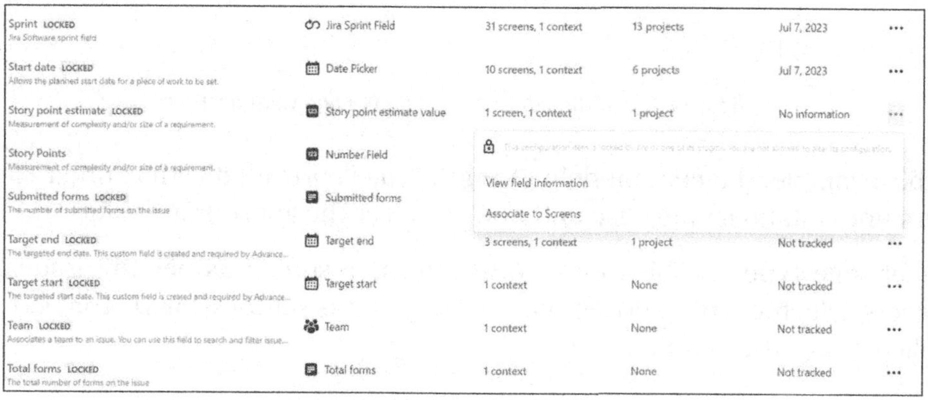

Figure 6.10: *Locked Fields in Jira*

In *Figure* 6.10, some fields are locked, whereas others such as Story Points are not locked.

Understanding Field Configuration

In Jira, a field configuration allows you to set the field's behavior. You can set this for both issue fields and custom fields.

It allows you to set:

- The description of the field that appears at the time of editing.
- Keep the field visible or hidden.
- Make the field required or optional.
- Decide the renderer to use for text fields.

Figure 6.11: *Configuring Fields*

Hide option: If a field is set as hidden in the field configuration, you will not be able to view the field in the issue view.

Required option: If the field is set as the required field, the user has to enter some value while creating it. So, if that field is not there on the project's screen, it may create problems for you.

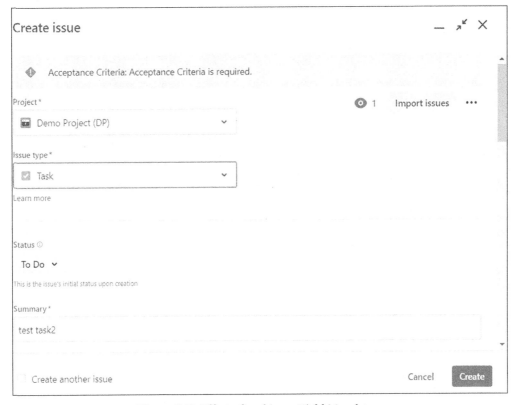

Figure 6.12: *Effect of making a Field Mandatory*

As shown in *Figure 6.12*, if the `Acceptance Criteria` field is made required, it has to be entered when creating any type of issue.

To overcome this problem, you can set field configurations that are different for different issues (Epics, Stories, Tasks, and so on.)

Renderers: It affects how a field's value is viewed. It is installed as a plugin. If you change the renderer, its view is changed. Changing the renderer doesn't affect the issue data.

For **example**: There are two types of text renderers as follows:

- **Default text Renderer**: It looks like a normal text field.
- **Wiki Style Renderer:** It looks like a field where you have all the options to format the text (Similar to the Description field in Jira).

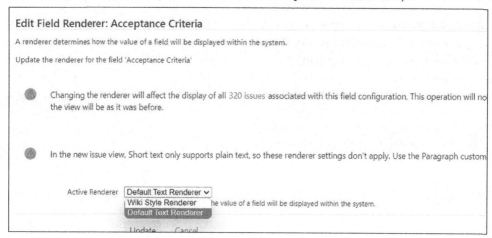

Figure 6.13: Editing Field Renderer for the field Acceptance Criteria

To see and set the field configurations:

1. Select ✿ > `Issues`.

2. Select `Field Configurations`.

3. Select `Configure`.

4. On this screen, you can set various fields as per requirement.

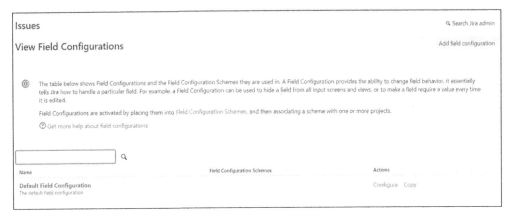

Figure 6.14: *Adding Field Configuration*

Field Configuration Scheme with an Example

Issue field configuration schemes allow you to apply a field configuration to all issues of a specific issue type. For example, when you want to change the fields that appear on all story issue types in a certain project, you can do it by configuring the field configuration schemes. The same field configuration can be used for multiple projects.

Steps to associate an Issue Type with a Field Configuration:

1. Access the issues section by clicking the gear icon and choosing `Issues`.

2. Under the `Fields` section, select `Field configuration schemes`.

3. Pick the desired field configuration scheme and click **Configure**.

4. Opt for `Associate an issue type with a field configuration`, then select the issue type and field configuration to link with this scheme.

5. Click **Add**.

Steps to associate a Field Configuration Scheme with a Project:

After establishing a link between a field configuration and an issue type within a field configuration scheme, you can integrate the scheme with a project to apply your changes.

1. Go to `Project` > `Project settings` > `Fields`.

2. Click `Actions` > `Use a different scheme`.

3. Choose the scheme you wish to associate with this project.

4. Click **Associate**.

Example:

We will create a field configuration, associate it with an issue type, and then associate it to a project.

To do this:

- Go to **Default field Configuration** in Jira Administration, and then select **Copy**.

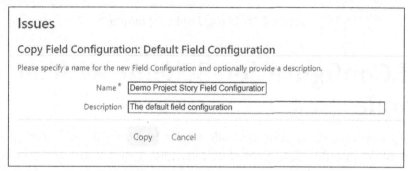

Figure 6.15: Creating a new Field Configuration

- We have created a new Field configuration named **Demo Project Story Field Configuration**. Now we can configure it by selecting **Configure**.

- In this step, you can make fields required, change the renderers, and add context to the fields.

Figure 6.16: Configuring fields of Demo Field Configuration

- Once the fields are configured, we can associate them with an issue type. To do that, we have to add a **Field Configuration Scheme**.

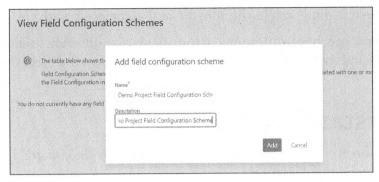

Figure 6.17: *Adding new field Configuration Scheme*

- After adding the scheme, associate it with an issue-type story.

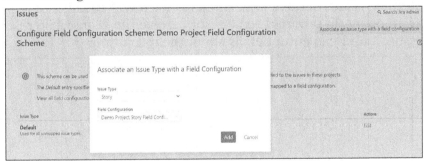

Figure 6.18: *Associating an Issue Type with a Field Configuration*

- Once it is associated with an issue type, associate it with a project.
- You can customize different field configurations for all the issue types.
- Go to the project settings of a project.
- Now select `Issues` >`Fields.`
- Go to the Actions drop-down and select `Use a different scheme.`

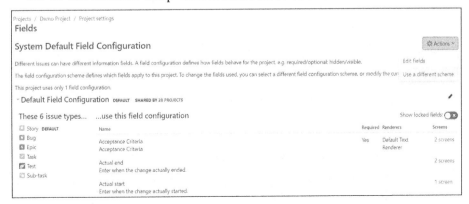

Figure 6.19: *Associating a field configuration scheme with a Project*

- Once it is done, select the scheme and associate it with the project.

This way you can have different custom fields for different issues. It can be customized and then a bunch of these associations form the Field Configuration Schemes.

Understanding Screens

In this section, we will understand about screens provided by Jira. Jira has three types of screens as follows:

- **Default screen**: This screen is used to customize the screens for create, edit, and view operations.

- **Resolve issues screen**: This screen is used while transitioning an issue from open /in progress to close or resolve the issue while resolving an issue. A user can enter details about the resolution.

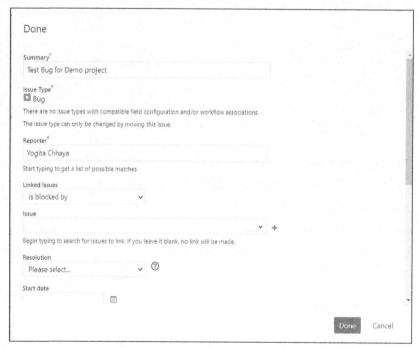

Figure 6.20: *Resolve Issue Screen*

- **Workflow screen:** This screen is used for:
  - ○ Reopen transitions from **Resolve and closed**.
  - ○ Close transition from resolved step. This screen has a smaller number of fields than the Resolve issues screen.

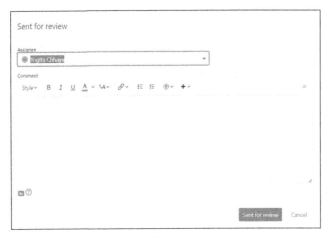

Figure 6.21: *Workflow Transition Screen*

How to Create or Configure Screen

1. Select ⚙ > `Issues`.

2. Select `Screens` > `Add Screen`.

3. Add a `Name` of the screen and a *Description* that describes when this screen should be used.

4. Select `Add.`

Figure 6.22: *Adding a screen*

We will learn how to add fields to configure a new screen.

A Summary field is mandatory on any Jira screen. So, the summary field cannot be kept empty when creating an issue in Jira.

Example: You can add tabs to the screen in Jira.

Let us understand how to add multiple tabs and what it looks like. We have added tabs on the screen for the bug issue type.

1. Select a screen you want to configure.

2. Select **Add tab** and **Add Acceptance Criteria**.

Figure 6.23: *Adding a field on the new tab*

3. Now, you can add the **Acceptance Criteria** field to this tab.

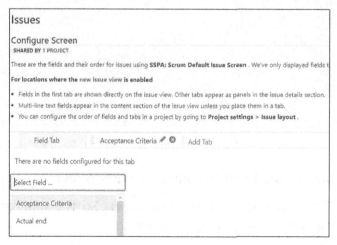

Figure 6.24: *Adding fields to a Screen*

4. By following the same process, you can add more tabs and add fields to the tabs. The new tab will appear when creating a new issue, and they will get added to the issue screen.

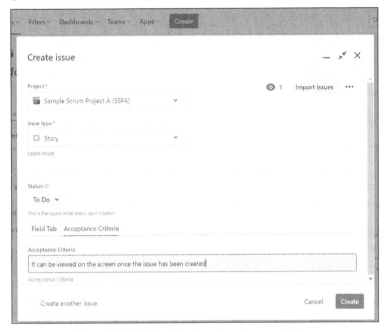

Figure 6.25: Tab added for Acceptance Criteria

Other tab for `Acceptance Criteria` can be viewed in *Figure* 6.25.

Figure 6.26: Entering Acceptance Criteria in the newly created tab

You can Edit, Copy, and Delete a screen as follows:

Editing a Screen

1. Access the issues section by clicking the gear icon and choosing Issues.

2. Select **Screens.**

3. Choose the relevant screen, select **Edit** to update the name or description.

Copying a screen

1. Access the issues section by clicking the gear icon and choosing **Issues.**

2. Select **Screens.**

3. Choose the relevant screen, select **Copy**.

Deleting a screen

1. Access the issues section by clicking the gear icon and choosing Issues.

2. Select **Screens.**

3. Choose the relevant screen, Select **Delete** a screen.

Delete screen option can be seen only if the screen is not associated with a project or it is not related to a workflow.

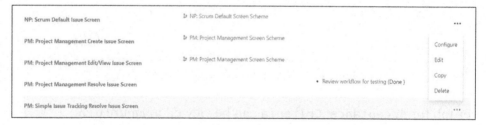

Figure 6.27: Options to Customize Screens

Creating Screen Schemes, Issue-type Screen Schemes, and associating them with a Project

We have learned how to create a screen in Jira, and now we will learn how to create a screen scheme. Let us first understand what a screen scheme is in Jira. A screen scheme is a combination of three types of screens for various issues.

Create, edit, and view issue screens

To understand this, select any project, and then go to project settings and select screens under issues. You can view the page for screens.

In the sample project **Scrum Project A**, two screen combinations are used. One set of screens is used for the Bug issue type and another set of screens is used for all other issue types (**Story, Epic, Task, Sub-task**).

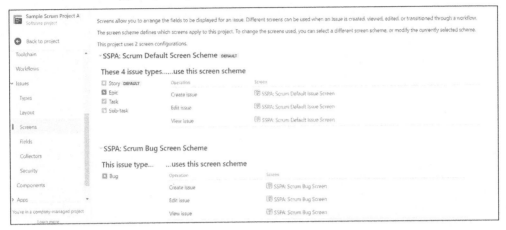

Figure 6.28: *Create, Edit, and View Screens*

Now we will learn the steps to create a new screen scheme in Jira software as follows:

1. Select ⚙ > **Issues**.

2. Select **Screen schemes** under **Screens** on the left navigation bar.

3. Select **Add Screen Scheme**.

4. Add the **Name** of the screen scheme, **Description**, and default screen. You can edit all the information later on.

5. Select **Add**.

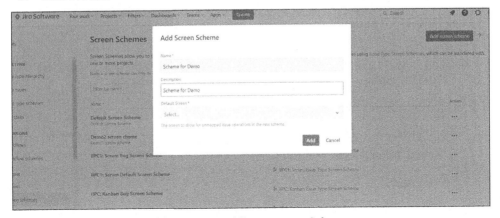

Figure 6.29: *Adding a screen Scheme*

Steps to Create an Issue-type Screen scheme

1. Access the issues section by clicking the gear icon and choosing **Issues**.

2. Choose **Issue-type screen schemes** under the screen schemes on the left navigation bar.

3. Click **Add Issue-type Screen Scheme**.

4. Add a **Name** of the Issue-type screen scheme, **Description**, and default screen scheme. You can edit all the information later on.

5. Select **Add.**

Figure 6.30: *Adding Issue-Type Screen Scheme*

Associating an issue type with a screen scheme

In a screen scheme, each issue operation - **Create, View**, and **Edit** - can be associated with a single screen. By default, it gets associated with the default screen.

1. Select ⚙ > **Issues**.

2. Select **Screen Schemes** from the left navigation bar.

3. Click on **Configure** next to the relevant screen scheme.

4. Choose **Associate** an issue operation with a screen.

5. Click the required issue operation (for example, **Create**, **Edit**, **View**) and the desired screen.

6. Select **Add.**

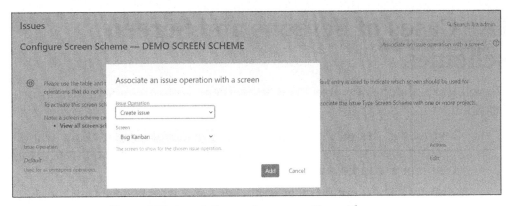

Figure 6.31: *Associating an Issue operation with a screen*

Associating an Issue-type screen scheme with a project

Once you've created the issue-type screens, you can now associate them with
a project. This will apply the screen scheme to all the issue types in the project.

1. Go to the project you want to configure.

2. Go to **project settings**.

3. In the left navigation bar, select **Issues**, and then select **Screen**.

4. On the right side, select **Actions**, and from the **Actions** dropdown, select
    Use a different scheme.

5. Now you can select and associate a screen scheme for the selected
    project.

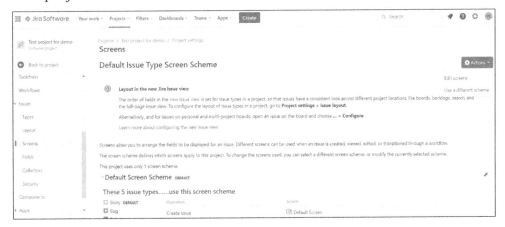

Figure 6.32: *Associating an Issue-type screen scheme with a project*

Use Cases of Screens and Screen schemes

We will learn about a few use cases for screens and screen schemes in Jira as follows:

- **Customized Issue Creation**: A software development team wants to capture specific information during issue creation, such as priority, components, and environment details.

  Solution: They create a custom screen with the relevant fields and associate it with a screen scheme. This screen scheme is then linked to the `Create Issue` operation, so that the desired fields are displayed when a new issue is created.

- **Sensitive Information Segregation**: An organization handles both internal and external projects, and they need to manage sensitive information separately for security reasons.

  Solution: By utilizing screen schemes, they can configure different screens for internal and external projects. This ensures that sensitive fields are shown only in the internal project context, helping maintain data confidentiality.

- **Workflow Transition Data Gathering**: During the `Code Review` workflow transition, a development team wants to gather code review details for each issue.

  Solution: They design a dedicated screen with fields like reviewer's comments and approval status. This screen is associated with a screen scheme that's linked to the `Code Review` workflow transition. Thus, every time an issue is sent for review through this transition, the relevant screen with code review fields is presented.

- **Global Template Implementation**: An organization wants to ensure consistency across different projects by customizing a standardized set of fields for all issues.

  Solution: They set up a default screen scheme that includes a predefined screen with mandatory fields applicable to all projects. When new projects are created, this default screen scheme is automatically applied, streamlining the process of ensuring consistent data capture.

Conclusion

We are now familiar with how to create and add custom fields, customize the screens, and associate a screen with issue operations and projects. We also understood the sequence to follow to create new issue-type screen schemes.

In the next chapter, we will learn about workflows and workflow schemes.

Points to Remember

- Choose appropriate custom fields so that the right information can be captured as per the process you follow.

- Fields can be of different types, such as Text fields, select lists, URL fields, and many more. You can select as per your requirements.

- Create different screens for different issue types and keep only the required fields.

- Create screen schemes and assign them to the issues to control which screen appears during create, edit, and view operation.

- The same screen scheme may not be useful for all the issue types as it may create confusion.

- A default screen having all the necessary fields can be used while creating an issue.

- Reuse the screens across multiple screen schemes so that it becomes easy to maintain.

- Arrange fields on the screen logically and set them as per the user's requirements.

- Test and validate screens and screen schemes so that the users can enter data easily.

- Keep a minimum number of fields on the screen and do the maintenance to remove the screens/fields that are not required.

- Jira provides many fields; however, try to customize it to simplify the process.

References

1. Description field is not visible.

https://community.atlassian.com/t5/Jira-Software-questions/Description-field-not-visible/qaq-p/2204554

2. Is it Possible to Change a Project Screen Scheme or Workflow for a Subset of Project Issues?

https://community.atlassian.com/t5/Jira-Software-questions/Is-it-Possible -to-Change-a-Project-Screen-Scheme-or-Workflow-for/qaq-p/2409599

3. Effect of changing screens, screen schemes and issue type screen schemes on existing data

https://community.atlassian.com/t5/Jira-Software-questions/Affect-of -changing-screens-screen-schemes-and-issue-type-screen/qaq-p/2281608

4. How to set multiple issue type screen schemes for a single project?

https://community.atlassian.com/t5/Jira-questions/How-to-set-multiple -issue-type-screen-schemes-for-a-single/qaq-p/287303

5. Do I need a Workflow scheme, an issues scheme, and a screen scheme for my one project?

https://community.atlassian.com/t5/Jira-Software-questions/Do-I-need-a -Workflow-scheme-an-issues-scheme-and-a-screen-scheme/qaq-p/2255115

CHAPTER 7

Configuring Workflows in Jira in Agile Projects

Introduction

Workflows play an essential role in every process as they represent the path a task follows from its creation to its completion. Jira workflows combine statuses and transitions within a process, applicable to various teams like business, Agile, and others. You have the ability to define and execute your processes using Jira workflows. For Agile teams, Jira offers predefined workflows, which can be customized by adding new statuses and transitions. Jira provides default workflows that you can duplicate and modify to fit your project's needs. You can create a workflow on your own or import a workflow from the marketplace.

You can link a workflow to a specific type of task, creating what's called a workflow scheme in Jira. This scheme can be linked to an entire project. By utilizing Jira workflows, you can incorporate conditions, validators, post-functions, and triggers to ensure a streamlined process.

Structure

In this chapter, we will discuss the following topics:

- Understanding workflows in Jira
- Components of workflow
- Creating a workflow with an Example
- Editing, Viewing, and Deleting workflows

- Global Transitions
- Adding a resolve issue screen to the Workflow transition
- Active vs. Inactive workflows
- Transitions, Conditions, Post-functions, and Triggers
- Workflow schemes
- Agile Boards and Workflows
- Mistakes to avoid while creating workflows
- Use cases with References

Components of Workflow

Workflow is a pictorial presentation of any process. It includes statuses, transitions, and resolutions. Jira has a unique feature that allows customization of the workflow steps to match the needs of the projects. Jira provides its built-in workflow with standard steps. You can also import a workflow from the Atlassian Marketplace. In this chapter, we will be covering topics applicable only to **Company-managed projects**.

Jira workflows mainly consist of three components:

- **Statuses**: They provide information about the current position of a work item or issue. For instance, an issue can progress through stages like Open, In Progress, Resolved, Closed, and Done. These stages are referred to as statuses in Jira.

- **Transitions**: When a work item or issue shifts from one status to another, it is termed as a transition. Transitions can either move in a single direction or go back and forth between two statuses.

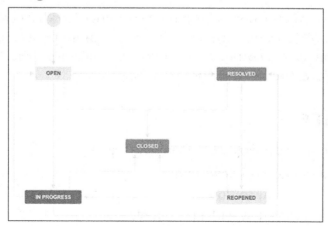

Figure 7.1: *Classic Default Workflow*

- **Resolutions**: Resolutions differ from statuses as they serve to indicate whether an issue has been resolved. If an issue remains unresolved, it can be categorized with statuses like `abandoned`, `won't fix`, or `incomplete`. Resolutions help the team in making informed decisions and effectively managing tasks. Jira also offers a built-in screen for transitioning issues to a resolved state.

Creating a Workflow with Example

In this section, we will learn to create, copy, import, and delete a workflow. Once a workflow is created, we can associate it with a workflow scheme.

Permissions required: Only Jira administrators who have the global permission to Administer Jira can create, edit, and delete workflows in Jira.

Here are the steps to create a new workflow:

1. Log in to your Jira instance with administrative privileges.

2. Navigate to the Issue section by selecting the gear icon and then clicking on Workflow.

3. Select `Workflows` > `Add workflow`.

Figure 7.2: Adding workflow

4. Enter a `Name` and `Description` of the workflow, and then click `Add`.

Figure 7.3: *Adding Name and Description of Workflow*

5. You can then use the workflow editor to add statuses and transitions.

Figure 7.4: *Adding Status*

6. Add all the required statuses as shown in *Figure 7.5*.

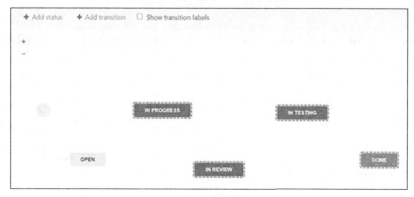

Figure 7.5: *Adding different Statuses*

7. Now, click on **Add Transition** and enter all the details: From **status, To status**, **Name, Description**, and **Screen**. It is not mandatory to enter the name of the Screen for each transition.

Figure 7.6: Adding transitions

8. Repeat the preceding process for all (forward and backward) the transitions.

9. The workflow has been created.

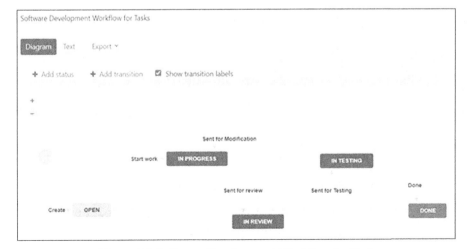

Figure 7.7: Software Development Workflow for Task

10. Click on the **Text** next to **Diagram** to view the workflow in Text mode. You can also edit the workflow in text mode.

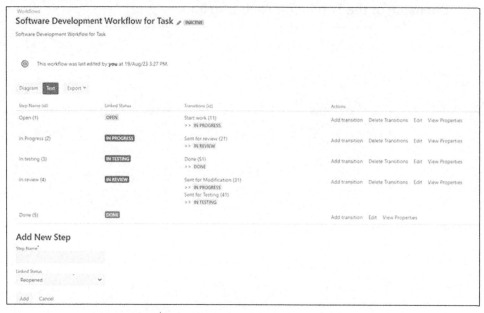

Figure 7.8: *Editing workflow in Text-mode*

We have created a workflow for software development issue-type tasks.

Editing, Viewing, and Deleting a Workflow

In this section, we will learn how to Edit, View, or Delete the workflow.

Here are the steps to Edit/view/Delete a workflow:

1. Log in to your Jira instance with administrative privileges.

2. Navigate to the **Issue** section by selecting the gear icon and then clicking on Workflow.

3. Select **Workflows**.

4. Select **Active workflows** or **Inactive workflows**.

5. Select the workflow that you want to **Edit/Delete/Copy**. Click on the required operation **(Edit/Delete/Copy)**.

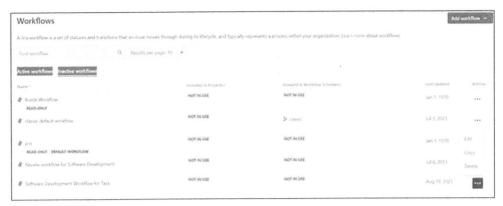

Figure 7.9: *Edit/Copy/Delete options for Workflow*

The Delete option can be seen only for those workflows that are not in use (not associated with workflow scheme/project).

Workflow.

Global transitions

Global transition allows any step in the workflow to transition to a particular workflow step.

Here are the steps on how to add a global transition in a workflow:

1. Log in to your Jira instance with administrative privileges.

2. Navigate to the **Issue** section by selecting the gear icon and then clicking on

3. Select **Workflows.**

4. Select **Inactive workflows.**

5. Select any status in the workflow.

6. Check the **Allow all statuses to transition to this one** in the window.

7. You can uncheck it to remove the global transition.

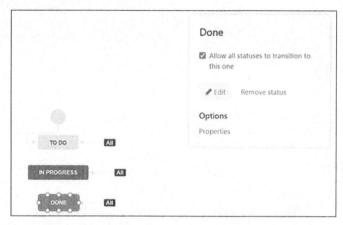

Figure 7.10: *Adding Global Transitions to a Status*

Associating a Workflow with an Issue type

In Agile projects, you have different issue types such as Epic, Story, Task, Bug, and so on. Story can have steps such as **Open**, **In Progress**, and **Done**, while Bug can go through steps such as **Open**, **In Progress**, **In Testing**, and **Done**. You can define **Workflow 1** for Story and **Workflow 2** for Bug, new workflow for other issue types, and so on. This allows you to have different workflows for various issue types.

Example: Here are the steps to associate a Workflow for Bug with an Issue-type Bug in a project:

1. We have created a **Workflow for Bug**, as shown in *Figure 7.11*.

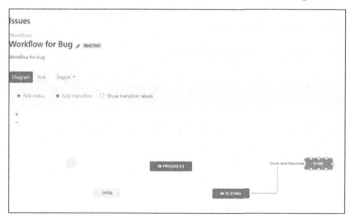

Figure 7.11: *Workflow for Bug*

2. Navigate to **All Projects > Project > Project settings**.

3. Click on **Workflows.**

4. Select **Add Existing.**

Figure 7.12: Adding a workflow for an issue-type Bug

5. Select the **Workflow for Bug** and click **Next**.

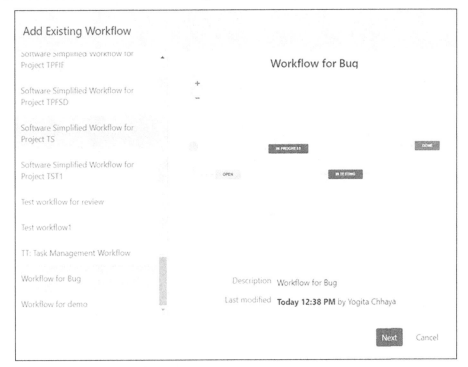

Figure 7.13: Associating Bug issue type with workflow

6. Select the issue-type as **Bug** and click on **Finish**.

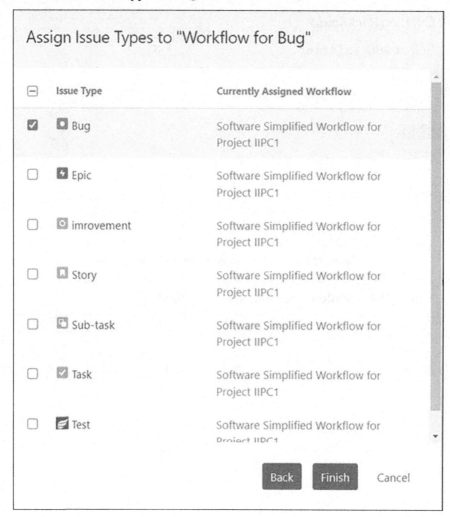

Figure 7.14: *Associating Bug Issue type*

7. The Bug issue type has been associated with the new workflow for Bug.

8. Click on **Publish** to publish the changes in the workflow scheme.

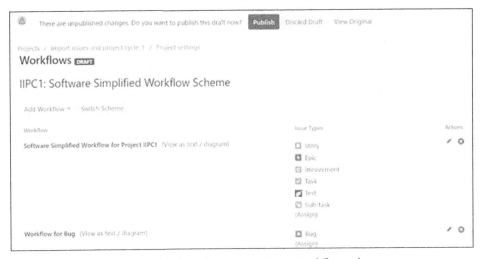

Figure 7.15: *Publishing changes in a Workflow scheme*

Jira creates a draft workflow when we make any changes to the existing workflow. It is necessary to publish the changes so that those changes become permanent.

In this example, we have associated a Bug issue type with a new workflow for Bug. All the other issue types are associated with the Software Simplified Workflow for project IIPC1.

Adding a resolve issue screen to Workflow transition

We will learn how to add a resolution screen when the Bug is transitioned to the Done status and add the details.

Jira provides inbuilt screens that can be added to workflow transitions for setting the resolution. In the workflow for Bug, the last transition is Done and Resolved.

Follow these steps to add the Resolve Issue screen on the Done transition:

1. Log in to your Jira instance with administrative privileges.

2. Navigate to the `Issue` section by selecting the gear icon and then clicking on **workflow**.

3. Select **Workflows**.

4. Select `Workflow for Bug` and select `Edit`.

5. Select **Add Transition** and add the details for the transition from **IN TESTING** to **DONE**.

6. Add the transition name as **Done and Resolved**.

7. Select the **Resolve Issue screen** from the dropdown.

8. Click **Save**.

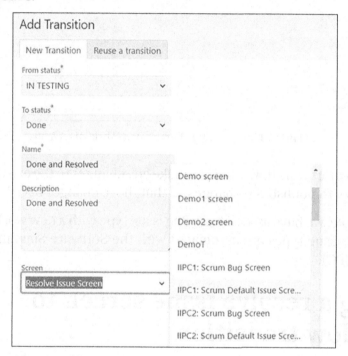

Figure 7.16: *Adding a Resolve issue screen on the Done and Resolved workflow transition*

9. We have added the **Resolve Issue Screen** on the **Done and Resolved** transition.

10. To test this transition, Open any Bug in the same project. Do all the transitions as defined in the workflow.

11. In the transition from **In Testing** to **Done**, you will be prompted to enter the details on the resolve issue screen.

12. Add the details such as **Resolution** and **Time spent**, and then click on **Done and Resolved**.

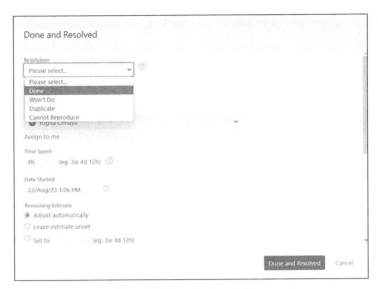

Figure 7.17: *Resolve issue Screen*

Workflow Schemes

Workflow schemes are like a bunch of different workflows associated with different issue types.

For example, project A has issue types such as **Epic**, **Story**, **Task**, **Sub-task**, and **Bug**. You can create a Workflow Scheme A containing different workflows for each issue type, which is exclusively for project A.

Project B has issue types such as **Story**, **Task**, and **Bug**. You can create a Workflow Scheme B containing different workflows for each issue type, which is exclusively for project B.

These schemes can be associated with projects. It helps organizations to save time by customizing schemes and utilizing the same for multiple projects.

In this example, we will copy a workflow scheme and then associate it with a project.

You can also create a new workflow scheme by selecting Add a workflow scheme.

Here are the steps:

1. Log in as a **Jira Administrator**.

2. Navigate to **Workflow Schemes** under **Workflows** in the Jira Administration section.

3. Select a workflow scheme from the **Active workflow** scheme and click on **Copy.**

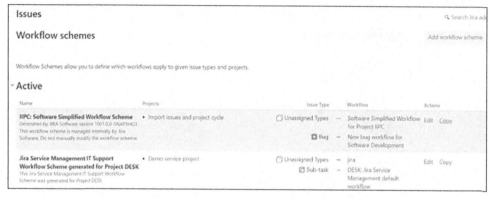

Figure 7.18: *Copying a Workflow scheme*

4. Jira provides **Active** and **Inactive** workflow schemes. Go to **Inactive** workflow schemes. The copied workflow scheme has been added to the inactive workflow scheme. Click on **Edit.**

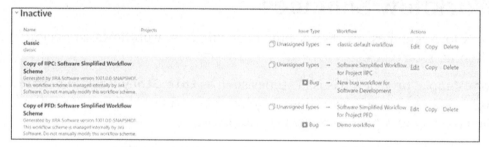

Figure 7.19: *Editing a Copy of Workflow scheme*

5. Edit the name of the copied scheme as **Demo Software Simplified Workflow Scheme.** Click to save the changes. Now, the newly created workflow scheme is ready to be associated with a project.

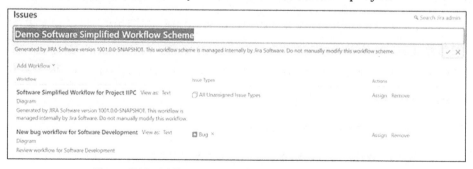

Figure 7.20: *Adding a Name of a new Workflow scheme*

6. Navigate to **Projects** > select **Project** > **Project Settings**. Select the project name that you want to associate with the Demo workflow scheme.

7. Select **Workflows** and then click on **Switch Scheme.**

Figure 7.21: *Switch scheme to Associate with other workflow schemes*

8. Click on **Associate**.

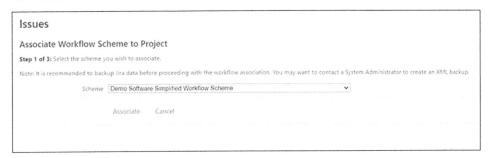

Figure 7.22: *Associating new workflow Scheme*

9. The **Demo Software Simplified Workflow Scheme** has been associated with the **Demo Project for Workflow Scheme**.

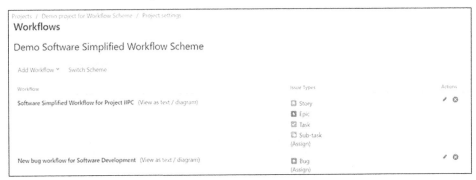

Figure 7.23: *New Workflow Scheme association with a Project*

As shown in *Figure 7.23*, the Bug issue type has been associated with the New bug workflow for Software Development. All other issue types have been associated with Software Simplified Workflow for project IIPC. To summarize, a workflow scheme is a combination of issue type and workflow associations, and it can be finally associated with multiple projects in Jira.

Conditions, Post-functions, Validators, and Triggers

Conditions: Conditions specify a few essentials for a transition to take place. If the requirements are not met to fulfill the condition, the transition is not allowed.

For example, a user must be in a **Developer** role to start the development task. Conditions control the transitions. A user cannot Start Work on the task until he is assigned a task.

Example: We will add a few conditions on transitioning of an issue. To do this, follow these steps:

1. Log in as a **Jira Administrator**.

2. Navigate to **Workflow** under **Workflows** in the Jira Administration section.

3. Select **Inactive workflows** and open the workflow in **Diagram** mode.

4. Select the transition **Start work** and click on **Conditions** to add a condition.

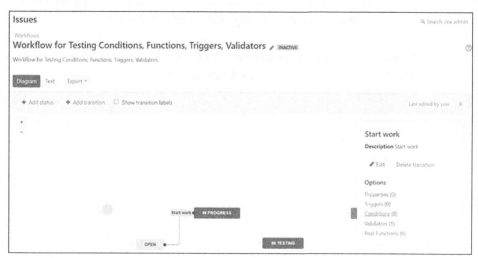

Figure 7.24: *Adding conditions on Start work transition*

5. Select the condition **User is in Project Role** and click **Add**.

○ Only Bamboo Notifications Workflow Condition	Only makes this transition available to the Bamboo build notifications.
○ Only Reporter Condition	Condition to allow only the reporter to execute a transition.
○ Permission Condition	Condition to allow only users with a certain permission to execute a transition.
○ Previous Status Condition	Condition to check if the issue has transitioned through a specified status or not.
○ ScriptRunner Script	Add a ScriptRunner Script Condition that evaluates a Jira Expression to determine whether to allow the transition.
○ Separation of Duties condition	Condition preventing a user to perform the transition, if the user has already performed a transition on the issue.
○ Sub-Task Blocking Condition	Condition to block parent issue transition depending on sub-task status.
○ User Is In Any Group	Condition to allow only users in a given group to execute a transition.
○ User Is In Any Project Role	Condition to allow only users in a given project role to execute a transition.
○ User Is In Custom field	Allows only users in a given custom field to execute the transition.
○ User Is In Group	Condition to allow only users in a given group to execute a transition.
○ User Is In Group Custom Field	Condition to allow only users in a custom field-specified group to execute a transition.
◉ User Is In Project Role	Condition to allow only users in a given project role to execute a transition.
○ Value Field	Allows to execute a transition if the given value of a field is equal to a constant value, or simply set.

Add   Cancel

Figure 7.25: Condition based on User project role

6. Select the User Role as **Scrum Masters**.

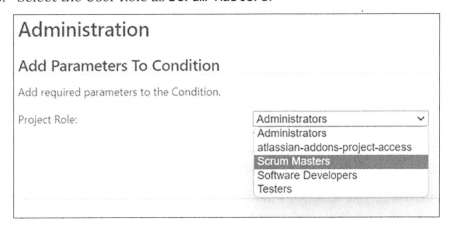

Figure 7.26: Selecting Project role for adding role-based condition

7. Select another condition, **Only the assignee of the issue can execute the transition** and click **Add**. We have now added two conditions.

Figure 7.27: Multiple conditions on a transition

8. Select the **Any of the following conditions** option, as shown in *Figure 7.28*. It allows the assignee of the task or scrum master to close the task.

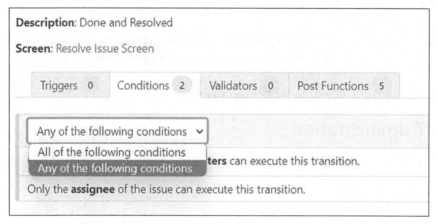

Figure 7.28: Selecting Any of the following conditions

There are many other conditions, which can be used to control the transition.

Post-function: Post-functions allow users to add extra functions after a transition has occurred. For example, setting or clearing a field value after a transition has occurred.

In this example, we will learn how to assign a task to the current user when an issue is created. Here are the steps:

1. Log in as a **Jira Administrator**.

2. Navigate to **Workflow** under **Workflows** in the Jira Administration section.

3. Select `Inactive workflows` and open the workflow in Diagram mode.

4. Click on **Post-Functions** and select the **Create** transition.

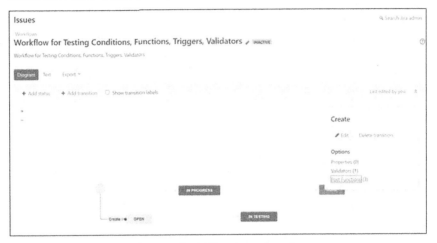

Figure 7.29: Adding post-function

5. Select the **Post-function Assign** to current user and click **Add.**

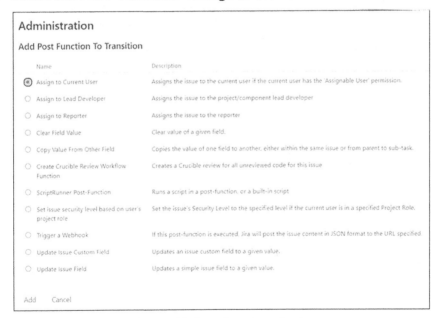

Figure 7.30: Post-function selection

Users can change the sequence of the post-functions by clicking on the up and down arrows. Additionally, users can also select to fire a generic event for an issue created, issue updated, and so on.

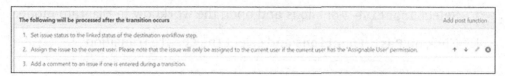

Figure 7.31: *List of post-functions after the transition occurs*

We have added a post-function on the **create** transition.

Validators: Validators serve as checkpoints to validate values. For instance, they can verify values within required custom fields or assess the presence of necessary permissions.

In this example, we will add a validator to check for Manage sprints permissions on the Start Work transition. Here are the steps:

1. Log in as a `Jira Administrator`.

2. Navigate to **Workflow** under **Workflows** in the Jira Administration section.

3. Select `Inactive` workflows and open the workflow in **Diagram** mode.

4. Select the **Start work** transition and click on **Validators.**

Figure 7.32: *Adding validators on start work transition*

5. Select **Permission validator** that validates the user permission.

Figure 7.33: *Selecting permission validator*

6. Select **Add** and select the **Manage sprints** permission. A user with this permission is allowed to start work in a sprint.

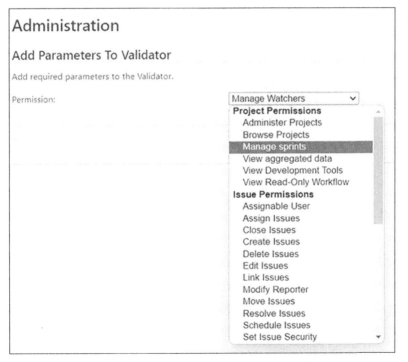

Figure 7.34: *Selecting Manage Sprints from the list of permissions*

We have added the validator to check for the Manage sprints permission. Similarly, users can add other validators such as parent status validator, date comparison, required field, and so on.

Triggers: The triggers help automate transitions as and when specific events occur in other systems. For example, Code review in the code repository. By doing so, triggers remove the necessity for your team to manually alter the process status when conditions are fulfilled.

Example: Here are the steps to add a commit created trigger on the Start progress transition:

1. Log in as a **Jira Administrator**.

2. Navigate to **Workflow** under **Workflows** in the Jira Administration section.

3. Select **Inactive workflows** and open the **Workflow for Code Review** in **Diagram** mode.

4. Select the transition **Start Progress** and click on **Triggers**.

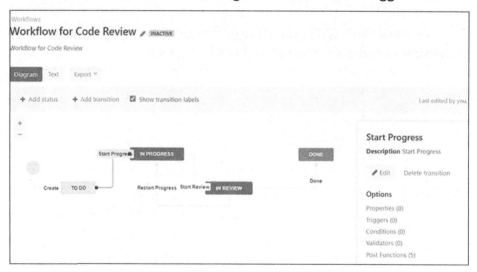

Figure 7.35: Adding triggers on start work transition

5. Click on **Add trigger**.

Figure 7.36: Adding Commit created trigger

6. Click on **Next** and then click `Add trigger`.

Figure 7.37: Adding trigger to automate transitions

7. Adding this trigger will automatically transition the issue when a pull request is created in a connected repository.

Figure 7.38: *Commit created trigger*

A trigger Commit created has been added. Similarly, triggers such as **Review Started**, **Review Abandoned**, and **Review Closed** can be added to the transitions **Start Review**, **Restart Progress**, and **Done transitions** in Crucible.

The names of the **Development Tools** that can be integrated with Jira for managing code reviews are as follows:

- Fisheye/Crucible
- Bitbucket
- GitHub
- GitHub Enterprise

Publish the Draft workflow after adding Conditions, Post-Functions, Validators, and Triggers if you are Editing an active workflow.

Do not add triggers on Global transitions. Instead, add the issue key in code-commit, branch, pull request, or review messages. There are many triggers that can be added, such as Review started, Review closed, and so on. Test the triggers while you are doing it for the first time by integrating them with the development tools.

Active vs. Inactive workflows

Active Workflow: A workflow is considered active when it is presently in use by one or multiple projects. When you make changes to an active workflow,

Jira initially generates a draft version of it. Once you've completed your edits, you can finalize your draft by publishing it and, if desired, retain the original workflow as an inactive backup.

There are limitations while editing a draft of an active workflow in Jira as follows:

- Existing workflow steps cannot be deleted.
- The associated status cannot be edited.
- Step IDs for the existing steps cannot be changed.
- You can modify the workflow description, but you cannot modify its name.

Inactive Workflow: An inactive workflow is one that is presently not being utilized by any projects. Since there are currently no issues undergoing transitions within an inactive workflow, you have the ability to directly modify the steps and transitions of the workflow.

To convert the inactive workflow into active workflow, associate it with an issue type, add the workflow to a workflow scheme, and finally associate the scheme with a project.

Workflows and Agile Boards

Jira has two types of workflows for software projects:

- Software Simplified workflow
- Jira (Customized) workflow.

In this section, we will understand the difference between these two types of workflows.

Software Simplified Workflow:

- It is a straightforward and minimalistic workflow process designed for small teams or simple projects.
- It involves only three steps: `To Do, In Progress`, and `Done` for the Scrum board. For the Kanban board, it has four steps: `Backlog, Selected for Development, In Progress, and Done.`
- Setting up the Software Simplified Workflow is quick and easy, making it suitable for teams without complex process requirements.
- There is less administrative work as the workflow involves a lesser number of transitions and statuses.
- Issues can be moved easily between columns.

- No transition screens will appear while moving the issues, and it sets the resolution automatically when the issues move to the final Done status.

Figure 7.39: Software Simplified Workflow

Jira Workflow:

- It is a highly customizable and adaptable workflow suitable for complex projects and teams of varying sizes.
- Jira workflows can have multiple steps, statuses, transitions, and conditions to customize the complex project process.
- Jira workflows support automation through conditions, validators, and post-functions, streamlining processes and reducing manual work.
- It can accommodate many workflow steps that are typically needed on a board.
- It has workflow conditions that do not allow issues to be moved between all columns.
- It displays screens on transitions, such as Resolve Issue, Close Issue, and Reopen Issue.
- Jira workflow can only be edited via workflow configuration.

Figure 7.40: *Customizable Jira workflow*

Mistakes to avoid while creating workflows

Here are some of the mistakes to avoid while creating workflows:

- **Avoid overcomplicating the workflow**: When designing the workflow, refrain from adding excessive steps, conditions, and validators. Additionally, ensure that adding required fields doesn't negatively impact other stakeholders. Strive for simplicity.

- **Consider the team's requirements**: Discuss any planned changes to the workflow with the team to understand their actual needs before implementing changes.

- **Involve all stakeholders during workflow creation**: Gather input from stakeholders, assess the feasibility of proposed changes, and then proceed with creating or modifying the workflow. Workflow changes can affect multiple individuals if schemes are shared across the organization.

- **Maintain relevant status names**: Utilize the provided statuses in Jira, adding new names that appropriately align with To Do, In Progress, and Done statuses.

- **Test the workflow and gather feedback**: Conduct thorough testing of the workflow and solicit feedback. Utilize a sandbox environment for testing or create a separate Jira project for testing purposes, inaccessible to others, to ensure smooth workflow testing and maintenance.

Conclusion

We are now familiar with how to create and add status, transitions, global transitions, Workflows, and workflow schemes. We have also understood active and inactive workflows, as well as how to associate a workflow with an issue type and how to associate a workflow with a project.

In the next chapter, we will learn about Jira Filters, Dashboards, Reports, and Analytics.

Points to Remember

- Workflows are the steps required to complete a process.
- In Jira, workflows can be created in both Diagram and Text modes.
- Design workflows with simplicity to minimize confusion.
- Maintain clear naming conventions for statuses and transitions.
- Utilize descriptive transition names to provide user guidance.
- Regularly review workflows to ensure alignment with current project practices.
- Harness features like Conditions, Validators, and Post-functions to automate processes and reduce manual effort.
- Conditions check for Transition viability, Validators ensure input validity, and Post-functions manage actions after transitions.
- Workflow schemes are associated with projects, allowing distinct workflows for different projects.
- Reusing workflow schemes across projects promotes consistency and efficiency.
- Changes to a workflow scheme can impact multiple projects; make modifications thoughtfully and communicate changes effectively.
- Two types of workflows exist: Software Simplified for smaller teams and less complex processes, and Customizable for intricate processes with lesser flexibility.
- Integrating Jira with other development tools enhances efficient code review management.

Links for Reference and Use Cases

1. How can I build a new workflow without affecting existing workflows, screens, and issues?

https://community.atlassian.com/t5/Jira-Software-questions/How-can-I-build-a-new-workflow-without-affecting-existing/qaq-p/2414148

2. How to define different statuses for specific issue types, create a workflow, and add to the workflow scheme?

https://community.atlassian.com/t5/Jira-Software-questions/Different-statuses-for-specific-issue-types-Workflow/qaq-p/2432098

3. If I remove an issue type from a Workflow Scheme, will the past issues be deleted?

https://community.atlassian.com/t5/Jira-Software-questions/If-I-remove-an-issue-type-from-a-Workflow-Scheme-will-the-past/qaq-p/2324428

4. Adding Workflows for a new issue type to Workflow Schemes.

https://community.atlassian.com/t5/Jira-questions/Adding-Workflows-to-Workflow-Schemes/qaq-p/2265392

5. Can I build a workflow in Production without affecting existing issues?

https://community.atlassian.com/t5/Jira-Software-questions/Can-I-build-a-workflow-in-Production-without-affecting-existing/qaq-p/2354907

6. How to activate the workflow I created?

https://community.atlassian.com/t5/Automation-questions/Workflow/qaq-p/2280162

7. How to activate a workflow?

https://community.atlassian.com/t5/Jira-questions/How-to-activate-the-inactive-workflow/qaq-p/1198597

8. How do I Edit the copied workflow scheme in the cloud?

https://community.atlassian.com/t5/Jira-Software-questions/Editing-a-copied-Workflow-in-the-cloud/qaq-p/1566531

9. Is it possible to give extended permissions to a user (project lead and project admin), so that they can change the edit workflow on their project without being site admin?

https://community.atlassian.com/t5/Jira-questions/Edit-workflows-jira
-cloud/qaq-p/946087

10. What is the right way to handle the Close Issue screen? Is it supposed to stand alone without being associated with a scheme?

https://community.atlassian.com/t5/Jira-questions/A-screen-for-quot
-Close-Issue-quot-transition/qaq-p/2352435

11. Jira workflow conditions are not applying for a specific user group with the All of the conditions option.

https://community.atlassian.com/t5/Jira-Software-questions/Jira-workflow
-condition-not-applying-for-specific-user-group/qaq-p/2339693

12. I have created a Kanban board and want to change the workflow scheme.

https://community.atlassian.com/t5/Jira-Software-questions/Modifying
-workflow-scheme/qaq-p/1867224

13. I want to copy a workflow scheme from Project 1 to Project 2. And afterwards, I should be able to alter the workflows in Project 2 without affecting Project 1.

https://community.atlassian.com/t5/Jira-Software-questions/How-do-I
-copy-a-workflow-scheme/qaq-p/1956132

14. Software Simplified Workflow vs. Custom workflow.

https://community.atlassian.com/t5/Jira-questions/Software-Simplified
-Workflow-v-Custom/qaq-p/1860651

15. How to gain permission to edit Software Simplified Workflow?

https://community.atlassian.com/t5/Jira-Software-questions/How-to-gain
-permission-to-edit-Software-Simplified-Workflow/qaq-p/1624932

CHAPTER 8

Filters, Dashboards, and Agile Reporting

Introduction

In the dynamic world of developing software applications and project management, Jira software is a helpful tool comprising three important parts: Filters, Dashboards, and Agile reports. These features help us to organize features, see how things are going, and understand how our team is doing.

Filters are like special tools designed for both basic search and advanced search. They help us to find the exact information from a big database created with projects. Dashboards help us to show important statistics in one place, much like a dashboard in a car shows speed, fuel, and more. Agile reports are helpful if we work in a certain way called 'Agile'. These reports tell us how fast we're working, what we have finished, and what is left, and get an idea about the obstacles. Jira also provides general reports that can be used by every kind of team.

In this chapter, we will learn about filters, dashboards, and agile reports. We will see how to use them to find important data, keep an eye on our projects, and work better together.

Structure

In this chapter, we will cover the following topics:

- Understanding Basic search and Advanced search in Jira
- Creating Jira filters
  - Step-by-step guide to creating and saving a Jira filter
  - Jira's built-in filters

- o Saving and Naming filters for easy access
- o Managing subscription, editing permissions, updating, copying, deleting filters
- Working with search results
- Creating filters using advanced search
  - o Step-by-step process to create a filter using advanced search
  - o Understanding JQL Functions, Fields, Keywords, and Operators
- Examples of important JQL queries for everyone
- Understanding the importance of Dashboards
- Step-by-step process to create a Dashboard and add Gadget
- Choosing a Dashboard Layout
- Copying, Sharing, and Deleting a Dashboard
- Adding and Customizing Gadgets to a Dashboard
- Example Dashboards and Gadgets
- Creating a Wallboard
- Introduction to Reports
- Steps to accessing Reports in Jira
- Understanding Agile reports
  - o Reports for Scrum Teams
  - o Reports for Kanban Teams
- Introduction and Overview of Atlassian Analytics
- Points to Remember
- Use cases and Reference

Understanding Basic search and Advanced search in Jira

Jira provides several ways in which you can search for an issue. Primarily, there are two methods: **Basic search** and **Advanced search**. Basic search works by selecting the search bar or navigating to issues and then setting the criteria to search for issues. On the other hand, advanced search involves writing queries in Jira Query Language (JQL). Basic search has some limitations that can be overcome by using advanced search. In this chapter, we will learn both types in detail.

Creating Jira filters

In this section, we will learn to create Jira filters using basic search options.

To find specific issues, follow these steps:

1. Navigate to **Search** > **All issues**.

2. Set the criteria for searching – **Type**, **Project**, **Assignee**, **Status.**

3. Enter the text to search for and click **More+**. Post clicks on *More+*, the user can choose any number of issue fields from the available list of issue fields.

4. Select **Search.**

Jira will provide you with the issues based on the set criteria for the search.

Step-by-step guide to create and save a Jira filter

Permission required: All Jira Users can create and save their own filters.

To create a filter in Jira, follow these steps:

1. Navigate to **Filters** in the main navigation bar and select **View all filters.**

Figure 8.1: *Creating filters step 1*

2. Select **Create filter.**

Figure 8.2: *Creating filters step-2*

3. Set the criteria for searching: **Type**, **Project**, **Status**, **Assignee**. You can toggle between basic and advanced search:

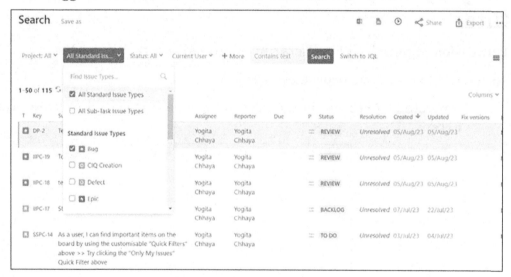

Figure 8.3: *Creating filters step-3*

4. Select **Search**, click **Save As**, enter the name of the filter, and click **Submit:**

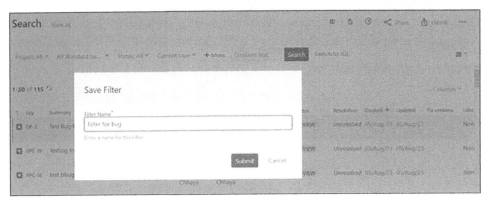

Figure 8.4: Creating filters step-4

The filter has been created and saved.

Jira's built-in filters

Permission required: All Jira users can access default filters.

Jira software provides a few ready filters. You can access these filters from the left navigation bar. The filters that users can access are listed as follows:

- My open issues
- Reported by me
- Open issues
- Done issues
- Viewed recently
- Resolved recently
- Updated recently

To access the built-in filters in Jira, follow these steps:

- Navigate to **Projects** > select a project > **Issues**, and then select the filter you want to access.
- Below the built-in filter, you can click **View all filters** to access all saved filters.

Managing subscription, editing permissions, updating, copying, deleting filters

In this section, we will learn how to edit, delete, alter permissions, subscribe, and mark filters as favorite.

Permissions required: To change the ownership of a filter and delete a filter, you must log in as a Jira Administrator with Administer Jira Global permission.

From the main Navigation bar, select `Filters` > `View all filters`.

Figure 8.5: *Viewing all filters*

On this page, Jira provides a list of all filters - private and shared by others.

Search for filter: You can enter the name of owners, projects, or groups to search for filters.

By selecting/clicking the name of the filter, it displays all issues of the selected filter.

On the same page, you can:

1. Open the search in Excel and Google Sheets.

2. Share the search by entering an Email address.

3. Export the search in different formats, such as Excel, CSV, and other formats.

4. Change the search criteria and then save it.

5. Mark as favorite by clicking the star symbol. Starred filters are your favorite filters.

6. Click on **Details** to view the owner and edit permissions and add details to subscribe to the filter.

Figure 8.6: *Options on a selected filter page*

Edit: On the `Filters` page, select the three dots and then select `Edit` to edit the name and description of the filter, and change who can edit and view the filter.

Permissions Required: Individuals with Administer Jira Global permission can see the Edit option.

Steps to Edit Filter:

1. Navigate to `Filters` > `View All Filters`. Find the filter you want to update.

Figure 8.7: *Viewing all filters*

2. Navigate to  on the right corner and select the same.

Figure 8.8: Selecting to Edit filter

3. Select `Edit`.

Figure 8.9: Editing Viewers, Editors, and other details of a filter

You can share a filter with:

-   **Project**: All members working on a specific project.
-   **Group**: It is a group defined in Jira.
-   **User:** A user whose name can be specified.
-   **Private**: It is a private filter for you, and others cannot view it.

Copy and Delete: Select the three dots and you will have options to copy or delete the filter:

Figure 8.10: Editing, Deleting, Copying, and other options of a filter

Working with search results

After conducting your issue search, you can take various actions as listed:

- Choose either the **List view** or **Detail view** of the issues according to your preference.
- Select and configure the columns that are visible or hidden.
- Sort the issues based on a column.
- Perform bulk edits on issues.
- Share your search results in different formats.
- Add the search results, that is, Jira filters, as a dashboard gadget.

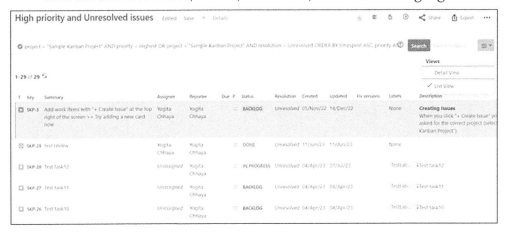

Figure 8.11: Working with search results

Creating filters using advanced search

The steps for performing advanced searches in Jira are similar to those for basic searches. Any basic search can be converted into an advanced search by clicking **Switch to JQL**. However, not all advanced searches can be converted back into basic searches.

With Jira's advanced search, you can specify search criteria and create structured queries using JQL. This advanced search feature utilizes keywords, operators, fields, and functions. For example, you can search for specific text or filter issues based on date and time criteria, among other options.

Step-by-step process to create an advanced filter

Permission required: All Jira Users can create advanced filters.

To create an advanced filter in Jira, follow these steps:

1. Navigate to **Filters** in the main navigation bar and select **View all filters**:

Figure 8.12: *Creating filter using Advanced search step-1*

2. Select **Create filter**:

Figure 8.13: *Creating filter using Advanced search step-2*

3. Set the criteria for searching - **Type**, **Project**, **Status**, **Assignee.** You can toggle between basic and advanced search. Select **Switch to JQL**:

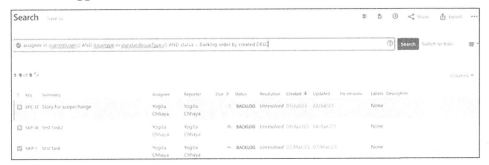

Figure 8.14: *Creating filter using Advanced search step-3*

4. Select search, click **Save As**, enter the name of the filter, and click **Submit.**

Figure 8.15: *Creating filter using Advanced search step-4*

The filter for Advanced search has been created and saved. You can modify new search criteria before saving the filter with the help of Jira Query Language.

Understanding JQL Functions, Fields, Keywords, and Operators

Any JQL query is written using specific Keywords, operators, Functions, and Fields. In this section, we will understand these with the help of examples.

Keywords: Keyword performs the following tasks:

- Combines multiple clauses to construct a query.
- Changes the logic of multiple clauses.
- Adjusts the logic of operators within the query.

JQL Keywords: Here are a few keywords in Jira: AND, OR, NOT, EMPTY, NULL, ORDER BY.

Examples

1. **AND**: It is used to combine multiple clauses of a query. Parenthesis can be used to control the order of the execution in a query.

   Example: Find all issues of project SSP that belong to closedSprint:

   ```
   project = "SSP" AND sprint IN closedSprints()ORDER BY created
   DESC
   ```

2. **OR**: It is used to combine multiple clauses. Parenthesis can be used to control the order of the execution in a query.

   Example: Find all issues of the type Bug or defect:

   ```
   issuetype = Bug or issuetype = Defect
   ```

Operators: Operators are the signs or words that compare the values on both sides of the expression. Only true results are used in the query after comparing the values. Examples of operators are Equals, Not Equals, and Greater than Equals.

Examples

1. **Equals** (=)

   Example: Find all issues in which the assignee is the current user.

   ```
   Query:  ASSIGNEE = currentUser()
   ```

2. **Not Equals** (!=)

    Example: Find all issues in which a project is not equal to the Sample Kanban Project:

    ```
    Query:    project! = "Sample Kanban Project"
    ```

3. **NOT IN**

    Example: Find all issues that are not of the type Bug or defect:

    ```
    Query:  issuetype not in (Bug,Defect)
    ```

Fields: It allows you to search for the values of the fields. Examples of fields are Assignee, Affectedversion, CreatedDate, Description, Due, Epic link, Fix version, Issue Key, and many more.

1. **Assignee**

    Example: Find all issues where the assignee was the current user.

    ```
    Query: assignee was currentUser()
    ```

2. **Description**

    Example: Find all issues where the description contains the word sprint

    ```
    Query: description ~ "sprint"
    ```

3. **Due**

    Example: Find all issues where the due is not empty

    ```
    Query: due is not EMPTY
    ```

Functions: A function is written using a word followed by parentheses. Parentheses may or may not contain some data. A function does calculations on Jira data or the numbers in parentheses. Function returns some values that are used in a query for searching issues.

Example Function: `openSprints()`, `componentsLeadByUser()`, `currentLogin()`, `earliestUnreleasedVersion()`, `endOfMonth()`, `parentepic()`, and many more:

1. Find issues that are assigned to future sprints.

    ```
    Query: sprint in futureSprints()
    ```

2. Find issues that do not belong to a released version.

    ```
    Query: fixversion in unreleasedVersions()
    ```

3. Find issues that are sub-tasks.

   Query: `issuetype in subtaskIssueTypes()`

4. Find issues that were created before 150 days.

   Query: `createdDate <150d`

Examples of important JQL for everyone

Here are some examples of important JQL queries:

1. Find all issues in a project that belong to the closedSprint.

   ```
   project = "SSP" AND sprint IN closedSprints()ORDER BY created
   DESC
   ```

2. Find issues in openSprints where the Status is not equal to done.

   ```
   Sprint in openSprints() and statusCategory != Done
   ```

3. Find out high-priority, unresolved issues and issue status is backlog.

   ```
   project = "Sample Kanban Project" AND priority = Highest AND
   resolution = Unresolved  and status = backlog
   ```

4. Find all issues in the next version to be released.

   ```
   fixVersion = earliestUnreleasedVersion(SSPA)
   ```

5. Find all issues for which time spent is equal to 1 day and issues are in unresolved status.

   ```
   timespent = 1d and resolution in (Unresolved)
   ```

6. Find all issues in which the current user is an assignee or reporter and the version is an unreleased version.

   ```
   (reporter= currentUser() or assignee = currentUser()) AND (fix-
   Version in unreleasedVersions())
   ```

7. Search all issues that are Created before 150 days and the status is not equal to To Do.

   ```
   createdDate <=150d and status != "To Do"
   ```

8. Select all Bugs assigned to me in a project, where the fixed version is either empty or not released.

   ```
   project = "Demo Project" AND issuetype = Bug AND assignee =
   currentUser()  AND (fixversion in unreleasedVersions() or fix-
   Version is EMPTY)
   ```

9. Search all issues that are of medium priority and in openSprints, sort by projects.

    ```
    sprint in openSprints() AND priority = Medium ORDER BY project
    ```

10. Find all issues where summary contains the word "kanban".

    ```
    project = "SKP" and summary ~ kanban ORDER BY created DESC
    ```

11. Setting precedence by using parentheses.

    Find all issues in Done status that belong to the project "DemoProject" OR assignee is the current user.

    ```
    status= Done and (project = "Demo Project" OR  assignee =
    currentUser() )
    ```

Understanding the importance of Dashboards

Dashboards are crucial for any project management tool. Jira dashboards help display project statistics and metrics. You can create dashboards and add gadgets to generate charts and other statistical analyses to track issues and projects. When you log in to Jira, you can first view the dashboard.

A user can create multiple dashboards specific to their requirements, such as different dashboards for various teams or projects. Jira dashboards provide statistics based on Jira filters. Therefore, it is essential to create the right filters and then add the appropriate gadgets to create dashboards. You can create dashboards and display them during daily stand-ups, retrospective meetings, or presentations to the top management. Jira also offers a feature called wallboard, which can be useful for displaying statistics on a TV screen and keeping everyone informed throughout the project.

Step-by-step process to create a Dashboard and add Gadget

Follow these steps to create a dashboard:

1. Login to Jira as admin and navigate to **Dashboards** in the top navigation bar.

2. Select dashboard and then select **Create** dashboard.

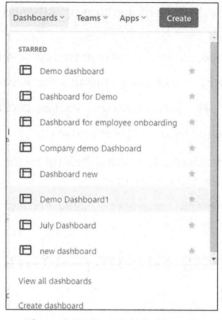

Figure 8.16: Creating dashboards

3. Enter all the details, such as Dashboard **Name, Description, Viewers**, and **Editors**, and click **Save**.

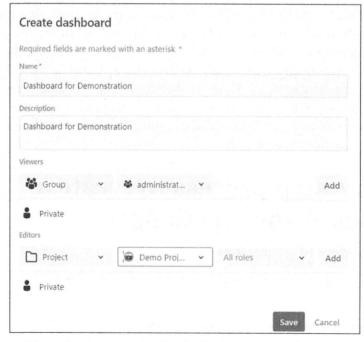

Figure 8.17: Entering the details of a dashboard and saving it

4. The dashboard has been created. You can change the layout, add gadgets after searching, and then click **Done**.

5. Click on **Add** after searching for the gadget. You can search for the gadget by typing the name of the gadget in the search gadget.

Figure 8.18: Adding a Gadget on a dashboard

Choosing a Dashboard Layout

Follow these steps to choose a dashboard layout:

1. Navigate to the top navigation bar and select `Dashboards.`

2. Select the dashboard.

3. Click on `Edit` and then select `Change layout.`

4. Select the layout as per your preference.

Figure 8.19: Choosing a Dashboard Layout

Copying, Sharing, and Deleting Dashboard

Follow these steps to copy, share, and delete a dashboard:

1. Navigate to the top navigation bar and select `Dashboards`.

2. Select `View all dashboards`.

3. Select the dashboard and click on three dots (`···`) on the right side.

4. You can copy the dashboard, rename, or share the dashboard, and delete the dashboard by selecting the required option.

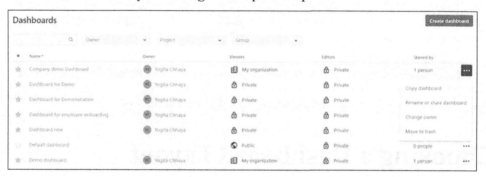

Figure 8.20: Choosing an option for a dashboard

Jira provides some standard Dashboard Gadgets. If you integrate Jira with an add-on, respective gadgets for that add-on get added and can be added to the dashboard.

Adding and Customizing Gadgets to a Dashboard

Follow these steps to add gadgets:

1. Navigate to the top navigation bar and select `Dashboards`.

2. Select the dashboard.

3. Select `Edit` on the right side. It will provide a list of multiple gadgets.

4. You can search for the gadgets by typing in the search bar. Select the preferred gadget and add the required details such as project/filter name, fields details, and save the gadget by clicking on `Done`.

Figure 8.21: *Adding and Customizing Gadgets*

Example Dashboards and Gadgets

Examples of dashboards and gadgets include:

- **Starred Filters**: This gadget lists the current user's favorite filters.
- **Two-Dimensional Filter Statistics**: It displays the data in table form. You can select x-axis and y-axis fields while configuring the gadget. This gadget can be used to keep track of the workload of a team, keep track of issues vs priority, and so on.
- **Sprint Health gadget**: It provides the overall statistics about the sprint such as Time elapsed, work completed, scope change in percentage, story point statistics, and name of the assignees in the sprint.

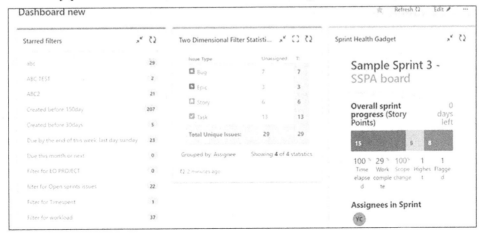

Figure 8.22: *Example Dashboard-1*

- **Issue Statistics**: It provides the percentage of different issue type for a selected project.
- **Pie Chart**: It displays a pie chart for a filter or a project. You can select which type of statistics to display. For example, you can select fields such as priority, assignee, labels, issue type, etc.
- **Sprint Burndown Gadget**: It displays the amount of remaining work in a sprint.
- **Workload Pie Chart**: It displays the matching issues based on the selected fields. You can select a filter or a project, and it displays data in the form of a pie chart.

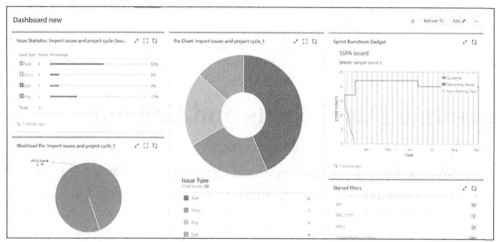

Figure 8.23: *Example Dashboard-2*

- **Projects Gadget**: It displays the information about all the projects and filters of each project.
- **Assigned to me**: It displays all issues assigned to the current user in all projects.
- **Jira Road map**: It displays upcoming versions of the project and a summary of the issues for that version.
- **Resolution time Gadget**: It displays the average number of days the issues were open for the selected period. It displays data in bar chart format.

Figure 8.24: *Example Dashboard-3*

Creating a Wallboard

Wallboard is a full-screen display of the Jira dashboard that can be done on a TV screen. It displays all the gadgets one-by-one and doesn't have any navigation menu on it.

Here are the steps:

1. Login to Jira and navigate to **Dashboards** in the top navigation bar.

2. Select **View all dashboard**s and select the dashboard that is required.

3. Select ⬛ and click **View as wallboard**.

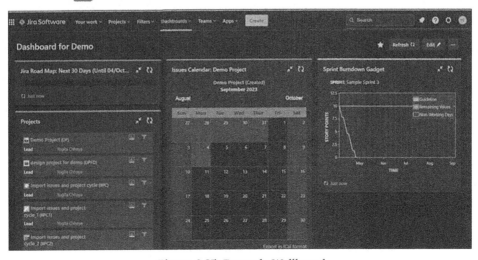

Figure 8.25: *Example Wallboard*

Introduction to Reports

Reports are an important feature in any project management tool. Jira provides a reporting feature for individuals, teams, and projects. Jira reporting helps teams manage time tracking, project management, and measuring agile metrics. By utilizing these parameters, project managers and teams can plan work in advance, track progress, and make data-driven decisions based on forecasts. You can also add plugins to get more detailed reports.

Steps to accessing Reports in Jira

Follow these steps to access the Jira reports:

1. Navigate to **All projects** and then select one project.

2. Click **Reports** on the left navigation bar.

3. You will be able to select various kinds of Jira reports.

4. Click the required report and select the parameters to view.

Jira provides different kinds of reports, and we will learn about Agile reports in detail.

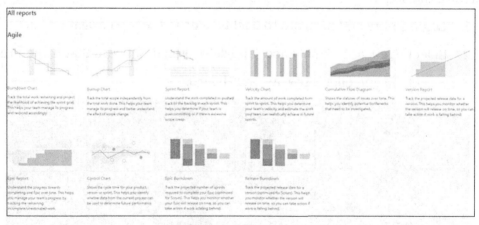

Figure 8.26: *Agile Reports in Jira*

Understanding Agile reports

In this section, we will understand all reports for Agile teams in detail.

Reports for Scrum Teams

There are eight reports for Agile Scrum projects as follows:

- **Burndown Chart** - This report is applicable to sprints within a project. It displays how much work is left in a sprint and provides an idea about achieving the sprint goal. By tracking the remaining work throughout the sprint, teams can manage changes in priority and plan the work to achieve the sprint goal. Users can select the sprints to view and also have the option to choose estimations in the board settings and on the reports page. The Burndown chart will only include the issues in the filter for the board. The Red line shows the remaining values, whereas the gray line is used to display the guideline.

Below the chart, it shows details about issues and information related to those issues, such as sprint start, issue burndown, sprint end, and scope changes. This helps in understanding the overall pattern of the iteration and its progress.

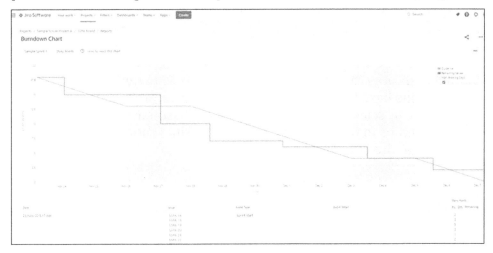

Figure 8.27: Burndown Chart

- **Burnup Chart:** This report is applicable to sprints within a project. It displays the sprint's completed work compared with its total scope.

The chart uses a vertical axis to measure the amount of work, which can be selected using various metrics like story points, issue count, or estimates. The horizontal axis represents time, measured in days. The gap between the lines on the chart indicates the remaining workload. When the project reaches completion, these lines will converge.

By closely observing the `Work scope` line, you can spot any instances of scope creep.

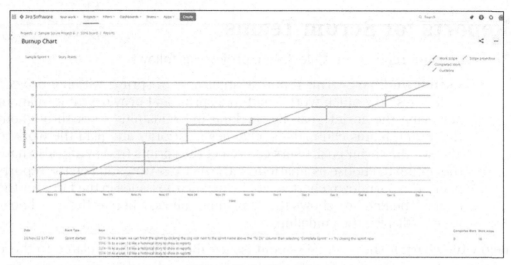

Figure 8.28: *Burnup Chart*

- **Sprint Report:** This report is applicable to sprints in a project. It displays the statistics regarding the completed and not completed issues, priority, status, and story points. This data can assist teams in understanding whether the teams are overcommitting or there is scope creep. The Red line indicates the actual work done, whereas the gray line indicates the guideline based on the estimation entered before the start of the sprint. Users can select the sprints to view and also have the option to select estimations in the board settings. The Sprint report will only include the issues in the filter for the board.

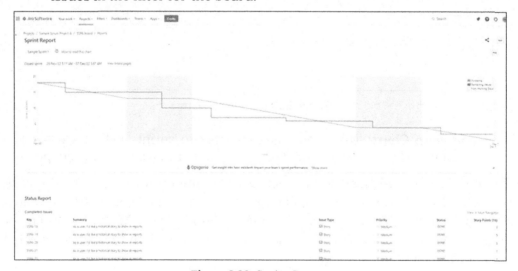

Figure 8.29: *Sprint Report*

- **Velocity Chart:** This report is applicable to sprints within a project. The velocity report is used to know the average amount of work a team can complete in a sprint. You can measure this in different ways, such as counting the number of tasks, measuring time in minutes, hours, days, or using the story points.

Jira keeps track of this over time and shows it in reports. These reports help the team figure out how much work they can do in future sprints. It helps managers plan how much work the team can realistically do in a certain amount of time.

There is a vertical line on the report, which is used to measure their work, in story points or time.

There are two types of bars on the report. Gray bars show how much work the team planned to do in a sprint before it started. Green bars show how much work the team actually finished in the sprint, and this is shown when the sprint ends.

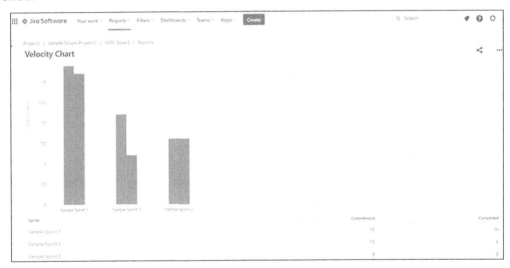

Figure 8.30: *Velocity Chart*

- **Version Report:** This chart is applicable to versions. It helps track the planned release date for a version and forecast whether the version will be released on time, allowing you to plan actions if the work falls behind. It provides a comprehensive view of the outstanding issues within a specific version and the overall amount of pending work for the entire version.

It includes the issues for a specific board but doesn't display archived versions. The horizontal axis starts on the date that is entered, taking the date of the first issue created if the date is not entered for the version.

The blue line indicates the Predicted Release date, which is based on the daily average velocity and the amount of estimated work remaining.

The Predicted Release Date (Optimistic) is the date by which you might expect the version to be complete (It is calculated by adding 10% to the average daily velocity). The Predicted Release Date (Pessimistic) is the date by which you might expect the version to be complete (It is calculated by subtracting 10% from the average daily velocity).

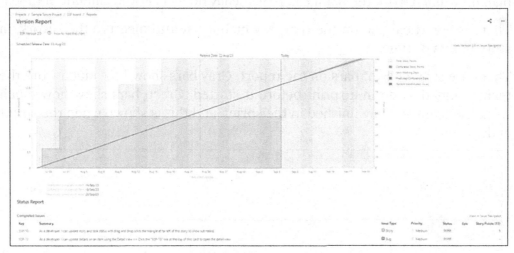

Figure 8.31: *Version Report*

- **Epic Report:** This report is applicable to Epics only.

The Epic Report provides an overview of an epic's issues, categorizing them as either finished, unfinished, or without estimates. This report is useful when planning tasks for an epic spanning multiple sprint.

You can use the Epic Report to see how much progress we've made on the epic and to keep track of how much work is still left to do. The way the report looks might change a bit if we're counting tasks instead of using a different method, like Story Points.

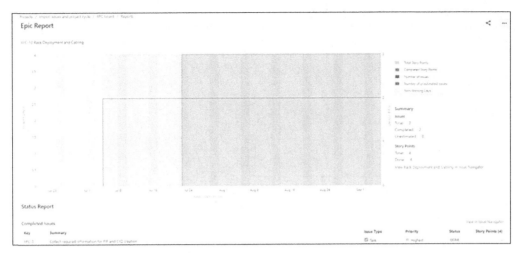

Figure 8.32: *Epic Report*

- **Epic Burndown Chart:** Epic Burndown report is specifically designed for agile scrum teams working in sprints, making progress tracking much more convenient. The Epic Burndown report provides insights into your team's progress with a specific epic. An epic is a user story that can be divided into smaller tasks. The report displays information based on the estimation method you have selected.

Here are a few ways you can make use of an Epic Burndown report:

- Monitor how fast your team is advancing through the epic.
- Observe how changes, such as tasks added or removed during the sprint, impact your team's overall progress.
- Forecast the number of sprints required to finish the epic, considering the past sprint data and the changes done in the ongoing sprints.

The estimated number of sprints needed is determined by assessing the work completed in the most recent three sprints. When calculating velocity, changes in scope are not considered, but they are taken into account when calculating the overall remaining work.

The Epic Burndown report can provide predictions solely based on estimated issues within your epic. If an issue is in a status that isn't mapped to a column, it won't be taken into account in the Epic Burndown report.

Figure 8.33: *Epic Burndown Chart*

- **Release Burndown Chart:** This report is applicable to project versions and is designed specifically for scrum teams. It presents data in accordance with the estimation statistics you've chosen. The Release Burndown report provides insights into your team's progress regarding tasks associated with a particular project release.

Here are a few ways you can make use of this report:

- Monitor the pace at which your team is working towards the project backlog.

- Assess how the addition and deletion of tasks during sprints have impacted your team's overall progress.

- Forecast the number of sprints required to complete the project version, drawing from insights gained from past sprints and changes made during those sprints.

  The estimated number of sprints needed is determined by assessing the work completed in the most recent three sprints. When calculating velocity, changes in scope are not considered, but they are taken into account when calculating the overall remaining work.

  The Release Burndown report can provide predictions solely based on estimated issues within your version. If an issue is in a status that isn't mapped to a column, it won't be taken into account in the Release Burndown report.

Figure 8.34: *Release Burndown Chart*

Reports for Kanban Teams

There are two reports for Agile Kanban projects as follows:

- Cumulative Flow Diagram
- Control Chart

Cumulative Flow Diagram: A Cumulative Flow Diagram (CFD) is a graphical representation in the form of an area chart, used to display the progress of work items within an application, version, or sprint. In this chart, the x-axis represents time, while the y-axis represents the number of issues. Each distinct colored region within the chart corresponds to a specific workflow status, mirroring the columns on your task board.

The CFD serves as a valuable tool for pinpointing bottlenecks in your workflow. If you observe a region within the chart expanding vertically over time, it typically indicates that the corresponding column on your board is experiencing a bottleneck.

In CFD, you can choose the **Refine** report option to select your desired filters. You can select different time frames and Date ranges. Changing the date range will highlight issues that occurred within those dates.

CFD provides data specific to a board (board's filter) and displays it based on column mapping. If any status is unmapped, it won't be shown on the chart. CFD also indicates if any issues have accumulated in a particular column.

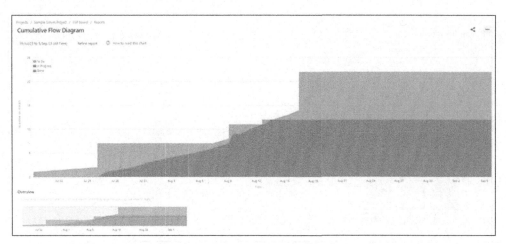

Figure 8.35: *Cumulative Flow Diagram*

Control Chart: The control chart is used to display the Cycle Time or Lead Time. It can be for a product, version, or sprint by tracking the duration each issue remains in specific status over a defined time interval. It provides key statistical measures, including the average, rolling average, and standard deviation based on this dataset.

A Control Chart serves as a tool to evaluate if the data gathered in the ongoing sprint is relevant for predicting future performance. The narrower the variance in issue Cycle Times, the greater the level of confidence in using the mean (or median) as a reliable indicator of future performance.

Important terms to understand are as follows:

- **Cycle Time**: It is the summation of the time from an issue passing through in progress, in review, and done statuses.
- **Lead Time**: It is the summation of the time from an issue passing through the backlog, in progress, in review, and done statuses.
- **The rolling Average**: Average of cycle times of A issues before the current issue +

  Average of cycle times of the current issue +

  Average of cycle times of A issues after the current issue

With the control chart, you can perform various actions, such as selecting a dot to view issue details, zooming in to highlight a specific time period on the chart, setting the desired time frame for data selection, and refining the report by selecting filters, swim lanes, and columns.

If your project's lead cycle time varies slightly from the average, it's generally not a concern. However, significant spikes beyond the average indicate the presence of pauses, obstacles, or waiting periods.

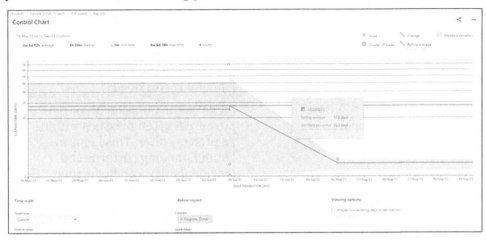

Figure 8.36: *Control Chart*

Other Reports

Jira software provides other reports, such as Issue Analysis Report, Forecast, and Management reports.

Type	Name of Report	Description
Issue Analysis	Average Age Report	Displays the average of the tasks that are unresolved within a project or filter, providing insight into the timeliness of managing your backlog
	Created vs Resolved issues Report	Compares newly generated issues to resolved ones over a specified timeframe, allowing you to understand the pattern of your overall backlog, whether it's expanding or contracting
	Pie Chart Report	It displays the search results from a specific project or a filter. This is based on selected statistics in the form of a pie chart. The users can see the breakdown of issues in each category selected

	Recently created issues Report	It shows the count of issues generated during a specific time frame for a project or filter and tracks how many of them were successfully resolved. This information assists in understanding whether your team is effectively managing the incoming workload
	Resolution Time Report	It gives the duration it takes to resolve a batch of issues within a project/filter. This helps in understanding patterns and incidents that can be further discussed and investigated
	Single Level Group by Report	Displays issues categorized by a specific field for a filter. This report helps you to organize search results based on a particular field and assess the overall status of each category
	Time Since Issues Report	Using a date and a project/filter, it shows when certain things happened with the issues. This can help you keep a watch on how many issues were created, updated, or more, in a particular time period
Forecast and Management	Time tracking Report	It displays the initial and current time estimates for tasks in the current project. This helps you figure out if the work on these tasks is going according to plan
	User Workload Report	It shows how much time is expected for all the unfinished tasks assigned to a user in different projects. This gives you a clearer picture of how busy that user is
	Version Workload Report	It displays how much time is needed to finish all the ongoing tasks assigned to a specific version, organized by users and the tasks themselves. This helps you see what still needs to be done for that version

Other	Workload pie chart Report	A report that presents project or filter issues in the form of a pie chart

Table 8.1: Other Reports in Jira Software

Introduction and Overview of Atlassian Analytics

Atlassian Analytics offers a solution to understand data, make data-driven decisions, and create dashboards for Atlassian tools and other data sources. Here is an overview:

- Atlassian Analytics helps teams make decisions using data. You can create interactive dashboards.

- You can use ready-made dashboards to find answers to your big questions. Or you can build custom views using a visual mode or a written SQL query editor.

- You can get deeper insights by looking at different types of data such as operations, finances, and customer info, all within Atlassian.

- It's a tool to analyze data from Jira software, Jira work management, and Jira Service Management.

- It allows you to perform custom data analysis with a visual SQL interface.

- You can connect to other databases like Snowflake, Amazon Redshift, Google Big Query, and more.

- In software projects, you can identify the causes of problems.

- In service projects, change management, and incident management, you can keep track of important metrics.

Here's how it works:

- Atlassian Analytics connects to a Data Lake so your data stays connected and updatable.

- You can choose and set up products, projects, and spaces to create charts from.

- You can write SQL queries if you want, but you can also make charts and dashboards without coding.

- You can pick different chart types and diagrams. Atlassian Analytics suggests chart types based on your data and queries.

- You can put the charts and dashboards into Confluence spaces. You can also comment on and tag them.

Conclusion

We are now familiar with searching issues in Jira using basic and advanced search, writing JQL queries, creating Dashboards, adding the right Gadgets to present the data, and tracking tasks and projects. In addition, we have also learned to access reports, understand the Agile metrics from various reports, and gain an overview of Atlassian Analytics.

In the next chapter, we will learn about Jira Automation Rules.

Points to Remember

- Give your filters appropriate names that reflect their purpose, making it easier to find and reuse them later.

- Share filters with your team to ensure everyone has access to the same set of criteria for issue searches.

- Learn Jira Query Language (JQL) to create more complex and correct filters, using operators like AND, OR, and NOT.

- Quick Filters on Agile boards allow you to quickly switch between different filters to view issues that match specific criteria.

- Use scheduled filter subscriptions to receive regular email updates with the results of your filter queries.

- Create your dashboards to suit your role or project by adding and arranging gadgets that display relevant and important information.

- Take advantage of gadget configuration options to fine-tune the way data is presented on your dashboard.

- Use the Filter Results and Two-Dimensional Filter Statistics gadgets to display filtered issue lists directly on your dashboard, providing quick access to specific sets of issues.

- Share filters and dashboards with team members or project stakeholders, allowing them to stay informed about project progress.

- Set appropriate permissions to control who can view and edit your filters and dashboards.

- Choose the report type that fits your needs best. Jira has different types, such as Burndown Charts, Control Charts, and Velocity Charts

- Many reports allow you to customize date ranges, issue types, and other parameters to focus on the data that matters most.

- Take the time to learn what metrics like velocity and burndown charts mean so you can make better decisions.

- Add gadgets like the "Filter Results" gadget or "Pie Chart" gadget within your reports to provide additional context and details.

- Periodically review and clean up your filters, dashboards, and reports to ensure they stay relevant and organized.

References

1. A JQL for: A piece of JQL I can add which will show me Jira tickets which were created before the first of the month but were closed and open on or after the first of the month . So for example tickets which were created before the 1st of November but were closed and still open on or after the 1st of November.

https://community.atlassian.com/t5/Jira-Software-questions/Filters -Advance-issue-search-JQL/qaq-p/1886105

2. Advanced search using JQL for epics without stories:

https://community.atlassian.com/t5/Jira-Core-Server-questions/Advanced -search-using-JQL-for-epics-without-stories/qaq-p/1049459

3. Deleting Filters in Jira Cloud:

https://community.atlassian.com/t5/Jira-Service-Management/Deleting -Filters-in-Jira-Cloud/qaq-p/2314822

4. Edit a private filter in Jira Cloud:

https://community.atlassian.com/t5/Jira-Software-questions/Edit-a-private -filter-in-Jira-Cloud/qaq-p/2294042

5. JQL Syntax for due date Quick Filter:

https://community.atlassian.com/t5/Jira-questions/JQL-Syntax-for-due -date-Quick-Filter/qaq-p/2175118

6. Using Quick Filters in Active Sprint board:

https://community.atlassian.com/t5/Jira-questions/Using-Quick-Filters-in-Active-Sprint-board/qaq-p/2226732

7. Is there a way in Jira Cloud to allow users to Share/Create filters & Dashboards & not boards:

https://community.atlassian.com/t5/Jira-Software-questions/Is-there-a-way-in-Jira-Cloud-to-allow-users-to-Share-Create/qaq-p/2393157

8. Are there any global settings for dashboards?

https://community.atlassian.com/t5/Jira-Software-questions/global-settings-for-dashboards/qaq-p/2131965

9. Are there any global settings for dashboards?

https://community.atlassian.com/t5/Jira-Software-questions/global-settings-for-dashboards/qaq-p/2131965

10. How to generate Dashboards according to the project needs?

https://community.atlassian.com/t5/Jira-Software-questions/How-to-generate-Dashboards-according-to-the-project-needs/qaq-p/2231361

11. I can access my projects but can no longer find my dashboards! I can go to the project board and see my issues. All I have now is a default dashboard:

https://community.atlassian.com/t5/Jira-Work-Management-Questions/What-happened-to-my-dashboards/qaq-p/2281858

12. Are Dashboards part of Jira or are they part of an add-on?

https://community.atlassian.com/t5/Jira-Software-questions/Are-Dashboards-part-of-Jira-or-are-they-part-of-an-add-on/qaq-p/2264722

13. I'd like to be able to copy and then modify a Jira software Dashboard gadget, instead of starting from scratch with a new one and adding the same fields again:

https://community.atlassian.com/t5/Jira-Software-questions/Can-Atlassian-enable-copying-a-Dashboard-gadget/qaq-p/2365482

14. I am looking to create a recurring dashboard that presents the health of the current/open sprint without having to change the sprint ID in my filter at the start of each sprint:

https://community.atlassian.com/t5/Jira-questions/Dashboard-dynamic
-sprint-dropdown/qaq-p/1870047

15. For each release, I have to have a dashboard for that particular release. This dashboard contains data from multiple filters. With each release, the only changing variable would be the "Fix version":

https://community.atlassian.com/t5/Jira-questions/Re-use-dashboards-by
-adding-dynamic-filtering-capability/qaq-p/1719508

16. Reports by Assignee:

https://community.atlassian.com/t5/Jira-Software-questions/Reports-by
-Assignee/qaq-p/2441865

17. Reports:

https://community.atlassian.com/t5/Jira-questions/Reports/qaq-p/2365294

18. Insights and sprint burndown feature:

https://community.atlassian.com/t5/Jira-Software-questions/Insights-and
-sprint-burndown-feature/qaq-p/2124121

19. Sprint Insights - the admins can see it but not the team members:

https://community.atlassian.com/t5/Jira-Software-questions/Sprint
-Insights-the-admins-can-see-it-but-not-the-team-members/
qaq-p/2365550

20. Reading Jira Sprint Report:

https://community.atlassian.com/t5/Jira-Software-questions/Reading-Jira
-Sprint-Report/qaq-p/2124012

CHAPTER 9

Jira Automation Rules

Introduction

Automation is employed to enhance the efficiency and productivity in project management. As the scope of software development and project management continues to expand, automation becomes indispensable for teams. It is not just a time-saver but also a game-changer, helping teams streamline their workflows, reduce manual effort, and minimize human error. Consequently, teams can shift their focus to more critical tasks, such as innovation and problem-solving. They can automatically assign tasks, transition issues through predefined workflows, send notifications, and set field values. Thus, automation serves as your behind-the-scenes assistant that makes your work life significantly smoother. In this chapter, we'll take a closer look at how this magical Jira Automation works and how you can make the most of it.

Structure

In this chapter, we will discuss the following topics:

- Understanding Automation in Jira
- Accessing the Automation rules on Jira Boards
- Knowing and Understanding Elements of Automation Rules
  - Triggers
  - Conditions
  - Actions
  - Rule Branching

- o   Smart Values
- o   Owner
- o   Rule Actor
- o   Scope
- o   Allowing rule trigger
- o   Notify on Error
- o   Audit Log
- o   Debugging Rules
- Templates and Automation Library
- Automation Playground
- Checking Usage
- Performance Insights
- Import and Export Jira Automation Rules
- Steps to Create an Automation Rule with Examples
- Essential Learning Examples

Understanding Automation Rules and its Importance

Automation helps you automate repetitive tasks. For example, it can involve creating multiple tasks, adding conditions, updating fields like assignee, and so on. It saves time for every team member. Writing an automation rule is a no-brainer because it is a no-code tool. Even people with a non-technical background can write automation rules, and it doesn't require any prior experience. It works with third-party tools and makes life easier. The rules are simple and easy to understand and can be created with drag and drop.

Accessing the Automation Rules on Jira Board

Here are the steps for accessing the Automation rules on the Jira Board:

1.   Navigate to **Project** > **Project Settings** > **Automation**:

Figure 9.1: *Navigating to Project settings*

2. Click **Automation** on the left panel. On the landing page, the user will see **create rule** and **Global administration** options:

Figure 9.2: *Options for accessing the Automation Rules*

3. Clicking **Global administration** gives the user a list of automation templates to choose from:

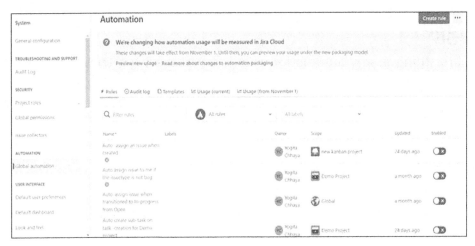

Figure 9.3: *Selecting Global Administration option*

4. Clicking **Create Rule** displays the first step to create a new automation rule:

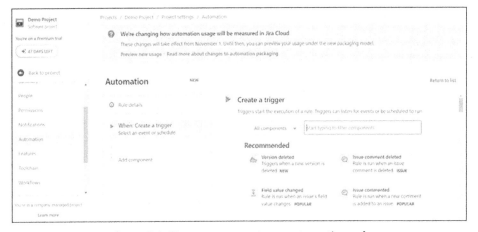

Figure 9.4: *First step to create an automation rule*

5. The first step is to add a trigger that will initiate the rule. You can add a condition, create a Branch, and conclude the rule by adding an action.

Knowing and Understanding Elements of Automation Rules

There are mainly three elements to create an automation rule: Triggers, Conditions, and Actions. In addition to that, there are a few basic things we will explore in this section.

Triggers

The first thing in any automation rule is to start with a trigger. Triggers are responsible for initiating the execution of the rule. There are events occurring in Jira, such as an issue transition, issue creation, or a change in field value. Triggers listen to these events. You can also trigger rules from add-ons such as Fisheye-Crucible, GitHub, and Bitbucket.

It is possible to set manual triggers that work based on a particular condition.

The issue triggers are as shown in *Figure 9.5*.

Figure 9.5: *Issue Triggers- Jira Automation Rule*

Conditions

Conditions enable you to refine the applicability of your rule. They must be satisfied for your rule to proceed. For example, you can configure your rule which will execute if the issues meet the specific JQL query. In the event that a condition is not met, the rule will halt, and any subsequent actions specified after the condition will not be executed.

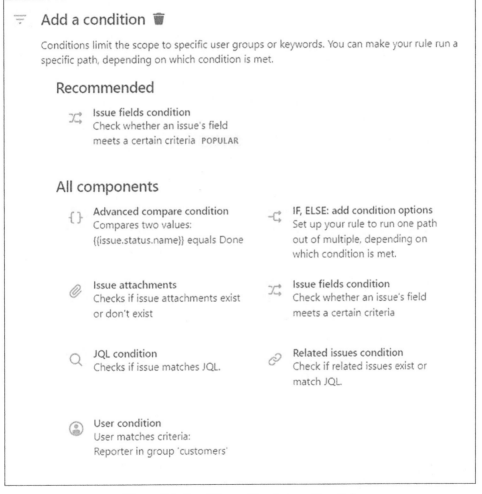

Figure 9.6: *Conditions –Jira Automation Rule*

Actions

Actions are the final stage of any automation rule. They ultimately allow you to take actions such as sending an email, closing tasks, or transitioning issues.

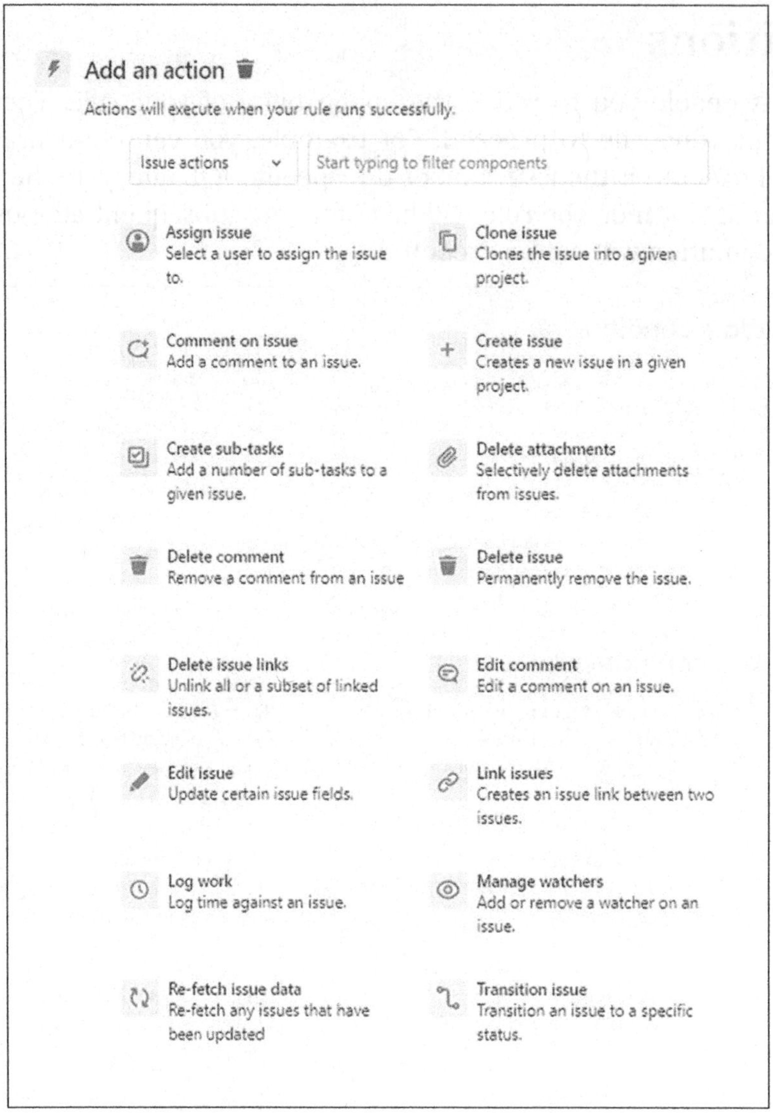

Figure 9.7: *Actions – Jira Automation Rule*

Rule Branching

When setting up automation rules, it is possible to create a separate section within the rule where actions can be performed on related issues. This concept is known as **branching**. Jira provides special conditions and actions to create extremely useful rules that can be applied to all the linked issues as well. It differs from the linear execution of rules and instead allows for the rule to diverge into multiple paths.

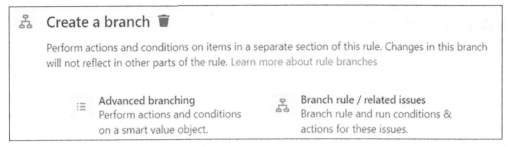

Figure 9.8: Rule branching

For instance, consider a rule triggered when an issue transitions to the **Done** status; this rule can also include a branch that carries out separate actions on the subtasks of that issue.

Branching Constraints:

- **Nesting**: It's important to note that branches cannot be nested within each other. This means you cannot have one branch contained within another.

- **If/else Condition**: The use of the If/else block condition is not supported in branching.

- **Isolation**: Each branch operates in isolation. Any modifications made within a branch do not affect the main rule or any other branches. For instance, if a branch includes a `Create variable` action, the created smart value can only be used within that particular branch and cannot be accessed in the main rule or other branches.

Example: In this example, story points of related issues, that is, sub-tasks under a parent task get added:

Figure 9.9: Example of Rule branching

Smart Values

Smart values allow access and manipulation of the issue data in Jira. We have provided the **Smart Values** list as mentioned below.

Jira Smart Values - Issues

The issue smart values are employed to retrieve details concerning the active issue of the rule, indicating the issue currently being processed by the rule.

Issue Fields	Smart Value and Properties	What it Returns
`{{issue.[property]}}`		Issue properties are helpful for accessing various information about the active issue
	`{{issue.description}}`	Content written in the description field
	`{{issue.key}}`	Issue-key is a combination of a project-key and an issue number
	`{{issue.project}}`	The project that issue belongs to
	`{{issue.status}}`	Status of the issue
	`{{issue.status.name}}`	Status of the issue
	`{{issue. Summary}}`	The summary of the issue
	`{{issue.versions}}`	Affect's version of the issue
	`{{issue.Issuetype.name}}`	Issue types such as Bug, Task, and Story
	`{{issue.resolution}}`	Resolution of the issue
	`{{issue.updated}}`	Date when the issue was updated
	`{{issue.Story Points}}`	The story point estimate of the issue's story (Applicable to company-managed project Jira Software Cloud)

	`{{issue.Story Points Estimate}}`	The story point estimate of the issue's story (Applicable to team-managed project Jira Software Cloud)
Issue Dates	`{{issue.created}}`	Creation date of the issue
	`{{issue.duedate}}`	Due date of the issue
Issue Users	`{{issue.assignee.displayName}}`	Name of the assignee of the issue
	`{{issue.reporter.displayName}}`	Name of the reporter of the issue
Issue Custom Field	`{{issue.[Custom Field].id}}`	Unique ID assigned by Jira to the Custom field
	`{{issue. [Custom Field]. description}}`	The text shown below the custom field when viewed in the Simple Search column
	`{{issue. [Custom Field].name}}`	The label visible on the left of the field
Issue Comments	`{{issue.comments.last.body}}`	Provides the body of the last comment
	`{{issue.comments.first.body}}`	Provides the body of the first comment
	`{{issue.comments.reverse.body}}`	Issue's comments in reverse order
	`{{issue.comments.size}}`	Number of comments added on the issue
	`{{issue.comments.author. displayName}}`	Provides the Comment authors
Issue Components	`{{issue.components.name}}`	Value of the component field of the issue
Issue's Epic	`{{issue.epic.key}}`	Epic's key, for example, TESTEPIC-23
	`{{issue.epic.status.name}}`	Epic's status, for example, Open
	`{{issue.epic.[Custom Field]}}`	Value in an Epic's custom field
Issue Fix Version	`{{issue.fixVersions.name}}`	The name of the fix version

	`{{issue.fixVersions.description}}`	The description of the fix version
	`{{issue.fixVersions.released}}`	True, if the fixed version is released; otherwise, False
	`{{issue.fixVersions.releaseDate}}`	Fix version's release date
	`{{issue.fix.Versions.archived}}`	True, if the fixed version is archived; otherwise, False
	`{{issue.latest}}`	Prints the issue-key and the status, for example, To Do, In Progress
	`{{issue.latest.description}}`	Provides the description of the status
	`{issue.parent.key}}`	Issue-key of the parent issue of sub-task
	`{{issue.parent.priority.name}}`	Priority of the parent issue of the sub-task
	`{{issue.parent.epic.summary}}`	Summary of the parent issue's epic
Issue property	`{{issue.properties}}`	Property of the issue such as some value stored that are used by add-ons and integrations
Issue security	`{{issue.security.name}}`	Provides Security level Name.
	`{{issue.security.id}}`	Provides Security level ID
	`{{issue.timetracking.timespent}}`	Time logged in the Time spent field
	`{{issue.timetracking.remainingestimate}}`	Value in the time remaining field
Issue Versions	`{{versions.name}}`	The name of the affects version
	`{{versions.description}}`	The description of the affects version
	`{{versions.archived}}`	True, if the affects version is archived; otherwise, False
	`{{versions.released}}`	True, if the affects version is released; otherwise, False
	`{{versions.releaseDate}}`	Affects version release date

Issue Watchers	`{{issue.watchers.displayName}}`	Name of the watchers for issue
	`{{issue.watchers.emailAddress}}`	E-mail ID of the issue watchers
lookupissues		It returns a list of issues from a JQL search
	`{{key}}`	Returns issuekey
	`{{url}}`	It provides the issueurl
	`{{summary}}`	It provides the issuesummary
	`{{assignee.displayName}}`	Provides the name of the Assignee
	`{{reporter.displayName}}`	Provides the name of the Reporter
	`{{status}}`	Status
	`{{issueType.name}}`	Name of the issue type
	`{{resolution}}`	Resolution status
	`{{fixVersion}}`	Projects the fixversion
	`{{created}}`	Date the issue was created
	`{{updated}}`	Date the issue was updated
	`{{Story Points}}`	For company-managed projects, it returns the story points of the issue
	`{{Story point estimate}}`	For team-managed projects, it returns the story points of the issue
Triggerissue	`{{triggerissue}}`	Refers to the issue that triggered the rule. All the properties applicable to issues are applicable to trigger issue
Attachment	`{{attachment.filename}}`	The filename of the attachment
	`{{attachment.mimeType}}`	The file format of the attachment
	`{{attachment.created}}`	Date and time of the attachment when it was added to the issue

	`{{attachment. [xxx]. size}}`	File size of a particular attachment
	`{{attachment.author}}`	Name of the user who added the attachment
	`{{attachment.author.accountId}}`	ID associated with the user
	`{{attachment.author.displayName}}`	Name displayed in the Jira Instance
	`{{attachment.author.active}}`	Returns TRUE, if the account is active; FALSE, if it is not active
	`{{attachment.author.emailAddress}}`	E-mail address associated with the user's name
	`{{attachment.author.timeZone}}`	It is the time zone registered in their account
	`{{baseUrl}}`	Gives the URL of the Jira instance
Changelog	`{{changelog}}`	This value accesses changelog and a list of changes for the field
	`{{changelog.summary}}`	Displays changelog information for the Summary field
	`{{changelog.issuetype}}`	Displays changelog information for the Issue type field
	`{{changelog.status}}`	Displays changelog information for the Status field
Comment	`{{comment}}`	It is used with issue Commented Trigger. This smart value will not work with other triggers
	`{{comment.body}}`	Content of the comment that prompted the rule
	`{{comment.author}}`	ID of the author of the comment
	`{{comment.created}}`	Date and time when the comment was created
	`{{comment.visibility.type}}`	Any restrictions on the comment, for example, Role

	`{{comment.visibility.value}}`	Label for Comment restriction if any
	`{{comment.properties}}`	It accesses comment property that are used by add-ons and integrations
	`{{comment.id}}`	The comment that prompted the rule is stored in this value
	`{{createdIssue}}`	Accesses the previous issue created in the rule All property used with issue smart value can be used with this
	`{{createdIssues}}`	A list of issues that have been created in the rule. It is used with Create sub-tasks, Create issue, and Clone issue actions. All property used with issue smart value can be used with this
Event Type	`{{eventType}}`	The type of event that prompted the rule. For Example: `Issue_commented`
Fieldchange	`{{fieldChange}}`	
	`{fieldChange.fromString}}`	It returns the previous value as displayed
	`{fieldChange.toString}}`	It returns the new value as displayed
	`{{fieldChange.from}}`	Previous raw value. For example: For a select field
	`{{fieldChange.to}}`	New raw value. For example: For a select field
	`{addedfieldChange.field}}`	It shows the field that has changed due to the addition of a value
	`{{addedFieldChange.fieldId}}`	The fieldId of the field that has changed due to the addition of a value

	`{{addedFieldChange.fieldType}}`	Returns the fieldType of the field that has changed due to the addition of a value
	`{addedfieldChange.valueIds}}`	Provides the ID/IDs of new value/values added
	`{{addedfieldChange.values}}`	Provides the new value/values added
	`{{deletedFieldChange.field}}`	Provides the field that value has changed due to deletion of a value
	`{{deletedFieldChange.fieldId}}`	The fieldId of the field that has changed due to the deletion of a value
	`{{deletedFieldChange.fieldType}}`	Provides the fieldType of the field that has changed due to deletion of a value
	`{{deletedFieldChange.valueIds}}`	Provides the iD/iDs of value/values deleted
	`{{deletedFieldChange.values}}`	Provides the value/values deleted
Rule	`{{rule}}`	Provides the information for the current rule
	`{{rule.name}}`	Name of the rule that is running
	`{{rule.actor}}`	The rule Actor
WebHook	`{{webhookData.[value].[childvalue]}}`	Enables access to the data transmitted with the incoming webhook, such as the request's body
	`{{webhookResponse}}`	Used with Send Web Request Action. Upon a successful request, you can access the response data from the webhook using the provided smart values
Worklog	`{{worklog}}`	Accesses worklog information of an issue that is recent
	`{{worklog.visibility}}`	When the worklog is restricted, it is available

	{{worklog.visibility.type}}	When the worklog is restricted, it is available
	{{worklog.visibility.value}}	When the worklog is restricted, it is available
	Other properties: {{worklog.comment}} {{worklog.started}} {{worklog.timeSpentSeconds}} {{worklog.timeSpent}}	

Table 9.1: Jira Smart Values – Issues

Jira Smart Values - Projects

The following smart values listed in *Table 9.2* can be used to access information regarding Jira projects:

	Smart Value and Properties	**What It Returns**
Projects	{{project.id}}	The ID of the project that activated the rule
	{{project.key}}	The project key associated with the project that activated the rule
	{{project.name}}	The name of the project associated with the project that activated the rule
	{{project.projectTypeKey}}	It returns the type of the project. For example: Software, Service Management, Software
	{{project.avatarUrls}}	It returns the avatar URL of the project that activated the rule

Table 9.2: Jira Smart Values – Projects

Jira Smart Values - Lists

The following smart values are available to access and format the value of items in a list when setting up a rule:

Smart Value	Property and Example	What it Returns
List	{{issue.fixVersions.name}}	Goes through a list and displays its contents. It can reference other methods and properties
List.average	{{issue.subtasks.Story Points. average}}	Returns the average of numbers within a list
list.distinct	{{lookupIssues.parent. distinct}}	This smart value returns all items from a list that are not repeated
list.isEmpty	{{issue.issuelinks.isEmpty}}	It shows true if the list is empty, or False if it is not
list. join(separator)	{{issue.fixVersions.name.join(" - ")}}	It produces a list of items separated by the specified characters
list.get(index)	{lookupIssues.get(0).summary}}	The element located at the given index, where 0 indicates the initial element in the array
list. getFromEnd(index)	{{issue.comments.getFromEnd(1). body}}	The element located at the specified index from the array's end, with 0 representing the last element
list.first	{{issue.comments.first.body}}	It returns the first element in the list
list.last	{{issue.comments.last.body}}	It returns the last element in the list
list.max	{{issue.subtasks.Due date.max}}	It returns the highest number in a list or returns the latest date in a list
list.min	{{issue.fixVersions.releaseDate. min}}	It returns the smallest number in a list or returns the earliest date in a list
list.size	{{issue.comments.size}}	It returns the size of the list
list.sum	{{issue.subtasks.Story Points. sum}}	It returns the sum of all values in a list

Table 9.3: *Jira Smart Values – Lists*

Jira Smart Values - Text Fields

The following smart values are available and applicable for text strings. It can be applied while creating new rules:

Smart Value and Properties	Example	What it Returns
`abbreviate(int maxLength)`	`{{issue.summary.abbreviate(4)}}` `-> Hell...`	Shortens the text to the specified character limit and appends "..." at the end. The maxLength parameter must be a minimum of four characters
`asNumber`	`{{issue.summary.asNumber}}` `-> Null`	Converts a given string into a number if feasible; otherwise, it returns null
`charAt(int index)`	`{{issue.summary.charAt(0)}} -> H`	Determines the character located at the designated position within the given text string
`capitalize()`	`{{issue.summary.capitalize()}} -> Hello world!`	Converts the first character to a capital letter
`concat(String str)`	`{{issue.summary.concat(" It's a beautiful day!")}}`	Appends a specific text string to the end of the resulting value

endsWith(String str)	`{{issue.summary.endsWith("World! ")}} -> true`	Verifies whether the text string concludes with the specified text and returns either true or false
equals(string)	`{{issue.summary.equals("hello world!")}} -> false`	Examines a text field to determine if it matches the provided string. If the strings are identical, it returns true. This can be employed in conditional logic
equalsIgnoreCase(string)	`{{issue.summary.equals("Hello world!")}} -> true`	Examines a text field to ascertain if it matches the provided string, without considering case sensitivity. If the strings are equal, regardless of the case, it returns true. This feature can be utilized in conditional logic
htmlEncode()	`{{issue.summary.htmlEncode}} -> Hello world!`	Encodes text to make it suitable for inclusion in HTML content

indexOf(String str)	`{{issue.summary.indexOf("Wo")}}` `-> 6`	Provides the position of the initial character in the specified text string
isAlpha()	`{{issue.summary.isAlpha()}} ->` `true`	Examines whether the text consists solely of letters and returns either true or false
isAlphanumeric()	`{{issue.summary.` `isAlphanumeric()}} -> true`	Verifies if the text comprises only letters or numbers and returns either true or false
isEmpty()	`{{issue.summary.isEmpty()}} ->` `false`	Evaluates whether the text is empty and returns either true or false
isNotEmpty()	`{{issue.summary.isNotEmpty()}}` `-> true`	Evaluates whether the text is not empty and returns either true or false
isNumeric()	`{{issue.summary.isNumeric()}} ->` `false`	Examines whether the text comprises solely numbers and returns either true or false
jsonEncode()	`{{issue.summary.jsonEncode}} ->` `Hello World!`	Encodes text to enable its inclusion in JSON calls

lastIndexOf(String str)	{{issue.summary. lastIndexOf("wo")}} -> 7	Provides the position of the final character in the specified text string
left(int length)	{{issue.summary.left(5)}} -> Hello	Returns the characters from the left side of the text string, starting from the specified position
leftPad(int length, String pad)	{{issue.summary.leftPad(14, "-")}} -> --Hello World!	Prepends characters to the beginning of the text until the total character count reaches the specified limit
match()		Executes a regular expression search and returns the first matching group (singular) found
quote()		Escapes the smart value into a literal text expression that can be used in a regular expression match using Pattern.quote()

remove(String remove)	{{issue.summary.remove("l")}} -> Heo Word!	Removes characters from text
replace(String target, String replacement)	{{issue.summary. replace("Hello","Goodbye")}} -> Goodbye World!	Substitutes all exact text matches with a specified replacement
replaceAll(String regex, String replacement)		Conducts a regular expression search and substitutes any matches with the specified replacement. $1 can be utilized to access a matching group in the replacement
reverse()	{issue.summary.reverse()}} -> !dlroW elloH	Inverts the order of characters within the text string
right(int length)	{{issue.summary.right(6)}} -> World!	Returns the characters from the right side of the text string, starting from the specified position
rightPad(int length, String pad)	{{issue.summary. rightPadPad (14,"-")}} -> Hello World!--	Appends characters to the end of the text string until the total character count reaches the specified limit

split(String separator)	{{issue.summary.split(" ").first}} -> Hello	Splits the text and returns the word specified by the word's position in the text string
startsWith(String str)	{{issue.summary.startsWith("World!")}} -> false	Evaluates whether the text string begins with the specified text and returns either true or false
substring(int start)	{{issue.summary.substring(7)}} -> orld!	Returns the characters following the specified number of characters
substring(int start, int end)	{{issue.summary.substring(1,3)}} -> el	Returns the characters located at the specified positions
substringAfter(String separator)	{{issue.summary.substringAfter("W")}} -> orld!	Returns the text following the initial occurrence of the provided separator
substringAfterLast(String separator)	{{issue.summary.substringAfterLast("o")}} -> rld!	Returns the text following the final occurrence of the provided separator
substringBefore(String separator)	{{issue.summary.substringBefore("W")}} -> Hello	Returns the text preceding the initial occurrence of the provided separator

substringBeforeLast(String separator)	{{issue.summary.substringBeforeLast("o")}} -> Hello W	Returns the text preceding the final occurrence of the provided separator
substringBetween(String open, String close)	{{issue.summary.substringBetween("e","d")}} -> llo Worl	Returns the text located between the specified parameters
toLowerCase()	{{issue.summary.toLowerCase()}} -> hello world!	Changes the text string to lowercase
toUpperCase()	{{issue.summary.toUpperCase(}}}} -> HELLO WORLD!	Changes the text string to uppercase
trim()	{{issue.summary.trim()}} -> Hello World!	Eliminates any leading or trailing whitespace from the value
urlEncode()	{{issue.summary.urlEncode}} -> See Encoding below.	Encodes text to allow them to be included as a URL param, for example, a link in an email
xmlEncode()	{{issue.summary.xmlEncode}} -> See Encoding below.	Encodes text to allow them to be included in XML data, for example, an outgoing webhook

Table 9.4: *Jira Smart Values – Text Fields*

Jira Smart Values - Users

The following list of smart values can be used to access user data and format it when creating new rules:

Smart Value and Properties	Example	What it Returns
`{{assignee}}`	`{{assignee.displayName}}`	Returns the assignee of the issue
`{{comment.author}}`	`{{comment.author.displayName}}`	It returns the name of the user who adds a comment on the issue
`{{creator}}`	`{{creator.displayName}}`	The person who created the issue and the creator cannot be changed
`{{initiator}}`	`{{initiator.displayName}}`	It returns the name of the user who prompted the rule
`{{reporter}}`	`{{reporter.displayName}}`	It returns the name of the reporter of an active issue
`{{Custom field}}`	`{{Scrum master.displayName}}`	If you have a custom field named scrum master, you can access the display name for the user

Table 9.5: *Jira Smart Values – Users*

Jira Smart Values - Conditional logic

The following list of smart values can be used when text fields are used and can provide output based on conditional logic:

Conditional Logic	Smart Value and Properties	What it Returns
If	`{{if(smartValue)}}`	It can be used with lookup issues actions and then add further action based on true or false results
equals	`{{equals(smartValue1, smartValue2)}}`	It returns TRUE, if the two inputs are equal, and FALSE, if the two inputs are not equal
exists	`{{exists(smartValue)}}`	It returns either TRUE or null

not	`{{not(smartValue)}}`	It returns either TRUE or FALSE. It can be used with Lookup issue action
and	`{{and(smartValue1, smartvalue2)}}`	It returns either TRUE or FALSE
or	`{{or(smartValue1, smartvalue2)}}`	It returns either TRUE or FALSE

Table 9.6: *Jira Smart Values – Conditional Logic*

Jira Smart Values - Date and time

The following list of smart values can be utilized to access and format date and time fields:

Smart Value and Properties	Example	What it Returns
`{{now}}`		It returns the current date and time
`{{[date].[dateformat]}}`	`{{now.shortDate}}` returns 11/10/23	You can provide data and time, and it returns in a format specified by you
`{{[date1].diff([date2]).[unit]}}`		It returns the difference between date1 and date2
`{{[date1].isAfter([date2])}}`		It gives a true result when date1 comes after date2, and false otherwise
`{{[date1].isBefore([date2])}}`		It provides a true outcome if date1 precedes date2, and false otherwise
`{{[date1].isEquals[(date2)]}}`		It gives a true result if date1 and date2 are identical, and false otherwise

`{{[date1].compareTo([date2])}}`		It compares date1 and date2. Gives -1, if date1 is earlier than date2 Gives 1, if date 2 is earlier than date1 Gives 0, if the two dates are the same
`{{[date].plus[Unit]([number])}}`	`{{sprint.startDate.plusDays(14)}}`	Accepts the provided date and time, adds the specified unit number, and provides the resulting date and time
`{{[date].minus[Unit]([number])}}`	`{{now.minusDays(5)}}`	Accepts the provided date and time, subtracts the specified unit number, and provides the resulting date and time
`{{[date].toBusinessDay}}`	`{{now.toBusinessDay}}`	Given a specific date, the function returns the following business day. If the input date falls on a business day, it will simply return that date
`{{ [date].toBusinessDayBackwards}}`	`{{now.toBusinessDayBackwards}}`	Accepts a provided date and outputs the business day immediately preceding it

`{{[date].`
`setTimeZone([timezone])}}`
	`{{now.`
	`setTimeZone("Australia/`
	`Sydney")}}`
		Takes a specified time and adjusts it to the given time zone without altering the actual time value. In other words, it displays the same time but in the specified time zone

`{{[date].`
`convertToTimeZone([timezone])}}`
	`{{now.convertToTimeZone`
	`("Australia/Sydney").`
	`shortTime}}`
		Accepts a specified time and converts it to the corresponding time in the given time zone

`{{[date].` `withDayOfMonth([date])}}`	`{{now.withDayOfMonth(15)}}`	Accepts a provided date and time and outputs the same date and time, but with the day of the month set to the input date
`{{[date].` `withNextDayOfWeek(["day"])}}`		Adjusts the date to the upcoming occurrence of the specified day. If the current day is already the specified day, it will advance to the next occurrence in the following week

{{[date].with[attribute] (input)}}	{{now.withYear(2005)}}	Accepts a provided date and time and adjusts either the date or time based on the description specified in the attribute

Table 9.7: *Jira Smart Values – Date and Time*

Jira Smart Values – Development

You can utilize the following smart values to access and format development information retrieved from a connected source code management tool:

Smart values	Properties	What it Returns
{{branch}}		It is a separate and independent line of development
	{{branch.name}}	It provides the branch name
	{{branch.url}}	It provides the URL of the branch
	{{branch.repository}}	Provides information related to the repository to which the branch is associated
{{createdBranch}}		Retrieve details about the latest branch that was created
	{{createdBranch.name}}	Provides the name of the branch
	{{createdBranch.url}}	Provides the URL of the recently created branch
	{{createdBranch.product}}	Provides the name of the product in which the branch was created
	{{createdBranch. repository.id}}	It provides the ID of the repository
	{{createdBranch. repository.name}}	It provides the name of the repository

	`{{createdBranch.` `repository.url}}`	It provides the URL of the repository
`{{createdBranches}}`		Retrieve information about all branches that were created in the rule, as a list
	`{{createdBranches.name}}`	Provides the names of the branches
	`{{createdBranches.url}}`	Provides the URL of the branches
	`{{createdBranches.` `product}}`	Provides the names of the products in which the branch was created
	`{{createdBranches.` `repository.id}}`	It provides the IDs of all the repositories
	`{{createdBranches.` `repository.name}}`	It provides the names of all the repositories
	`{{createdBranches.` `repository.url}}`	It provides the URLs of all the repositories
`{{commit}}`		A commit signifies a specific change made to a file or a group of files
	`{{commit.hash}}`	Provides the SHA1 hash of the commit
	`{{commit.shortHash}}`	Provides the truncated SHA1 hash of the commit
	`{{commit.message}}`	Provides the content of the commit message
	`{{commit.url}}`	Provides the URL of the commit
	`{{commit.isMergeCommit}}`	If a commit is a merge commit, the value returned is True
	`{{commit.timestamp}}`	It provides the details of the date and time when the commit was done
	`{{commit.repository}}`	It provides additional information related with the repository

	{{commit.repository.name}}	It provides the name of the repository
{{Pull request}}		A pull request represents suggested modifications prior to their incorporation into an official project
	{{pullRequest.title}}	It provides the title of the pullrequest
	{{pullRequest.url}}	It provides the URL of the pullrequest
	{{pullRequest.state}}	It provides the name of the state of the pullrequest
	{{pullRequest.createdDate}}	It provides the details about the date and time when the pullrequest was created
	{{pullRequest.updatedDate}}	It provides the details about the date and time when the pullrequest was updated
	{{pullRequest.sourceBranch}}	It provides information about the source branch for the pullrequest
	{{pullRequest.sourceBranch}}	It provides the name of the source branch
	{{pullRequest.sourceBranch.url}}	It provides the URL of the source branch
	{{pullRequest.destinationBranch}}	It provides the name of the destination branch
	{{pullRequest.destinationBranch.url}}	It provides the URL of the destination branch
	{{pullRequest.destinationBranch.repository}}	It provides information about the destination branch repository
{{build}}		A build signifies the transformation of files into their final usable form
	{{build.name}}	It provides the name of the build
	{{build.url}}	Provides absolute URL of the build

	`{{build.state}}`	It provides the state of the build; for example, In progress, Cancelled, and so on
	`{{build.refs}}`	Provides the references for the build. This compilation of metadata can be linked with a build and might include branch and tag names, among other details
`{{deployment}}`		A deployment denotes the procedure through which a product is released within a specific environment
	`{{deployment.name}}`	Provides a user-friendly deployment name
	`{{deployment.url}}`	Provides absolute URL of the deployment
	`{{deployment.state}}`	Provides the state of the deployment
	`{{deployment.environment}}`	Provides details associated with the deployment environment
	`{{deployment.environment.type}}`	It Returns production
`{{repository}}`		It is a collection of source code and related metadata
	`{{repository.name}}`	Provides the repository name
	`{{repository.url}}`	Provides absolute URL of the repository
`{{environment}}`		An environment signifies a unique ecosystem where products are deployed
	`{{environment.name}}`	Returns the name for the environment provided by the user
	`{{environment.type}}`	Provides the environment type

{{sprint}}		Accesses details pertaining to the sprint that activated the rule
	{{sprint.id}}	Provides sprintID
	{{sprint.name}}	Provides the name of the sprint
	{{sprint.isStarted}}	Returns true if the sprint has begun, and false if it has not started yet
	{{sprint.isClosed}}	Returns true if the sprint has been closed and false if it hasn't
	{{sprint.startDate}}	Provides the sprint's start date
	{{sprint.endDate}}	Provides the sprint's end date
	{{sprint.completeDate}}	Provides the date when the sprint was marked as complete
	{{sprint.originBoardId}}	Provides the ID of the board to which the sprint is associated
	{{sprint.goal}}	Provides the goal of the sprint
{{version}}		Accesses details related to the version that activated the rule
	{{version.name}}	Provides the name of the version
	{{version.id}}	Provides the ID of the version
	{{version.description}}	Provides the description of the version
	{{version.archived}}	Returns a true value if the version has been archived, and false if it has not
	{{version.startDate}}	Provides the start date of the version

	`{{version.released}}`	Returns a true value if the version has been released, and false if it has not
	`{{version.releaseDate}}`	Provides the release date of the version
	`{{version.project.key}}`	Provides the project key associated with the project to which the version belongs

Table 9.8: *Jira Smart Values – Development*

Jira Smart Values - Math Expressions

The following smart values can be utilized to insert and format numerical values when configuring a rule:

Numerical Operations	Smart Values	What it Returns
Abs		It provides the absolute value of a number. Absolute value of -4 is 4
Round		Provides a number rounded to the nearest integer. For example, 3.7 is rounded to 4
Floor		Provides the lower value of a number. For example, 2.8 returns 2
Ceil		Provides the upper value of a number. For example, 3.2 returns 4
Plus/Minus		Addition or subtraction of one numerical smart value with another can be done
Multiply		Multiplication of one numerical smart value with another can be done
Divide		Division of one numerical smart value with another can be done
Numerical comparisons		
Greater than	`gt(value)`	Accepts a numerical smart value, and checks whether it is greater than the specific value

Greater than or equal to	gte(value)	Accepts a numerical smart value, and checks whether it is greater than or equal to the specific value
Equal to	eq(value)	Accepts a numerical smart value, and checks whether it is equal to the specific value
Less than	lt(value)	Accepts a numerical smart value, and checks whether it is less than the specific value
Less than or equal to	lte(value)	Accepts a numerical smart value, and checks whether it is less than or equal to the specific value
Format numerical values		
format		Converts a given number into a US locale. For example, 234523456 becomes 234,523,456
format(input)		Converts a number into the given locale
formatWithLocale(input)		Converts a number into the given locale. For example, "fr_FR", 234123456 becomes 234 523 456
asPercentage		Converts a number into a percentage format according to the US locale
asPercentage(locale)		Converts a number into a percentage format according to the given locale
asCurrency		Converts a number into a currency format based on the US locale
asCurrency(locale)		Converts a number into a currency format according to the given locale

Table 9.9: *Jira Smart Values – Math Expressions*

To verify what a smart value returns:

1. Create a rule with a manual trigger and check the Log:

   a. Select the manual trigger.

     b. And set the action as Log.

2. Navigate to the **issue** and select **Rule executions**.

3. The value will be displayed in the audit log.

Owner

Owner is the person who creates the rule in Jira. This is the rule creator who will be notified in case of an error.

Rule Actor

When configuring a rule, project admins and site admins have the option to change the rule actor, allowing automation rules to be perceived as being executed by a real team member. For instance, if an automation rule adds a comment to all issues in a sprint, a team lead may want to configure it so that the comment is added by them, rather than by the Automation for Jira user.

You must be a project admin to configure project-based automation rules, and you must be a site admin to configure global automation rules. Both project admins and site admins can select the name of an actor, as shown in *Figure 9.10*

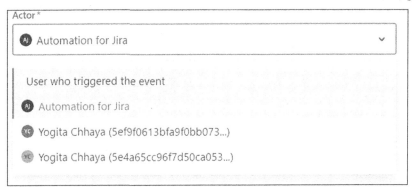

Figure 9.10: Selecting Actor of an Automation rule

The person selected as the actor will receive notifications for a specific automation rule. In the **History** tab, Jira will indicate that issue changes/updates have been made by the actor defined during the configuration of the automation rule.

Global admins can select anyone as the actor for the automation rule, while project admins can choose either themselves or Automation for Jira as the actor. They (project admins) cannot designate others as actors.

Project admins are expected to act as the actor for automation rules to make any changes in the rule. This does not apply to global administrators.

Scope

Scope can only be edited or added globally in automation. It decides where the rule will apply and includes the following options:

- **Single Project**: The rule applies to a specific project based on the selection.
- **Multi-Project**: The rule applies to multiple projects based on the selection.
- **Project Type**: The rule applies only to specific project types (for example, Business projects, Service Management projects, Software projects).
- **Global**: The rule applies to all projects in Jira.

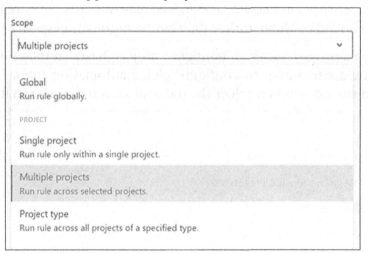

Figure 9.11: Defining Scope of an Automation Rule

Allowing Rule Trigger

The rule can be triggered by other rules, if it is selected:

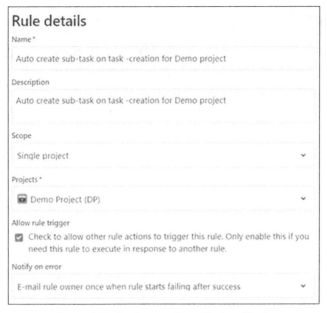

Figure 9.12: Setting to allow Chain of Rules

Notify on Error

It defines how frequently the rule owner can be notified by email:

Figure 9.13: Defining frequency of the notifications on Error

Audit Log

After creating a rule, navigate to the **Audit log** to review its execution status. The log will indicate whether the rule ran successfully or generated errors. You can also check the log during the execution of any rule.

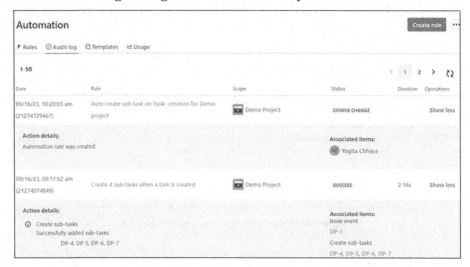

Figure 9.14: Understanding Audit log

Debugging Rules

If a rule is generating errors and not behaving as expected, follow these steps to debug the rule:

1. Check the Audit log:

    a. Review the displayed errors and examine any provided suggestions and instructions on how to resolve them.

    b. Compare the entries in the audit log with the comments on the issues.

    c. Ensure that all fields are correctly associated with the screens; otherwise, the rule will not fulfill its intended purpose.

    d. Before executing the rule, verify and update the data in Jira, and validate the filter query.

2. Debugging smart values:

    a. You can check the correctness of the smart values using a log.

    b. Additionally, there is a function called **Debug** that can assist you in debugging.

    c. Surround your smart value with **{{#debug}}**. Utilize it and verify it in the log.

  3. Test the Rule:

    a. Disable the rule, make a copy of the rule, and then check it so that you have a copy of the original rule.

    b. Test the rule using either a manual or scheduled trigger.

Templates and Jira Automation Library

Jira provides ready-to-use templates for Automation rules. Select templates on the Global Automation page to view all the templates available in Jira.

Scroll down on this page, and you will see the option to select the automation library. Within the library, you can explore example rules and create your own rules.

Jira Automation Playground

Navigate to the site for the Jira Automation playground. You can explore multiple automation rule templates and create your own rules based on these rules.

Checking Usage

Users can obtain information about how many automation rules have been executed compared to the actual limit. Each version has a defined limit for the number of automation rule executions. Rules can trigger until you have reached the limit.

Figure 9.15: *Viewing Usage of Automation Rules in Jira*

Note: There is a limit to creating a number of automation rules on your Jira Cloud site based on your subscription. Jira does not allow the execution of more rules than the allowed number. You can find out the details by checking usage.

Performance Insights

To get the performance insights of the automation rules, select ▪▪▪ on the right side and select `View performance insights`.

Figure 9.16: *Performance Insights*

Jira provides you with the date-wise total number of executions, number of errors, and number of successes in the form of a chart. Below the chart, it also provides detailed information in the form of a table.

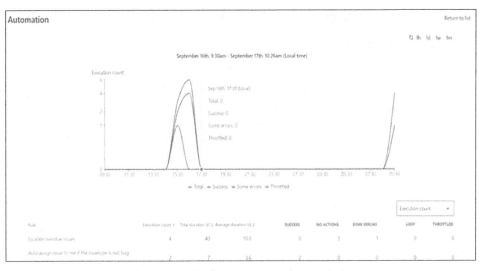

Figure 9.17: *Performance Insights statistics*

Using these insights, you can also check the statistics about the performance of each and every automation rule.

Import and Export Jira Automation Rules

Permission required: Jira administrator with **Administer Jira** global permission.

Jira administrators can perform the following actions:

1. Import rules from one Jira cloud site to the other Jira cloud site.

2. Export rules while moving from server to Jira cloud.

Export rules to a JSON file:

1. Navigate to **System** > **Global Automation**.

2. On the automation screen, navigate to top-right corner ▦> **Export rules**

3. It will download a JSON file with all the automation rules.

4. Once the file is downloaded, you can import the data to any site.

Import rules to a Jira site:

1. Navigate to **System** > **Global Automation**.

2. On the screen, navigate to the top-right corner ▦> **Import rules**.

3. Select **Upload JSON** or drop file to import data.

4. Select the **automation rules** and select the projects for the rules selected.

5. You can optionally select to import rule owners. If it is not selected, the person importing rules will be set as the rule owner:

   a. It is not required to make any changes to the JSON file if you are importing from a Jira cloud site. Ensure that the users are also there in your Jira site.

   b. If you are importing the data from the server/data center, then you have to change the account IDs of the rule owners manually.

6. Select **Let us do this** to finish the process.

Steps to Create an Automation Rule with Example

Permissions required:

1. A project admin can create automation rules in Jira that are specific to a project.

2. A site admin with **Administer Jira** global permission can create global automation rules that are applicable to all projects in Jira.

Example: We will create an automation rule to auto-assign an issue to the user who created an issue.

Creating an automation rule in Jira involves several steps. Here is a step-by-step guide to help you create an automation rule:

1. **Login to Jira**: Access your Jira account and ensure you have the necessary permissions to create automation rules. You need administrative or project-level permissions.

2. **Navigate to Project Settings**: If you want to create a project-specific rule, go to the project where you want to set up the automation.

   If you want to create a global rule, go to the **global Jira settings**.

3. **Access Automation Rules**: In the project settings, select an **Automation** option and Click it.

In the **global settings**, you can find automation under **System** or a similar menu. Click **Automation**.

4. **Create a Rule**: Click on the **Create Rule** to start the rule creation process.

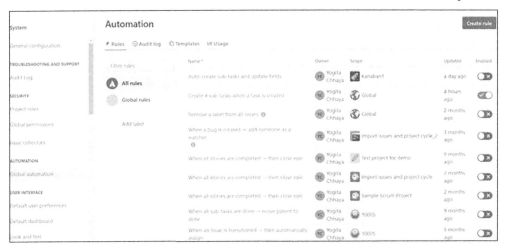

Figure 9.18: Creating Automation rule in Jira

5. **Select a Trigger**: Choose a trigger that initiates the automation. Triggers can include events such as issue creation, issue transition, or custom events.

   Configure the trigger settings, which may include specifying conditions for when the trigger should activate.

   In this example, we have selected the **Issue created** trigger.

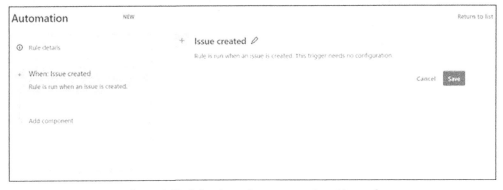

Figure 9.19: Selecting trigger to create a New rule

6. **Define the Conditions:**

   If needed, set conditions that determine whether the rule should be applied. Conditions are used to filter which issues the rule should affect.

   In this example, we have to add the condition to check whether the Assignee is empty.

   Select the **Add a condition** > **issue fields condition** > **Assignee** > **is empty**, as shown in *Figure 9.20*, and **Save**.

Figure 9.20: *Adding issue condition to create a new rule*

7. **Add Actions:**

   Specify the actions that should be performed when the trigger and conditions (if any) are met. Actions can include: Commenting on issues, Assigning issues to users, Changing issue fields, Sending notifications, Linking issues, Transitioning issues, and more.

   Configure the action settings according to your requirements.

   Here, we have selected the Action to assign the issues to the user who triggered the event.

Figure 9.21: *Adding action to create a new rule*

8. **Name Your Rule:**

    Give your rule a name that describes its purpose or functionality. This makes it easier to identify and manage multiple rules.

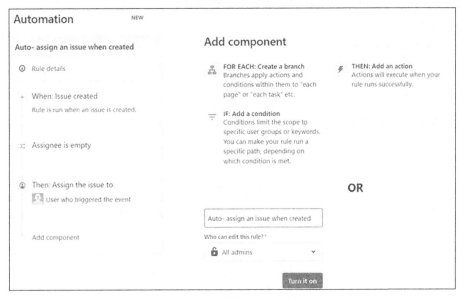

Figure 9.22: Naming a rule

9. **Select who can edit this rule:**

    Determine who can edit this rule and select the right option.

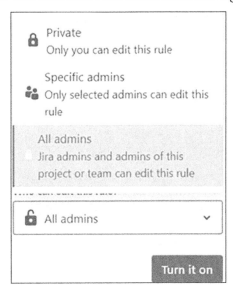

Figure 9.23: Selecting Editors of the Rule

10. **Save and Activate**:

Once you've configured all the rule components, save the rule.

Depending on your Jira configuration, you may need to activate the rule explicitly.

11. **Test the Rule**:

It's a good practice to test the rule with sample issues to ensure it behaves as expected.

12. **Maintain and Update**:

As your project evolves, review and update automation rules to reflect changes in your workflow or requirements.

That's the general step-by-step process for creating an automation rule in Jira. The specific options and features available may vary depending on your Jira version and configuration.

Essential Learning Examples

1. **Auto-create sub-tasks and update fields:**

Trigger: Issue created

Condition: Issue type is task

Action: Create sub-tasks

Figure 9.24: *Auto-create sub-tasks and update fields*

In the preceding example, we can check the automation rule by creating a task and confirming whether the sub-tasks are created and a summary field is updated. We can check the same by selecting the audit log of a rule.

Log Detail

Figure 9.25: Audit Log – Auto-create sub-tasks and update fields

2. **If/else rule to auto-assign issues:**

   Trigger: Issue created

   Condition: If the issue type is not a bug, assign it to me. Otherwise, if the issue type is Bug, then assign the issue to a member of the software developers project role.

   Action: Assign to the person as mentioned in the condition

Figure 9.26: If/else rule to auto-assign issues

This rule is designed to automatically assign all issues, except for bugs, to the specified name. If the issue type is a bug, it will be assigned to a person from the developers' group based on a balanced workload.

Log Detail

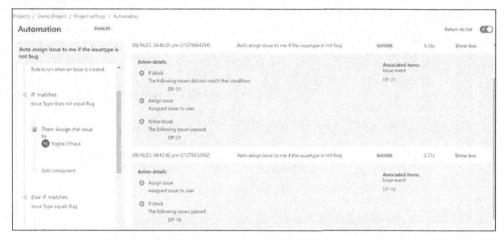

Figure 9.27: *Audit Log - If/else rule to auto-assign issues*

3. **Due date is in three days from now-send reminder:**

   Trigger: Schedule a trigger daily

   Trigger is based on JQL - project = **DP** and due <= **2023-09-20**

   Action: Send an Email reminder

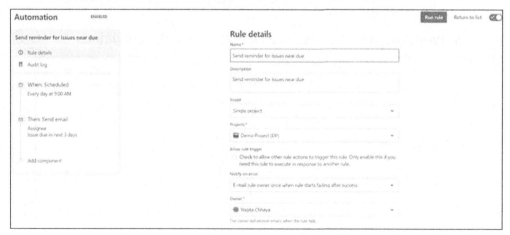

Figure 9.28: *Due date is in three days from now-send reminder*

This rule will send a reminder email to all the assignees of the issues daily. It will check the results of the filter query selected. Filter query can be configured to address the requirement.

Log Detail

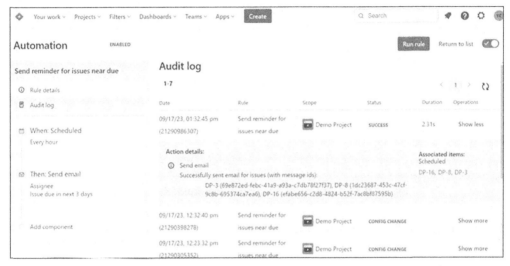

Figure 9.29: *Audit Log -Due date is in three days from now-send reminder*

4. **Add comment using smart values when an issue transitions from Todo to InProgress (Helpful to understand various smart values):**

    Trigger: Issue Transition to In Progress

    Action: Add a comment using various smart values

Figure 9.30: A rule to understand Smart Values

This rule, on execution, adds comment using smart values when an issue transitions from Todo to InProgress.

Log Detail

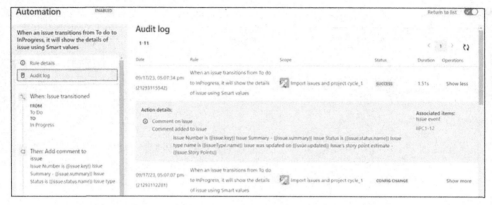

Figure 9.31: *Audit Log – A rule to understand Smart Values*

Comment using Smart Values on the Jira issue:

Figure 9.32: *Comment – A rule to understand Smart Values*

5. **When an issue remains for five days without an update → send a notification to the Assignee:**

Figure 9.33: *Notify Assignee for issues not updated more than five days*

When this rule is triggered, it will send an email to the assignee and leave a single comment on the issue.

Log detail

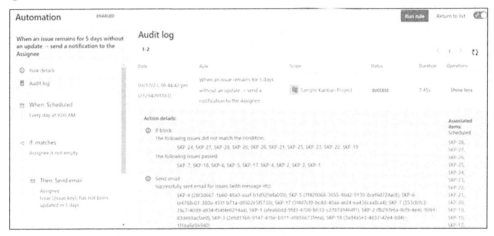

Figure 9.34: *Audit Log - Notify Assignee for issues not updated more than five days*

6. **When an issue is transitioned to InProgress, set the start date value to the Current date:**

   Trigger: Issue Transitioned to InProgress

   Action: Then Edit issue field Start date

   We have selected the

Start date as: `{{now.convertToTimeZone(issue.reporter.timeZone)}}` , which will set the start date for any time zone as set by the reporter.

Figure 9.35: *Set the start date as the Current date on transition to InProgress*

This rule will set the start date for any time zone as set by the reporter, for any task that transitions from To Do to InProgress.

Log Detail

Figure 9.36: *Audit Log - Set the start date as the Current date on transition to InProgress*

7. **Sum up story points when field value changes:**

    Trigger: When value changes for Story points

    Condition: Issue type equals Sub-task

    Branch Rule: Related issues - For parents

    Action: Edit issue field with a story point

Smart value for story point to add: `{{issue.subtasks.Story Points.sum}}`

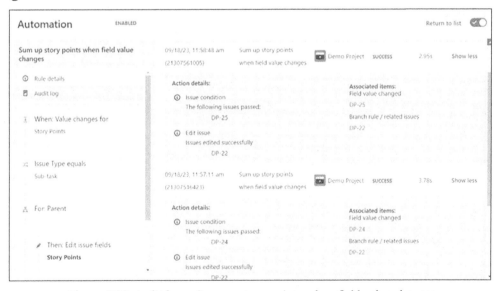

Figure 9.37: Sum up story points when field value changes

Whenever story points are added to a sub-task, they are automatically added to the parent task, ensuring that it remains in sync without any manual work.

Log Detail

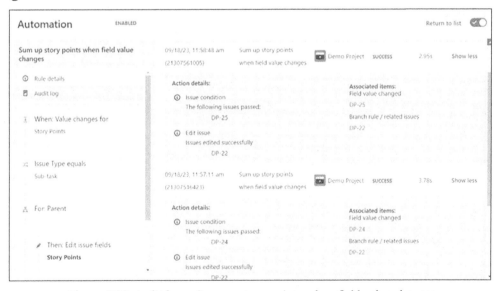

Figure 9.38: Audit log - Sum up story points when field value changes

8. **When assignee updated, transition to InProgress**

    Trigger: Assignee Updated

    Condition: Assignee is empty

Action: Transition to InProgress

Figure 9.39: *When assignee updated, transition to InProgress*

This rule automatically transitions any issue to InProgress when the assignee is updated.

Log Detail

Figure 9.40: *Audit Log – When assignee updated, transition to InProgress*

Conclusion

We are now familiar with the elements of automation rules in Jira Agile projects, creating various automation rules, testing them before implementation, checking the log details, and debugging a rule. Additionally, we have learned about smart values, how to find them, and how to utilize them in the automation rules.

In the next chapter, we will learn about how to manage Team-managed projects.

Points to Remember

- Start by identifying the specific tasks or processes you want to automate.
- Think about the rules you need and how they can work together.
- Align your automation strategy with your business and operational processes.
- Choose an appropriate trigger that defines when the rule should run (for example, issue created, issue transitioned, field updated).
- Set conditions to specify under what circumstances the rule should be executed.
- Conditions help filter the issues to which the rule applies (for example, project, issue type, custom fields).
- Use compare conditions early in the rule chain to filter out unnecessary actions.
- Place conditions requiring more processing towards the end of the rule chain.
- Decide the action the rule should do, such as sending an email or updating data.
- Utilize available built-in actions and consider custom scripts for advanced actions.
- Configure any additional parameters or settings specific to the chosen trigger and actions.
- Decide whether the rule should apply globally or to specific projects or issues.
- Restrict the scope of your rules and avoid global rules whenever possible.
- Consider the order of your automation rules, as they are executed in sequence from top to bottom.
- Always test new rules in a test environment before implementing them in production.

- Monitor rule execution to verify that they perform as expected.

- Regularly review and refine your automation rules as your processes and requirements change.

- Ensure that users who can create automation rules have appropriate permissions.

- Maintain backups of your Jira configuration, including automation rules, to prevent data loss.

- Consider the scalability of your automation rules to ensure they can handle increased workloads.

- Document your automation rules, including their purpose and conditions, for future reference.

Links for Reference and Use Cases

1. Is it possible to use the "Issue created" trigger to move to another status?

https://community.atlassian.com/t5/Jira-Software-questions/jira-automation-rules/qaq-p/2395457

2. How do I manually trigger an automation?

https://community.atlassian.com/t5/Jira-Software-questions/How-do-I-manually-trigger-an-automation/qaq-p/1575271

3. Manually Triggered Automation Rule - User who triggered the event

https://community.atlassian.com/t5/Jira-Software-questions/Manually-Triggered-Automation-Rule-User-who-triggered-the-event/qaq-p/2428674

4. Automation rule for Reminder mail

https://community.atlassian.com/t5/Automation-questions/Automation-rules/qaq-p/2368644

5. Setting up automation rules

https://community.atlassian.com/t5/Jira-Software-questions/Setting-up-automation-rules/qaq-p/2400624

6. Jira Automation - Edit issue fields / User who triggered the event

https://community.atlassian.com/t5/Jira-Software-questions/Jira-Automation-Edit-issue-fields-User-who-triggered-the-event/qaq-p/2276774

7. Automation vs Global Automation vs Multi-Project Automation

https://community.atlassian.com/t5/Jira-Service-Management/Automation
-vs-Global-Automation-vs-Multi-Project-Automation/qaq-p/2109238

8. Automation for Version Release Trigger

https://community.atlassian.com/t5/Jira-Software-questions/Automation
-for-Version-Release-Trigger/qaq-p/2362507

9. How to recognize the proper Custom Field name to use it in formula

https://community.atlassian.com/t5/Jira-Service-Management/how-to
-recognize-the-proper-Custom-Field-name-to-use-it-in/qaq-p/2338611

10. Example of automation rules that use "Start of sprint" as trigger?

https://community.atlassian.com/t5/Jira-Software-questions/Please-share
-example-of-automation-rules-that-use-quot-Start-of/qaq-p/2413147

11. Jira Automation: Complete Guides on how to Sum Up Story Points between Subtasks/Stories/Epics

https://community.atlassian.com/t5/Automation-discussions/Jira
-Automation-Complete-Video-Guides-on-how-to-Sum-Up-Story/td
-p/1741948

12. Document for Smart values

https://support.atlassian.com/cloud-automation/docs/smart-values-in-jira
-automation/

Resources

1. Jira Automation Library

2. Jira Automation Playground

    https://www.atlassian.com/software/jira/automation-template
    -library/rules#/rule/140662/25000692

3. Smart values in Jira automation

    https://support.atlassian.com/cloud-automation/docs/smart-values
    -in-jira-automation/

Chapter 10

Managing Team-Managed Projects

Introduction

Jira offers mainly two types of projects: **Team-managed projects** and **Company-managed projects**. Team-managed projects provide a higher degree of autonomy, allowing users to configure project settings without affecting other teams or projects. Typically, this project type is helpful for small teams where customization is not the only important thing. Another important aspect is granting permissions to everyone equally, that is, fewer restrictions. These types of projects are helpful for beginners who are in their learning phase of project management tools. However, selecting the right template is of utmost importance in Jira. In this chapter, we will learn how to create team-managed projects tailored to your team's requirements. This includes creating sprints, boards, defining statuses, configuring workflows, establishing automation rules, and accessing and understanding reports.

Structure

In this chapter, we will discuss the following topics:

- Understanding Team-managed projects
  - Features
- Setting up Team-managed project
- Adding People, Roles, and Access levels
- Enabling Agile features
- Issue types in Team-managed project

- Creating Custom Issue Types
- Configuring an Issue Type's Workflow
- Defining Status
- Creating Transitions
- Transition Properties
- Adding or Removing Workflow Rules
- Managing Backlog
- Sprint Operations
- Agile Board Features
- Understanding Insights
- Timeline View
- Reports
- Migrating from team to company-managed projects
  - ○ Things to keep in mind if you migrate from company-managed to team-managed
  - ○ Things to keep in mind if you migrate from team-managed to company-managed

Understanding Team-managed projects

Team-managed projects are easy to create and manage by anyone in the team. They are designed for smaller teams and projects that do not require extensive customization.

Features

Here are a few important features of Team-managed projects:

- There is no need to involve a Jira administrator to create and modify the project configuration.
- Teams and members can decide and control their own projects and processes.
- Project administrators can have total control over project configuration and modification.
- It provides a separate space for project teams without affecting other teams and projects, as the changes done in the team-managed project configuration do not impact other projects.
- Team-managed projects can be created quickly and easily.

- Create them when only access-level permissions are needed.
- Add issue types, statuses, transitions, and boards.
- Customize the workflow for each issue type.
- Set rules for workflows to control transitions and actions.
- Use the timeline feature for planning and generating reports.

Setting up Team-managed projects

Permissions: Any logged-in user can create a team-managed project by default. Jira Administrators can restrict it by managing permissions for a group.

Here are the steps to create a Team-managed project in Jira:

1. Navigate to **Projects** > **Create project**.

2. Select **Software Development** under **Project Template**.

3. Select one of the three options: **Scrum**, **Kanban**, and **Bug tracking** software.

Figure 10.1: *Selecting an Agile Project Template*

4. Understand the information on the respective page and then select **Use template**.

Figure 10.2: *Scrum Project Template*

5. Select the project type as **Team-managed.**

Figure 10.3: *Features of Team-Managed and Company-Managed Project*

6. Decide the name of the project and enter it.

7. Jira will generate a key for the project key. It can be changed while creating a project. Project key is also used to identify all the issues.

8. Select **Create**.

Adding People, Roles, and Access levels

In this section, we will understand how to add people, what are roles, and what are access levels in team-managed projects.

Permissions required: A person with an Administrator role in a project can set access levels and define roles in team-managed projects.

Adding people: You can add people to your project only if they are added by the Jira administrator to your site. If you cannot find their names or e-mails, you need to tell your Jira administrator to enter their names.

Access levels: The access level of your project determines who has the ability to search, view, and modify the project and its associated issues in your Jira site.

Team-managed software projects have three access levels as follows:

1. **Open**: When a project is set to Open, anyone in your Jira site can view, create, and edit issues within the project. In this access level, Jira automatically assigns the member role to anyone who logs into your Jira site and accesses the project.

2. **Limited**: If a project is designated as Limited, anyone within your Jira site can view and provide comments on issues within the project, but they are unable to edit or create new ones. Jira assigns the **Viewer** role to individuals who log into your Jira site and access this project at this access level.

3. **Private**: In cases where a project is marked as Private, it is exclusively visible to Jira administrators and people specifically added to the project. These users can see the project in their project directory and its associated issues in search results.

Here are the steps to change Project access:

1. Navigate to the **Project** > **Project settings** > **Access.**

2. Select **Change Project Access.**

3. Select the level of project access and select **Change**.

Roles: In team-managed projects, roles define the people who work in your project. In real-world scenarios, people are assigned various roles in your project work, such as Scrum masters, members, or architects.

These roles help you to control people's access and actions within your project. Different roles may require specific access levels to your team's content, or you might want to restrict certain roles' capabilities. For instance, you may wish to grant exclusive sprint planning and management privileges to your team's Scrum masters.

Team-managed software projects have three default roles as follows:

1. **Administrator**: Admins have extensive capabilities, including adjusting settings, adding other admins, managing features, customizing issue types, and creating rules on the board. Admins require Jira Software product access to fully utilize this role.

2. **Member**: Members are team members who can create, edit, comment, and manage issues, along with collaborating on project tasks. Members need Jira Software product access to work on a project.

3. **Viewer**: Viewers have limited privileges and can search for and view issues within your project but have restricted capabilities beyond that. You can assign this role to any registered user on your Jira site without requiring additional product access.

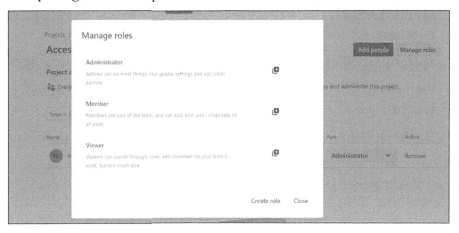

Figure 10.4: *Adding people and managing Role*

You have the flexibility to create custom roles to further tailor individuals' access to your project, allowing for greater customization.

Here are the steps to change the project role:

1. Navigate to the **Project** > **Project settings** > **Access.**

2. In the table, choose the dropdown menu for **Role**.

3. Select the right role to be assigned to the person.

Enabling Agile Features

In team-managed projects, all the features are not enabled by default. Follow these steps to enable the agile features.

1. Navigate to **Projects** > **project settings**.

2. Select **Features**.

3. Enable the features by selecting them.

You can enable the following features:

1. **Timeline**: It is a place from which you can manage epic.

2. **Backlog**: Plan work items, sprints, and prioritize them.

3. **Board**: View, track, and manage all tasks in the sprint as it progresses.

4. **Reports**: Find agile metrics and keep track of your projects to plan accordingly.

5. **Issue-navigator**: Access issues and create filters based on specific criteria.

6. **Sprints**: A predefined time frame that you can set when creating it.

7. **Estimation**: It can be in Story points or in time affecting reports and insights.

8. **Releases**: Helps define a list of features to be released to the client.

Additionally, you can enable requests, code, security, deployments, on-call settings, and project pages from the features page.

Figure 10.5: *Enabling Agile features*

Issue types in Team-managed project

In team-managed projects, Jira provides the issue types as listed here:

Epic: Jira has the issue type `Epic` to manage larger work items. It is a parent issue type. You can create other child issue types such as `Story`, `Bug`, and `Task` under Epic.

Figure 10.6: *Epic issue type in Team-managed project*

Story: It is an issue type used by agile teams to explain features required by the customer and includes the final goal of that feature.

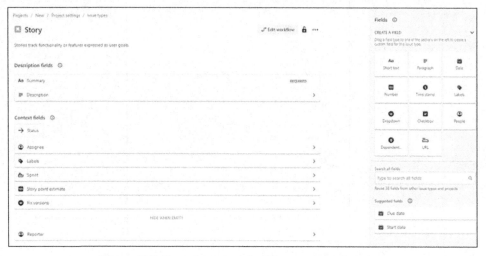

Figure 10.7: *Story issue type in Team-managed project*

Bug: It is an issue type used by agile teams to track the problems faced related to software functionality, user interface problems, or total failure of the software application.

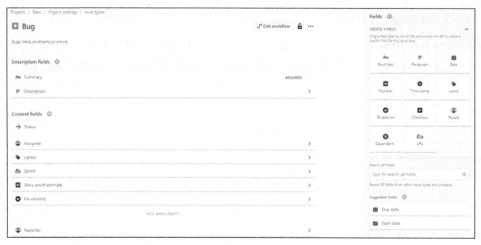

Figure 10.8: *Bug issue type in Team-managed project*

Task: It is an issue type used by agile teams to create issues when bigger issues are broken down into smaller ones, non-technical activities, or training tasks.

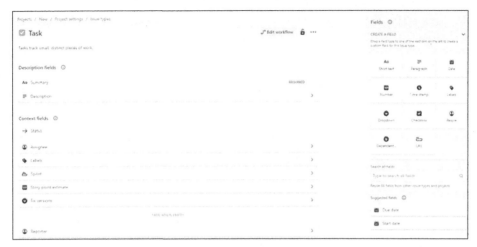

Figure 10.9: *Task issue type in Team-managed project*

Subtask: It helps agile teams to break down complicated tasks into smaller tasks. All tasks – **Bug**, **Story**, and **Task** – can be broken down into subtasks. Subtasks can be viewed on agile boards in team-managed projects.

Figure 10.10: *Subtask issue type in Team-managed project*

Creating custom issue types

To create custom issue types in team-managed projects, perform the following steps:

1. Navigate to **Project** > **Project settings** > **Issue types**

2. Click on **+** Add issue type and then select **Create issue type**.

3. Enter the details of the issue type, such as **Name**, **Description,** and an **Icon**.

4. Hit **Create**.

Figure 10.11: Creating standard issue type in Team-managed project

Make fields required for issue type

In a team-managed project, you set the fields as mandatory. To do that, perform the following steps:

1. Navigate to **Project** > **Project settings** > **Issue types**.
2. Select the issue type for which you want to make fields mandatory.
3. Click the **Required** checkbox for the fields that are to be made mandatory.
4. Click **Save changes**.

Once it is defined as required, new issues of that issue type cannot be created without those fields.

Figure 10.12: Making fields required

Configuring an issue types' workflow

Jira provides a simple workflow for all issue types. To change the workflow of the issue type, follow these steps:

1. Navigate to **Project** > **Project settings** > **Issue types**.

2. Select the issue type from the sidebar.

3. Click on **Edit workflow**.

4. Change the workflow steps.

5. Hit **Update workflow** to save the changes.

6. Select only those issue types for which the new workflow has to be applied.

7. Select **Save.**

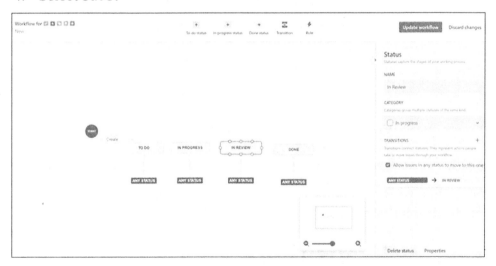

Figure 10.13: Configuring Workflow in a team-managed project

Defining Status

Statuses represent the state of the work item or an issue.

Permissions required: To add/delete status in a team-managed project, you must have an administrator role in the Jira project.

Here are the steps to Add/Create a Status:

1. Navigate to your **Project** > **Project settings** > **Issue types**.

2. Select the issue type from the sidebar and select **Edit workflow**.

3. Select the category from the top toolbar (**To Do**, **InProgress**, **Done**) and name the status.

4. Select **Add.**

Figure 10.14: *Adding Status to an issue type's workflow*

Similarly, you can **Edit/Delete** the Status in a team-managed workflow.

Finally, when you have completed editing the statuses, click on **Update workflow** to confirm which issue type it is for.

Creating Transitions

Transitions tell us about the purpose of changing the status.

Permissions required: To add/delete status in a team-managed project, you must have an administrator role in the Jira project.

Here are the steps to Add/Create a transition:

1. Navigate to your **Project** > **Project settings** > **Issue types**.

2. Select the issue type from the sidebar and select **Edit workflow**.

3. Select **transition** from the top toolbar.

4. A window will pop up. Enter the details **From status**, **To status**, and **Name** of the transition.

5. Select **Create**.

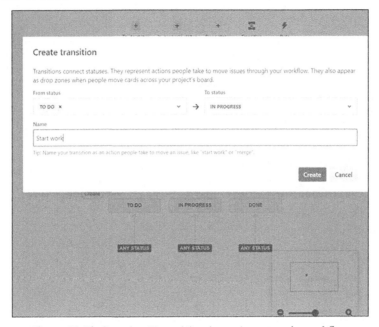

Figure 10.15: *Creating Transition in an issue type's workflow*

Similarly, you can Edit or Delete the Transition in a team-managed workflow.

Finally, when you have completed editing the transitions, click on **Update workflow** to confirm which issue type it is for.

Transition Properties

You have the option to use workflow properties to impose limitations on both workflow statuses and transitions.

Here are the steps to add a Transition Property:

After creating a transition, you can incorporate the following transition property:

1. Navigate to **Projects > Project settings > Issue types**

2. Select the **Issue type** and then select **Edit workflow**.

3. Select a specific **Transition** from the top navigation bar.

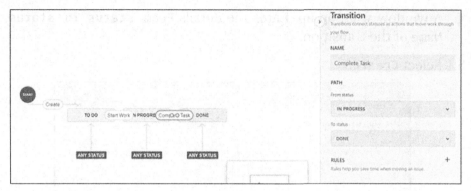

Figure 10.16: *Selecting a transition to add transition properties*

4. Select **Update workflow** on the top navigation bar.

Figure 10.17: *Selecting Update Workflow*

5. Select **Properties** from the bottom of the page.

Figure 10.18: *Selecting properties to add transition properties*

6.	Enter the value of the key and value and click **Save**.

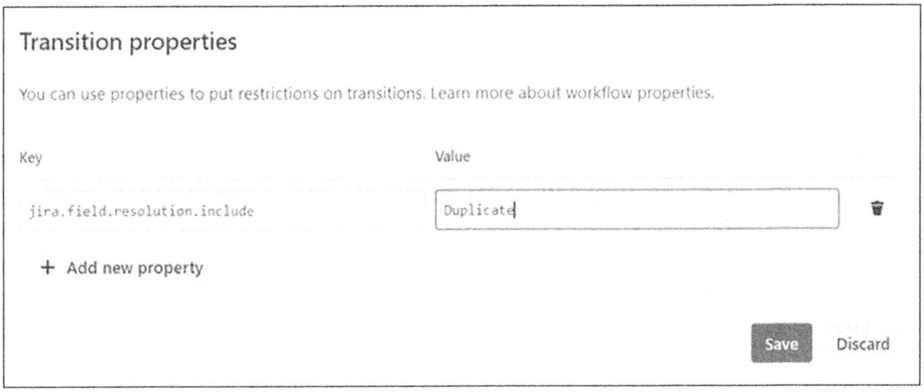

Transition properties

You can use properties to put restrictions on transitions. Learn more about workflow properties.

Key

jira.field.resolution.include

Value

Duplicate

+ Add new property

Save Discard

Figure 10.19: *Entering kay value for a Transition Property*

7. By saving this property, Jira will allow a **Duplicated** status as a valid status for the transition from **In Progress** to **Done**.

8. Select **Update workflow** from the top navigation bar.

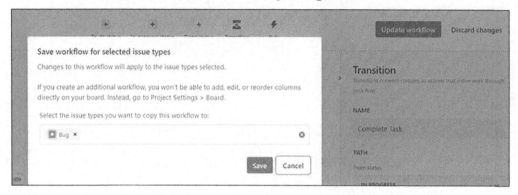

Figure 10.20: *Updating workflow after adding a transition property*

9. This property has been saved for the Bug issue type.

Example Status Properties

1. **jira.issue.editable**

    You might prefer to prevent editing an issue when it's in a specific status. For instance, once an issue reaches the **Done** status, you may wish to limit editing to avoid any data modifications after the work is completed.

    Use cases:

    *   When an issue is in a specific status, you can make it editable by using the key **jira.issue.editable** and setting it to true.
    *   When an issue is in a specific status, you can restrict editing by using the key **jira.issue.editable** and setting it to **false.**

2. **jira.permission.***

    If you wish to impose limitations beyond the permission scheme, you can achieve this with the **jira.permission** workflow property. By employing this permission, you can limit specific actions to selected users according to your preferences.

    The standard format of this property is **jira. permission.[subtasks.] {permission}.{user}.[.suffix].**

    1. **jira.permission** is used to start the property.

2. `[subtasks.]` is not mandatory and is applicable to subtasks for restricting the permission.

3. `Permission` is the permission you want to restrict. It is applicable to these permissions:

`Create`, `move`, `edit`, `transition`, `viewworkflowreadonly`, `viewversioncontrol`, `close`, `resolve`, `link`, `delete`, `scheduleissue`, `viewvotersandwatchers`, `modifyreporter`, `setsecurity`, `assign`, `assignable`, `commenteditall`, `comment`, `attachdeleteall`, `attachdeleteown`, `commentdeleteall`, `commentdeleteown`, `managewatcherlist`, `attach`, `work`, `worklogdeleteall`, `worklogeditall`, `worklogeditown`.

4. `User:` The user whose permission we want to restrict could be the `assignee`, `reporter`, `application role`, `project role`, `group`, or `lead`.

5. `[.suffix]` is a number used to apply the same property multiple times. It is optional.

Use cases:

- Permit modifications to the reporter field only for the user named `userxyz` when the issue is in a specific status. Use the key `jira.permission.modifyreporter.user` and the value as `userxyz`.

- Add a property such that only the reporter can transition the issue when it is in a specific status. Use the key as `jira.permission.transition.reporter` and enter the value as `empty`.

Example of Transition Properties

If you wish to prevent a specific resolution from being available on an issue during a particular status, you can utilize the `jira.field.resolution` property to limit it.

Use cases:

- If you want to allow a resolution `Won'tFix` on a transition, edit the key as `jira.field.resolution.include` and the value as `resolution ID` of the resolution. If there are multiple resolutions to be added, include the IDs separated by commas.

- If you want to deactivate a resolution 'Won'tFix' on a transition, edit the key as `jira.field.resolution.exclude` and the value as `resolution ID` of the resolution. If there are multiple resolutions to be disabled, include the IDs separated by commas. This will make it unavailable.

Adding or Removing Workflow rules

Workflow rules are helpful to restrict transitions, validate permissions, and take actions.

Permissions required: To add/delete workflow rules in a team-managed project, you must have an administrator role in the Jira project.

Here are the steps to add a Workflow rule to a transition:

1. Navigate to your **Project >Project settings > Issue types**.
2. Select the issue type from the sidebar and select **Edit workflow.**
3. Select **Rules** from the workflow toolbar.
4. Select the required rule from the options provided in the list and click **Select.**
5. Select the transition on which you want to add a rule from the **For transition** dropdown.
6. Enter the details of the rule and click **Add.**
7. Test the rule by creating a test issue and verify the workflow rule.

Similarly, you can **Edit/Delete** a workflow transition rule.

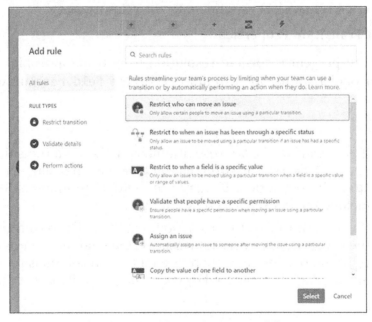

Figure 10.21: Adding Rules to a Workflow

There are three types of rules, which can run in the following order:

1. `Restrict transition`: It runs before someone tries to transition an issue.

   For example:

   - `Restrict who can move an issue`
   - `Restrict when a field has a specific value`

2. `Validate details`: It makes sure that details are correct while transitioning an issue.

   For example:

   - `Validate that people have a specific permission`

3. `Perform actions`: Perform an action that you may have to do manually.

   For example:

   - `Assign an issue`
   - `Update an issue field`
   - `Copy the value of one field to another after moving an issue using a particular transition.`

Managing Backlog

For Scrum teams, a backlog is a place where teams can create issues, enter the details, prioritize issues, and associate with an Epic or Version after creating the same.

For the teams that work in Kanban style, there is no backlog. However, the teams can still plan and prioritize work by activating backlog and sprint in project settings in Jira. This is called the Kanplan way of working.

Add issues to the Backlog

You can add issues in the backlog or the sprint by clicking on `+ Create issue`. If you add issues in an active sprint, it is considered as a change in the scope of work and gets reflected in the reports.

Figure 10.22: *Backlog view of a Scrum Team-managed project*

Reorder issues

You can reorder issues in the backlog and it should be done based on priority and how important it is.

Features on backlog view: There are many small but interesting features. Right-click on the issue and utilize the following features:

1. **Move**: Move the issue to other sprint or top of the backlog, bottom of the backlog, move up, or move down as per priority.

2. **Copy issue link**

3. **Copy issue key**

4. **Add flag**: It will add a flag to mark that the issue is important.

5. **Assignee**: Add assignee

6. **Add parent**: Unlink the issue and add another parent link

7. **Story Point Estimate**: Add story point

8. **Split issue**: If the issue is too big, you can split it into two tasks.

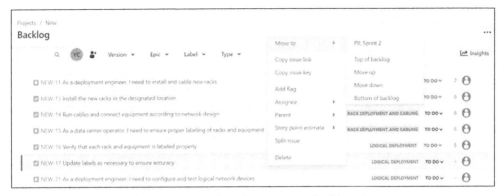

Figure 10.23: *Various features on a backlog view*

Display the Epic Panel and Versions

The Epics panel can be enabled and disabled on the backlog view as follows:

- Click on **Epics** dropdown and select to **enable/disable** the Epic panel.
- It displays all the Epic names that are created in a project.
- Select **+Create epic** to create new Epics and enter the details.
- Drag and drop the issues in the backlog to associate issues with an Epic.
- Epics can also be created from the **Create** issue button in the top navigation bar.
- Epics can be created from the **Timeline view**.

Figure 10.24: *Enabling Epic panel in Backlog view*

Version panel can be enabled and disabled on the backlog view as follows:

- Click on **Version** dropdown and select to **enable/disable** the Version panel.
- It displays all the version names that are created in a project.
- Select **+Create version to** create new Versions and enter the details.
- Drag and drop the issues in the backlog to associate issues with versions.
- Versions can also be created from the **Create issue** button in the top navigation bar.

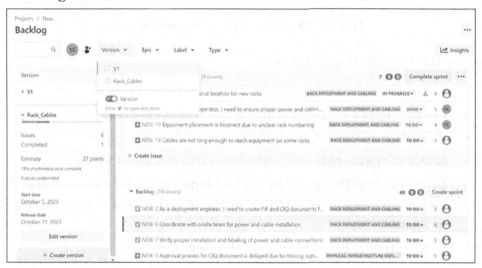

Figure 10.25: Enabling Versions panel in Backlog view

Custom filters in Backlog

You can create custom filters in the backlog view as follows:

- To create a custom filter, navigate to ▦ on the right corner and select the same.
- Select **Manage custom filters**.
- Enter the name and description of the filter and JQL query.

These filters can be displayed in **Timeline view**, **Backlog view,** and **Board view**.

Figure 10.26: *Creating Custom filters*

Bulk change features on Board

In the backlog view, you can select multiple issues and make bulk operations such as

Bulk change, add **story point estimate**, edit **parent** link, **Add** flag, edit **Assignee,** and **Move** issues.

Figure 10.27: *Bulk change features on Backlog*

Sprint operations

In this section, we will learn about how to create a sprint, edit sprint, reopen sprint, and delete a sprint.

Create Sprint

Sprint: It is a predefined time interval during which a scrum team does the development work. It can last from 1-week to 4-week time.

Go to the `Product Backlog` page and create a sprint as shown in *Figure* 10.28:

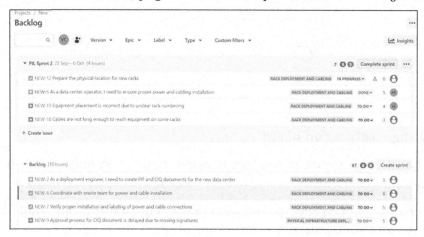

Figure 10.28: *Creating Sprint*

Edit Sprint: Using this option, you can enter the details of the sprint. To edit sprint, navigate to ▪▪▪ near `Complete sprint` and select it. You will get the option to edit sprint.

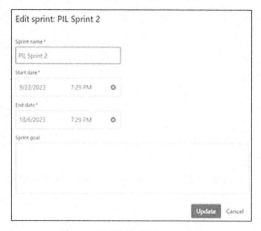

Figure 10.29: *Editing sprint*

Team can start the sprint once all the details are entered.

Figure 10.30 shows the **Start sprint**, **Edit sprint,** and **Create sprint** options.

Figure 10.30: *Various sprint operations*

Agile Board Features

In the team-managed project board, select ... on the right side where you have the options to **edit sprint**, **manage workflow**, **manage custom filters**, and **Configure board**.

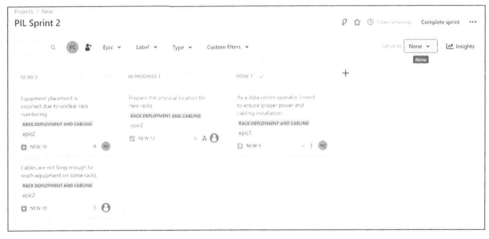

Figure 10.31: *Scrum Board*

By selecting the **Configure board**, you can customize the board for the following features.

1. Add **`Columns and statuses`** for the workflow

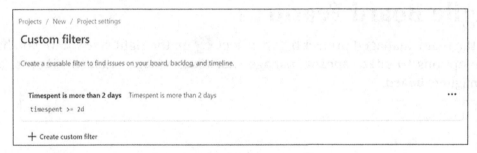

Figure 10.32: *Adding Columns and Statuses*

2. Add **`Custom filters`**.

Figure 10.33: *Adding Custom filters*

3. Add the images for cards on the boards

Figure 10.34: *Adding images for cards*

4. Enable or Disable the `Timeline` view and set the `Child-level issue scheduling`

Figure 10.35: *Enabling Timeline view*

5. Change settings for `Insights on backlog` and `board view`.

Understanding Insights

Permissions: To configure the insights for backlog or board, you must be the board administrator of that specific board OR you must be a project administrator for the location of the board.

Configure Insights for backlog: To enable or disable insights on backlog, follow these steps:

1. Navigate to a **Project** > **Project settings** > **Board**.

2. Select the **Backlog insights** from the **Board settings** menu. By default, insights is enabled. You can disable it by selecting toggle if you don't want to show it on your board.

It can also be set from the insight's panel directly.

Figure 10.36: *Enabling backlog Insights*

Configure Insights for board: To enable or disable insights on board, follow these steps:

1. Navigate to **Project** > **Project settings** > **Board**.

2. Select the **Board insights** from the **Board settings** menu. By default, insights is enabled. You can disable it by selecting toggle if you don't want to show it on your board.

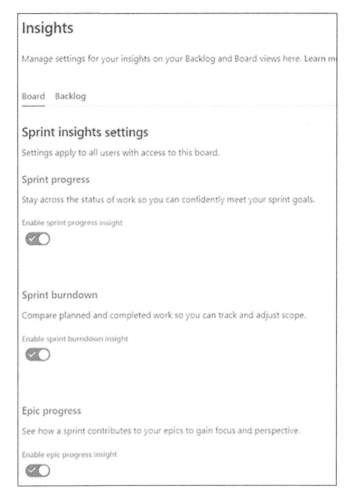

Figure 10.37: Enabling board Insights

Understanding Insights for backlog

Jira provides insights within the backlog view. Users can observe parameters like **Sprint commitment** and **Issue-type breakdown**. These insights prove invaluable for sprint planning, based on historical data to determine both commitment and where to allocate more attention across issue types. It provides this data based on the estimation statistics such as story points, issues completed, or work logged in the last sprints.

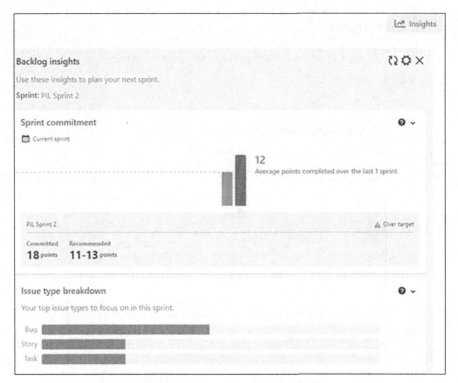

Figure 10.38: *Backlog Insights*

Understanding Insights for board

Users can access various parameters, such as issues requiring attention, **Sprint progress**, **Sprint burndown** chart, and **Epic progress**. These features help the Scrum master and the team in making informed decisions guided by data-driven insights.

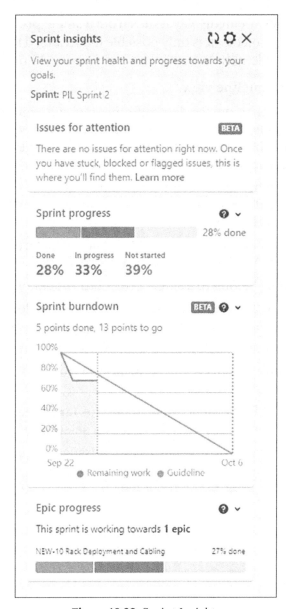

Figure 10.39: *Sprint Insights*

Timeline View

It is a planning tool that teams can use to plan the work for long-term projects. The timeline is the same for both company-managed and team-managed projects. It shows issues in Gantt chart-like format, helping teams plan, track, and manage dependencies for a project. It is available in all plans for Jira software.

Note: The timeline view can display issues from a single project only. If you want to manage multiple projects, it is only possible in Advanced Roadmaps. Advanced Roadmaps are available with Jira software Premium and Enterprise.

Important tips for Timeline view

- In Timeline view, on the left side, people can view **Epics, Stories, Tasks,** and **Bugs,** along with a summary and status of the issues. Additionally, they can create issues and schedule the same by entering all the necessary details.

- People can schedule issues using either bars or by entering the **Start date** and **Due date** in the **issue view**. A Jira Administrator has to add the date fields on the issue view.

- It can display parent issue types (**Epic**) and standard issue types (**Story, Bug,** and **Task).** You cannot plan subtasks from the timeline view.

- All issues must belong to a single project to appear on the **Timeline view**.

- Issues have to be under an Epic, which should be defined in your project through JQL (Jira Query Language).

- A timeline cannot display more than 5000 issues and 500 parent issues.

- You can enable **child-level scheduling** from **Board Configuration** or from the **Timeline view**.

- To enable child-level scheduling from the **Timeline view**, select the [...] near **Export** on the top right corner and select **Configure Timeline.**

- Dependencies show the order in which issues will be worked upon. This is also called issue-linking, which allows people to indicate if something is blocking the progress of the issues.

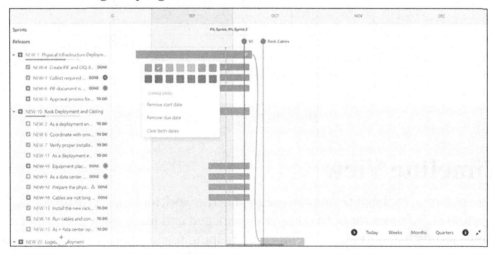

Figure 10.40: Timeline view in Team-managed project

Reports

There are four reports in Team-managed software projects. We will learn about all in this section.

Enabling reports: To enable the reports, follow these steps:

1. Select all projects and navigate to your team-managed software project.

2. Click on `Project settings` > `Features` > `Reports`.

3. Enable reports in the selected project.

To view the reports, you must have enough data in the project. In addition, you also need to enable the `Sprints` to view `Sprint burndown charts`, `Burnup,` and `Velocity reports`.

*   **Burndown Chart** - This report is applicable to sprints within a project. It displays how much work is left in a sprint and provides an idea about achieving the sprint goal. By tracking the remaining work throughout the sprint, teams can manage changes in priority and plan the work to achieve the sprint goal. Users can select the `sprints to view` and also have the option to choose `estimations statistics` on the reports page. The red line shows the remaining values whereas the grey line is used to display the guideline.

The following chart (*Figure* 10.41) shows details about issues and information related to those issues, such as sprint start, issue burndown, sprint end, and scope change. This helps in understanding the overall pattern of the iteration and its progress.

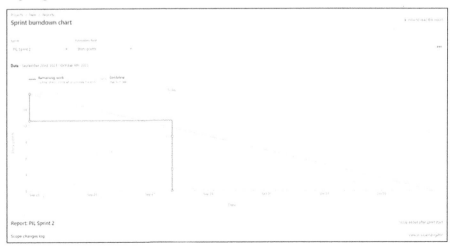

Figure 10.41: *Sprint Burndown chart*

- **Burnup Chart:** This report is applicable to sprints within a project. It displays sprint's completed work compared with its total scope.

The chart uses a vertical axis to measure the amount of work, which can be selected using various metrics like story points, issue count, or estimates. The horizontal axis represents time, measured in days. The gap between the lines on the chart indicates the remaining workload. When the project reaches completion, these lines will converge.

By closely observing the `Work scope` line, you can spot any instances of scope creep.

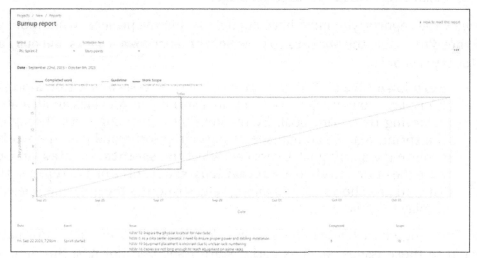

Figure 10.42: *Burnup Chart*

- **Cumulative Flow Diagram:** A Cumulative Flow Diagram (CFD) is a graphical representation in the form of an area chart, used to display the progress of work items within an application or sprint. In this chart, the x-axis represents time, while the y-axis represents the number of issues. Each distinct colored region within the chart corresponds to a specific workflow status, mirroring the columns on your task board.

The CFD serves as a valuable tool for pinpointing bottlenecks in your workflow. If you observe a region within the chart expanding vertically over time, it indicates that the corresponding column on your board is experiencing a bottleneck.

CFD provides data specific to a board and displays it based on column mapping. If any status is unmapped, it won't be shown on the chart. CFD also indicates if any issues have accumulated in a particular column. It also provides a date selection for the chart to be displayed.

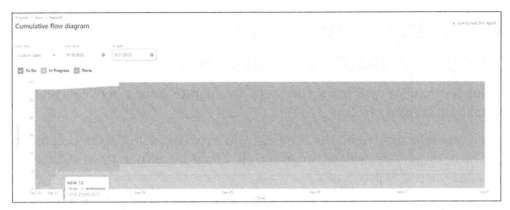

Figure 10.43: *Cumulative Flow Diagram*

- **Velocity Chart:** This report is applicable to sprints within a project. The velocity report is used to know the average amount of work a team can complete in a sprint. You can measure this in different ways, like counting the number of tasks, measuring time in minutes, hours, and days, or using the `story points.`

Jira keeps track of this over time and shows it in reports. These reports help the team figure out how much work they can do in future sprints. It helps managers plan how much work the team can realistically do in a certain amount of time.

There is a vertical line on the report which is used to measure their work, in story points or time.

There are two types of bars on the report. Gray bars show how much work the team planned to do in a sprint before it started. Green bars show how much work the team actually finished in the sprint, and this is shown when the sprint ends.

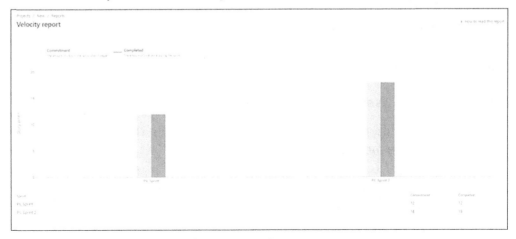

Figure 10.44: *Velocity Report*

Migrating from team to company-managed projects

In this section, we will learn the steps to migrate issues between team and company-managed projects.

To migrate issues between the projects, you have to create destination projects to which the issues will be migrated. It could be either team-managed or company-managed projects.

Here are the steps to create a Team-managed project in Jira:

1. Navigate to **Projects** > `Create project`.

2. Select `Software Development` under `Project Template`

3. Select one of the three options: `Scrum,` `Kanban,` and `Bug tracking software`

4. Understand the information on the respective page and then select `Use Template`

5. Select project type: `Team-managed` or `Company-managed` (as per your requirement)

6. Decide the name of the project and enter it.

7. Jira will generate a key for the project key. It can be changed while creating a project.

8. Select `Create`.

Search and move issues to the destination project

Follow these steps to search for the issues and then bulk move issues to the destination project:

1. Navigate to `Issues` and select `All issues`.

2. Select the filter that is already created or filter the issues using basic search to be moved.

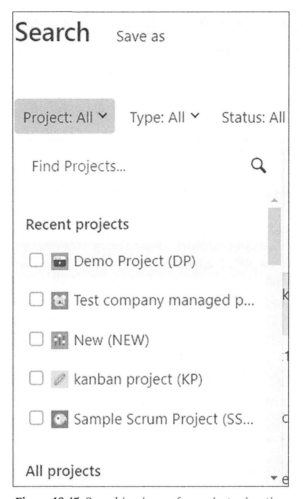

Figure 10.45: *Searching issues for project migration*

3. Navigate to ··· on the right side, select **Bulk change all**. It will open **the Bulk change** page.

4. Select the issues to be moved and then select **Next.**

5. Select **Move issues** and click **Next.**

6. Select **source project** and **issue type** to move from, and **destination project** and **issue type** to move to.

7. On the last screen, click **Confirm.**

Points to remember if you migrate from company-managed to team-managed

Team-managed and Company-managed projects are quite different. When you migrate issues, make sure you read the following points and take corrective actions:

- **Sprints**: Sprints (Active, Completed, or Planned) will not move from company to team-managed projects. All past sprints will not appear on the timeline. The issues in company-managed projects get added to the backlog of team-managed projects.

- **Components**: If you migrate with components fields, the information is lost as they are unique to projects.

- **Custom Fields**: If you migrate data from `Company` to `Company-managed`, custom field data is not lost. However, if you migrate from Company to team-managed one, custom field data other than the global custom field is lost. You have to recreate those custom fields.

- **Story points Estimation**: The data related to story points estimation will be lost. You can start by enabling the `Estimation` feature in your destination team-managed project.

- **Reports**: Velocity project data comes from sprints. As past sprints data is lost, velocity reports cannot be viewed after migration.

- **Report History**: All the history related to reports is lost, and Velocity report and Burn-up chart will not be migrated.

- **Project and issue keys**: Issue keys of the new migrated issues will be updated as per the new project. Any linked issue keys also will be reflected.

- **Versions and Releases**: All version information is lost after the migration, regardless of whether the releases and versions feature is enabled in your team-managed project.

Points to remember if you migrate from team-managed to company-managed

Team-managed and Company-managed projects are quite different. When you migrate issues, make sure you read the following points and take corrective actions:

- **Board statuses**: If you have defined statuses and workflows in a team-managed project, you have to add the same to the new company-managed project. Only Jira administrators have permission to customize workflows and statuses.

- **Custom Fields**: Jira administrator needs to create custom fields in the new company project and add them to the screens and in field configuration as the data is lost in the migration process.

- **Issue Types**: Jira administrator needs to create issue types that were created in the team-managed project. Additionally, the administrator has to create/edit the issue-type scheme to associate it with the company-managed project.

- **Project access**: Jira administrator has to create permission schemes in company-managed projects. In company-managed projects, there are detailed permissions using which one can control access to projects and many other things.

- **Project and Issue keys**: Issue keys of the new migrated issues will be updated as per the new project. Any linked issue keys also will be reflected.

- **Reports**: The data for issues will remain as it is, but the Velocity and Burn-up chart will be lost.

- **Story points Estimation**: The data for this field is lost. The custom field used for story points in company-managed projects (story points) is different from the field used in team-managed projects (story point estimate).

Conclusion

We are now familiar with creating team-managed projects, boards, statuses, transitions, and workflow. We have learned how to migrate between team-managed and company-managed projects. We have also learned how to access reports and understand agile metrics.

In the next chapter, we will learn Must know Features, Tips and Tricks, Advanced Roadmaps, and an Overview of Jira Product Discovery.

Points to Remember

- Team-managed projects can be created by anyone in your team and there is no need to have a dedicated Jira Administrator to customize the same. One should have an Administrator role in a project to configure the project.

- There are project access levels and roles in team-managed projects. You can define who can do what in Jira.

- Defining and assigning roles and permissions for team members ensures that everyone has the appropriate level of excess and responsibilities.

- Team-managed projects are quick and easy to set up. Learn to create and customize using project settings.

- You can add issue types, create workflows for each issue type, add custom fields, create sprints, boards, and access reports in team-managed projects

- Understand the various issue types available, such as task, story, and bug, and use them to categorize and track work items.

- Create and customize workflows that reflect your team-managed project management workflows. Define how issues move through different statuses.

- Create Kanban and Scrum boards to visualize and manage the progress of work items. Configure them to match with your team's workflow

- If using Scrum, create a sprint to plan and track work. Add the user stories and tasks that are ready for development to your backlog.

- Utilize epics to group related user stories or tasks together. This helps in organizing larger work items.

- Add Custom fields that are useful to capture additional details for issues and projects.

- Configure notifications to keep team members informed about updates in the project

- Automation rules defined can be applied to both company-managed and team-managed projects equally. It can be either a global rule or specific to a team-managed project.

- Create dashboards and access reports to provide visibility into project progress, keep a watch on team performance, and find out key agile metrics.

- Integrate Jira with other tools your team uses for seamless communication and data synchronization.

- If applicable, manage software releases and versions within Jira. This is crucial for tracking software development progress.

References and Use Cases

1. I can't seem to get the Epic Link or Parent Link added to the card. Is that possible?

https://community.atlassian.com/t5/Jira-Software-questions/Epics-Team-Managed-Project/qaq-p/2238144

2. Can I add a Team-managed project board on a Company managed project board?

https://community.atlassian.com/t5/Jira-Software-questions/Team-managed-project-board/qaq-p/2439056

3. Team-managed projects/issues in board

https://community.atlassian.com/t5/Jira-Software-questions/Team-managed-Projects-Issues-in-Board/qaq-p/2429689

4. Disable team-managed projects

https://community.atlassian.com/t5/Jira-Software-questions/Disable-team-managed-project/qaq-p/1680083

5. Workflow statuses and team managed backlogs

https://community.atlassian.com/t5/Jira-Software-questions/Workflow-statuses-and-team-managed-backlogs/qaq-p/1831858

6. SwimLane in team-managed projects

https://community.atlassian.com/t5/Jira-Software-questions/SwimLane-in-team-managed-projects/qaq-p/2338868

7. Team Managed Projects - Can't edit a custom field's context to Global

https://community.atlassian.com/t5/Jira-Software-questions/Team-Managed-Projects-Can-t-edit-a-custom-field-s-context-to/qaq-p/2351783

8. If I move the issues from the team-managed to a newly created company-managed project, will the sprint be created automatically?

https://community.atlassian.com/t5/Jira-Software-questions/Migrating-team-to-company-managed-project/qaq-p/2005271

9. Does the migration of team managed project to Company managed project erase Team managed project?

https://community.atlassian.com/t5/Jira-Software-questions/Does-the-migration-of-team-managed-project-to-company-managed/qaq-p/2259024

10. Move issues between two team-managed projects

https://community.atlassian.com/t5/Jira-Software-questions/move-issues-between-two-quot-team-managed-quot-projects/qaq-p/2428796

11. How to migrate all the issues at once from a team-managed to a company-managed project.

https://community.atlassian.com/t5/Jira-Software-questions/How-to-migrate-all-the-issues-at-once-from-a-team-managed-to-a/qaq-p/2025499

12. Issue-level security in Team Managed project

https://community.atlassian.com/t5/Jira-Service-Management/TEAM-MANAGED-PROJECT/qaq-p/2203961

13. How do I transfer a team-managed project from one organisation to another?

https://community.atlassian.com/t5/Jira-Software-questions/How-do-I-transfer-a-team-managed-project-from-one-organisation/qaq-p/2156348

14. Team-managed projects have multiple boards?

https://community.atlassian.com/t5/Jira-Software-questions/Team-managed-project-have-multiple-boards/qaq-p/1682741

15. Custom notifications for Team managed projects

https://community.atlassian.com/t5/Jira-questions/Custom-notifications-for-team-managed-projects/qaq-p/1987442

CHAPTER 11

Jira Best practices and Must-know Features in Advanced Roadmaps

Introduction

Jira offers various ways to create projects and Agile boards. People can create projects based on sample data, selected filters, or by using multiple boards. We will learn about all the different ways to create boards. Advanced Roadmaps allow you to combine issues from boards, projects, and filters to create an all-in-one plan that can include multiple teams working together. By using this Roadmap feature, you can plan and estimate release dates for cross-project initiatives, perform resource planning, and align your plans with your organization's goals. Jira Product Discovery is a tool specifically designed for product managers to capture and prioritize ideas, as well as connect and align all the teams using other Jira family of products. In this chapter, we will learn about various Administrator roles in Jira.

Structure

In this chapter, we will cover the following topics:

- Dos and Don'ts for Product Owner
- Dos and Don'ts for Scrum Master
- Dos and Don'ts for Software Developers
- Must-learn Features for Jira Administrators
  - Import issues in Jira
  - Creating a project with Sample data
  - Creating a project with multiple boards
- Understanding Various Administrator Roles in Jira
- Understanding Advanced roadmap
  - Viewing a Sample Plan
  - Creating a Plan
  - Timeline View
  - Dependency Report
  - Setting up Teams
  - Creating Releases
  - Creating Cross-project Releases
  - Adding Filters
  - Configuring issues hierarchy above Epics
- Overview of Jira Product Discovery
  - All Ideas View
  - Impact Assessment View
  - Impact vs. Effort View
  - Roadmap View
  - Timeline View
  - Delivery Status View

Dos and Don'ts for Product Owner

In this section, we will explore how a product owner can adapt to the Agile way of working in Jira. We have discussed the features of Jira and the processes that the Product Owner and their team need to follow:

1. As a Product Owner, ensure that features, improvements, and bugs are entered into the product backlog.

2. Include all necessary details in the backlog, such as additional fields and Acceptance Criteria in the issues.

3. Backlog refinement is an ongoing activity that aids in effective Sprint planning, defining Sprint goals, and user stories estimation. The stakeholders - PO, SM, Developers, Testers, UI/UX engineers, and BA - will participate in this process, which aids in the sprint planning meeting.

4. The Product Owner or their team can enter tasks, stories, and other issue types either from the timeline view or directly from the backlog view.

5. The PO can utilize or make the best use of Jira bulk import functionality.

6. The product backlog includes a ranking feature. The Product Owner and the Scrum team can rank issues by dragging and dropping them. Alternatively, you can right-click on an issue and move it to the top, bottom, or directly into a sprint.

7. Make use of Epics, Versions, and priority settings in Jira. Create Epics and releases, and enter the correct priority details. People can associate issues by dragging and dropping them into Epics and versions.

8. Acceptance criteria and other necessary fields for stories can be created with the help of a Jira Administrator. Mentioning this information can be helpful for everyone involved.

9. The Product Owner could hold Sprint demos and retrospectives to discuss progress and identify areas for improvement. The outcomes can be documented by creating Jira issues with action items and owners.

Dos and Don'ts for Scrum Master

In this section, we have covered several key points that the Scrum Master should ensure before initiating the sprint. We have also discussed the necessary steps for all sprint-related activities, helping teams to obtain accurate Agile metrics from Jira:

1. Check the product backlog before the Sprint Planning Ceremony so that you can plan for the next sprint.

2. Ensure the product backlog is groomed before the sprint planning meeting. Seek assistance from the product owner to refine the backlog.

3. Once the backlog is ready, move issues to a sprint. This can be done through drag and drop or by right-clicking on the task and sending it to the sprint.

4. Before starting the sprint, enter story points and priority. Then move the stories and tasks to your sprint. Also, make sure the issues are assigned to people who can actually work on them. Avoid moving unassigned issues.

5. Enter data such as story points, assignee, and priority by opening the issue in the right window. At this point, everyone should be clear about their roles.

6. After this, move the issues to the sprint. You can check the **Workload by Assignee** by clicking on 🔳 below the sprint name.

7. The workload will display the number of issues and story points assigned to each person. Cross-check this with the team's capacity.

8. Additionally, click on **Insights** and verify if the commitment aligns with the velocity. Insights are based on historical data. Take corrective actions if necessary.

9. Select to start the sprint and enter details such as **Start date**, **End Date**, and **Sprint Goal**.

10. Once you start the sprint, the Scrum team can track the journey of the Jira issue(s) on the Scrum and Kanban boards. Scrum Master should ensure the team members are moving the Jira tasks as per the defined project workflow.

11. As a Scrum Master, monitor if any issue remains in a status for more than 2-3 days. You can configure this in the board settings.

12. Check with the team about any impediments such as server issues or team member absences. Verify these details using the board's insights. Technical challenges in coding can also hinder progress. The Scrum Master could lead daily stand-up meetings to understand roadblocks that are preventing the team from making progress.

13. Ensure that all tasks transition to the final status, which is **Done**. Only when all tasks are in the **Done** stage can you complete the sprint.

14. After completing the sprint, view the **BurnDown** chart. The red line should align closely with the grey line.

Dos and Don'ts for Software Developers

In this section, we have discussed the following important tips for developers working in Agile teams:

1. When creating issues in Jira, make sure user stories or tasks are well-defined and include clear acceptance criteria. This helps you and your team understand what needs to be done and reduces misunderstandings.

2. Ensure that tasks are properly prioritized and assigned to the right team members. This prevents confusion and helps everyone focus on their responsibilities.

3. Utilize Jira's Agile features such as boards, sprints, swim lanes, advanced roadmaps, and more. These tools help you visualize and manage work efficiently.

4. When creating tasks in Jira, make sure they are SMART. SMART stands for: Specific, Measurable, Achievable, Relevant, Time-bound. Setting realistic due dates serves as an alarm to the team members. Use clear and concise summaries and descriptions. Assign tasks to the appropriate team members and set due dates.

5. Jira allows for comments and discussions on tasks. Use this feature to communicate effectively with team members, product owners, and testers. Ask questions, seek clarifications, and provide updates. Clear communication ensures everyone is on the same page and helps in resolving issues faster.

6. Avoid creating vague or incomplete issues. Provide detailed descriptions, steps to reproduce, and any relevant attachments. Insufficient information can lead to misunderstandings and delays in resolving problems.

7. Avoid neglecting to update the status of your tasks, log work hours, or add comments. Regular updates provide visibility to your team and stakeholders, helping everyone understand the progress and potential roadblocks.

8. Avoid ignoring notifications from Jira, especially mentions and comments directed at you. Stay engaged with the platform to respond promptly to queries, feedback, or discussions. Ignoring notifications can lead to miscommunication and hinder collaboration.

9. Assess the necessary add-ons for code review, test management, and scaling agile processes. Utilize the full range of features offered by these add-ons to ensure a seamless application development experience.

Must-learn Features for Jira Admins

In this section, we will learn small features that are helpful for new Jira Administrators and users.

Importing issues in Jira

We will learn step-by-step process of importing issues in Jira. People can import issues using Import Wizard or from the issues page.

Permissions required: You should have `Administer Jira` Global permission. OR for other users, `Create issue` project permission and `Make Bulk Changes` Global permission is required.

1. Prepare your CSV file.

2. Make sure your CSV file follows the correct format. The first row should contain the field names (for example, `Summary, Description, Assignee`, and so on), and subsequent rows should contain the corresponding data.

3. Ensure that the fields in your CSV file match the fields in Jira. Jira has standard fields like `Summary, Description, Assignee`, and so on. Your CSV columns should align with these Jira fields.

4. Log in to your Jira account with the Jira Administrator permissions.

5. Navigate to `Jira Settings` > `System` > `External System Import` > `CSV`.

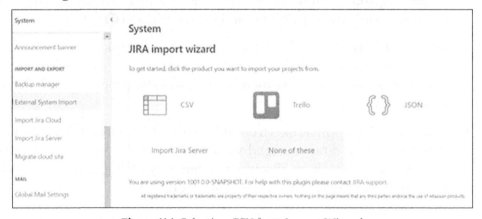

Figure 11.1: *Selecting CSV from Import Wizard*

6. Click on **Choose File** or a similar button to upload your prepared CSV file.

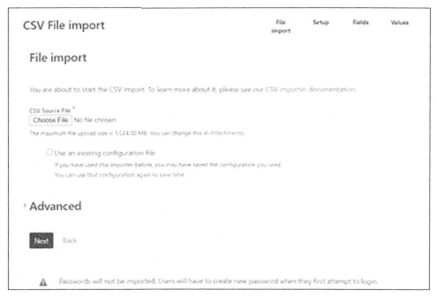

Figure 11.2: *Choosing file for CSV import*

7. Jira will attempt to map your CSV columns to Jira fields automatically. Review these mappings and make adjustments if necessary. Ensure all crucial fields are mapped correctly.

Figure 11.3: *Mapping Jira fields with CSV file fields*

8. Set import options such as how to handle duplicates, which project the issues should be imported into, and other relevant configurations.

9. Start the import process. Jira will process your CSV file, creating issues based on the data provided.

10. After the import, Jira will provide a summary report. Check for any errors or warnings related to the imported data.

11. If there are errors, review the CSV file and Jira's error messages to identify and correct the problematic entries. Then, re-import the corrected data.

12. Go to the relevant Jira project where you imported the issues.

13. Verify that the imported issues appear correctly in the project. Check their details to ensure all necessary information has been imported accurately.

By following these steps, you can successfully import issues into Jira using a CSV file, ensuring that your data is accurately transferred and ready for use in your project management processes.

Creating a project with Sample data

In this section, we will learn to create a project with sample data in Jira. This feature is helpful when evaluating and understanding Jira software features for Agile projects.

Here are the steps to create a project with Sample data:

1. Navigate to your created **Scrum/Kanban** project.

2. In the left navigation bar, click on the drop-down for that board. Jira will display the option to **Create** a board.

3. Select `Create a Scrum board with sample data` or `Create a Kanban board with sample data`.

Figure 11.4: *Options to Create a board*

4. By selecting any of the options shown in *Figure* 11.4, Jira will ask to create a project with the **Scrum/Kanban** Board.

Figure 11.5: *Details of a project created with Sample data*

5. Select **Create board**.

Creating a project with sample data is helpful to everyone.

Creating a project with multiple boards

In this section, we will learn to create a board from multiple projects or filters in Jira. It is essential to define in which project it will be created. The steps are as follows:

1. Navigate to your created **Scrum/Kanban** project.

2. In the left navigation bar, click on the drop-down for that board. Jira will display the option to **Create Board**.

3. Select **Create a board**.

4. Select **Create a Scrum** or **Kanban board**.

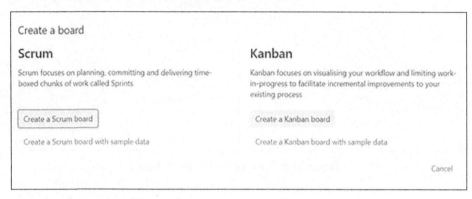

Figure 11.6: Options to *Create a board*

5. Select the option as shown here:

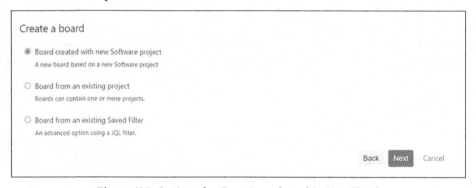

Figure 11.7: *Options for Creating a board in Jira Cloud*

6. Selecting the first option allows users to create a project with a Board.

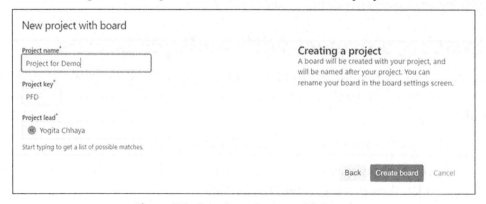

Figure 11.8: *Creating a Project with Board*

7. Select **Board from an existing project**. Select **Board from Multiple projects**. Additionally, add the name of the project or your profile to indicate the place where the board will be created. Follow the next steps to create a **Board from an existing Saved filter.**

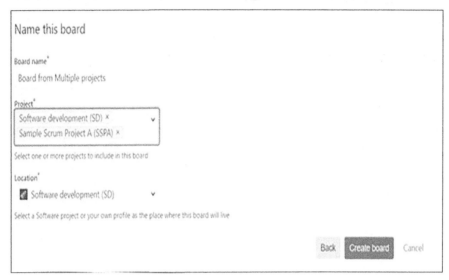

Figure 11.9: *Creating a Board based on Multiple projects in Jira*

8. Select **Board from an existing filter to** create a board from a filter. Select the filter name. Additionally, add the name of the project or your profile to indicate the place where the board will be created.

Figure 11.10: *Creating a board based on Selected Filter*

We can create a board from multiple projects or a filter and save it in a particular project or our profile, which helps to decide the permissions on that board.

Understanding Various Administrator Roles in Jira

There are two types of user management views in Jira:

- Original
- Centralized

To check, go to your organization at **admin.atlassian.com** and select the directory. If the **Users** and **Groups** are found under the directory, then you are using centralized user management.

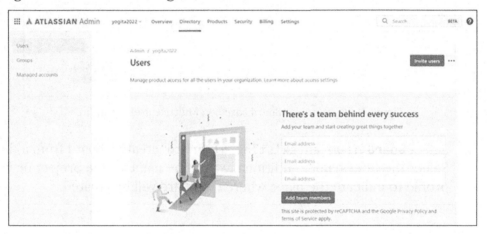

Figure 11.11: *User Management in Jira*

If the **Users** and **Groups** are found under products, then you are using Original User Management.

Centralized User Management

- **Org Admin:** You become an organization admin when you create an organization. Org admins administer users and groups for the organization's products and have access to the organization's settings, which can be found at admin.atlassian.com. It is recommended that you always have more than one Org Admin, as only the org admin can add or manage the org admin role.

They are the highest-level admin and can perform any type of administration tasks in Atlassian administration. Org admins are the only admins who have access to the admin tasks. This role has limited access to managing billing activities.

- **User access Admin**: User access admins are responsible for managing users and groups for a specific product from admin.atlassian.com. There can be one or multiple people performing the role of User access Admin for multiple products. However, they cannot log in to those products.

- **Product Admin**: A product admin can manage administration settings for a specific product. They do not have access to Atlassian administration. The same person can be a product admin for more than one product.

Original User Management

- **Org Admin:** You become an organization admin when you create an organization. Org admins administer users and groups for the organization's products and have access to the organization's settings, which can be found at **admin.atlassian.com**. It is recommended that you always have more than one Org Admin, as only the org admin can add or manage the org admin role.

  They are the highest-level admin and can perform any type of administration tasks in Atlassian administration. Org admins are the only admins who have access to the admin tasks. This role has limited access to managing billing activities.

- **Product Admin**: A product admin can manage administration settings for a specific product. They cannot access Atlassian administration. The same person can be a product admin for more than one product.

- **Site Admin:** This role is only available in the original user management. A site admin manages users, groups, and administration settings for the site they have been assigned to and any products within the site. They have access to any content on their assigned site. It allows limited access to manage billing.

- **Trusted User:** It is only available if you have the original user management. They have access to all products for the site to which they are assigned. They can invite users to their site's product from the Teams menu in Jira. While they don't have access to Atlassian Administration, they can access the administration areas for their site's products.

Understanding Advanced Roadmap

The Advanced Roadmap is a feature for teams to plan and track multiple projects with multiple teams working on them. It includes features such as planning, dependency management, releases, sandbox, and views.

It is available as part of Jira Premium and Enterprise Versions. The features are as follows:

- **Hierarchy Levels**: Users can add additional hierarchy levels above the Epic. It allows large organizations to strategically plan according to their goals and track progress using the roadmap.

- **Dependencies**: It has a feature to check and track dependencies outside the plan.

- **Sandbox Environment**: Create plans and check their effects in a sandbox environment. Plans are not implemented in Jira until you save them.

- **Plan as per Velocity and Capacity:** It allows people to plan based on the team's velocity and Capacity.

- **Plan for all Scenarios**: It allows planning based on all possibilities by adjusting the scenarios.

- **Permissions required**: All the configuration settings can be managed by individuals having Jira Software Administrator permissions.

Viewing a Sample Plan

Plan is a combination of issues from multiple projects and teams. It includes the tasks to work towards an organizational goal.

You can find the `Plan` button in your top navigation bar if you have the Advanced Roadmap feature available. Within the plan, you can create a new plan or a sample Plan with sample data. A sample plan can help understand all the features of the Advanced Roadmap.

Figure 11.12: *Creating Plan or Sample Plan*

People can create a sample plan that consists of issues from multiple boards and multiple teams.

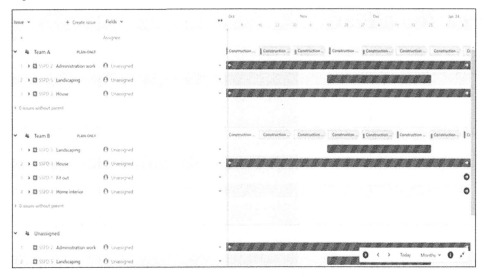

Figure 11.13: *A Sample Plan*

Timeline View

In the timeline view, you can see dependency details between issues. When you hover over an issue in the basic timeline view, you can view specific dependency details, such as **is blocked by** or **is blocking.** You can modify the settings in **View Settings** to display lines for dependencies. By clicking the lines, you can view the details.

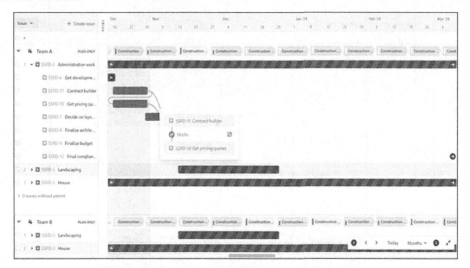

Figure 11.14: Viewing Dependencies in a Sample Plan

Creating a Plan

In this section, we will learn about important settings while creating a plan. Here are the steps to follow:

- Navigate to **Plans** and select **Create plan**.
- Enter the name of a plan.
- Access can be **Open** or **Private**. By default, access is set to **Open**.
- By setting the **Open** access, roadmap users can view and edit the plan. It can be restricted later.
- If you set the access as **Private**, only you can view the plan and share it with other users and groups.

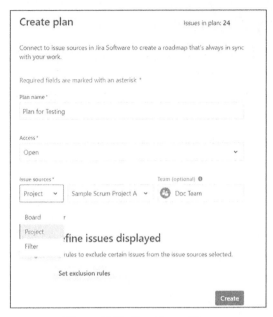

Figure 11.15: *Creating a Plan*

- You can also `Set exclusion rules` in **Advanced Roadmap**. It is optional.
- The rules can be set to exclude issue types, statuses, Releases, and any issues completed more than a set number of days.
- Select **Create** once all the settings are done.

Figure 11.16: *Setting Exclusion rules*

Dependency Report

Select the **Dependencies Report** under the **Roadmap view**. In this report, you can view only those issues with dependency details. You cannot modify dependencies from this view; however, you can keep track of all issues that are dependent on others.

Figure 11.17: *Dependency report*

Setting up Teams

To add a Team, select **Teams** tab from the Left navigation bar.

Figure 11.18: *Setting up Teams*

Select **Add team** from the right side. You can add a new team or add an existing team from an organization. While creating a new team, it can be a plan-only team or available across organizations.

Set the **`Issue source`**, **`Planning style`**, **`Capacity`**, and **`Sprint length`**.

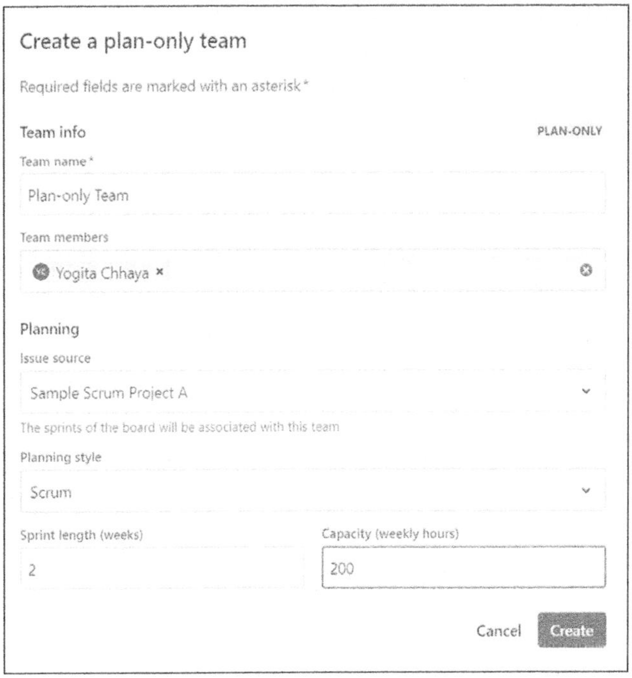

Create a plan-only team
Required fields are marked with an asterisk *
Team info
PLAN-ONLY
Team name *
Plan-only Team
Team members
Yogita Chhaya
Planning
Issue source
Sample Scrum Project A
The sprints of the board will be associated with this team
Planning style
Scrum
Sprint length (weeks)
2
Capacity (weekly hours)
200
Cancel
Create

***Figure 11.19**: Entering details of a Team*

Creating Releases

You can create a new release by selecting **`Releases`** in the left navigation bar and then choosing **`Create release`**. Enter the name and description of the new release along with the details of the start date and release date.

Jira Software
Releases
Create release
Cross-project release
Sample Scrum P
Cancel

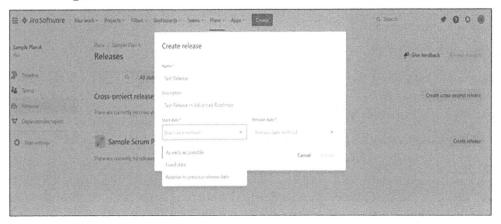

***Figure 11.20**: Creating releases*

Once you have created a new Release, it is not yet saved in Jira. Go to the timeline view and check for any obstacles and then select `Review changes`. You can save the changes or discard changes from this page.

Figure 11.21: *Review Changes*

Creating Cross-project Releases

You can also create Cross-project releases. It allows you to create releases across multiple Jira projects. This way you can release projects that are related to each other.

Figure 11.22: *Creating Cross-project Releases*

You can use this feature to check for obstacles and review changes. It is particularly helpful for syncing the dates of related releases.

Adding Filters

You can apply filters in the Timeline view to filter issues based on **Issues, Releases, Assignees, Teams, Sprints, Projects, Priorities, Issue types, Components, Labels, Dependencies, Reporters**, and **Statuses.**

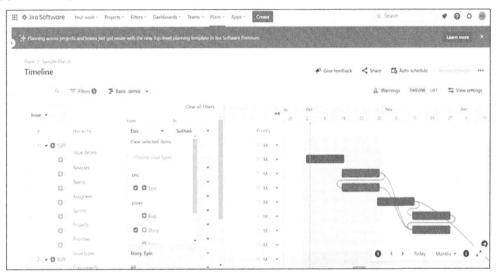

Figure 11.23: *Adding Filters on Timeline view*

Views: After applying a filter, you can save the view. You can make a new view of your plan and change the view settings. This new view will inherit the filters and settings of the currently selected view.

Create a new view

Make a new view of your plan, and change the view settings to tell a different story. This new view will inherit the filters and settings of the currently selected view.

Title *

Capacity planning

Choose a name that others will recognize

    Make default for everyone
    Use as initial view for everyone

                                                    Cancel   Save

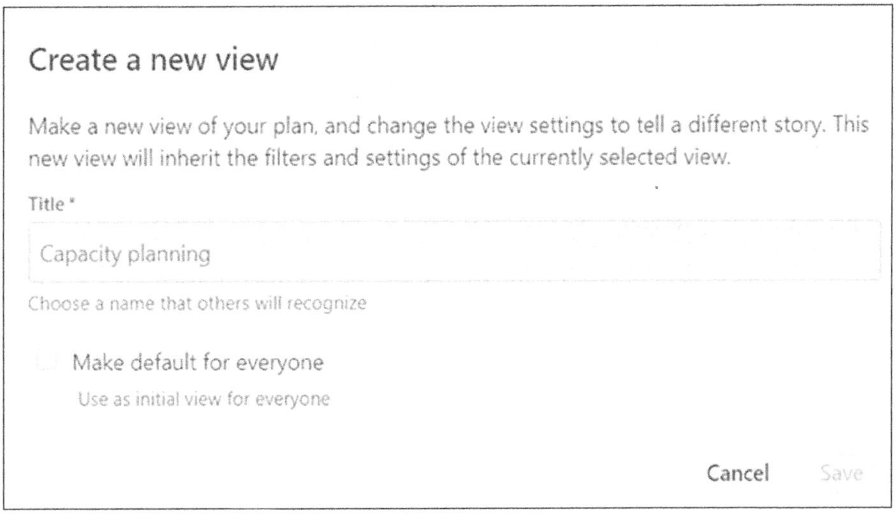

Figure 11.24: *Creating new views*

Adding Custom Fields on Timeline

You can add custom fields by selecting from the **Fields** drop-down. This way you can add and view the values of multiple fields on the Timeline view.

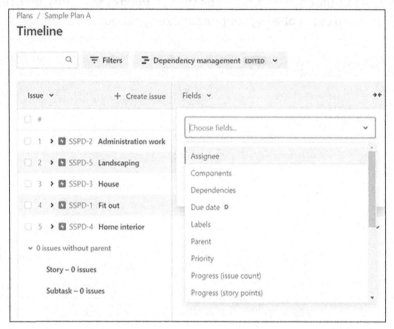

Figure 11.25: *Adding various Custom fields on Timeline view*

View Settings

You can set different parameters from View Settings as mentioned here:

- Adding color based on selected parameter
- Sort issues
- Group issues
- Dependency style
- Enable roll-ups in your plan

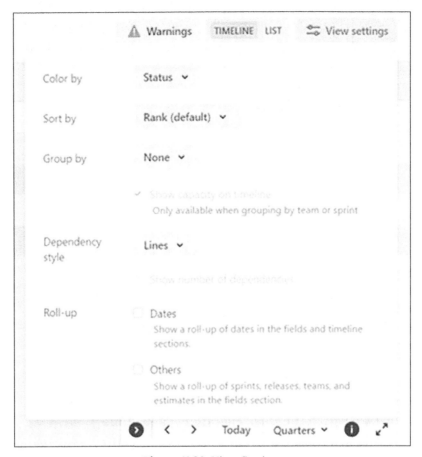

Figure 11.26: *View Settings*

Configuring issues hierarchy above epics

Advanced Roadmaps has a feature to add issue types above epic level. Here are the steps:

- To add a new issue type, navigate to the cog icon and select **Issues.**
- Navigate to the **Issue type scheme** and select the Issue type scheme for a specific project.
- Select `Add Issue Type`.
- Add the name and description of the new Issue type.
- Select **Standard Issue Type** and Choose `Add`.
- Save the changes.

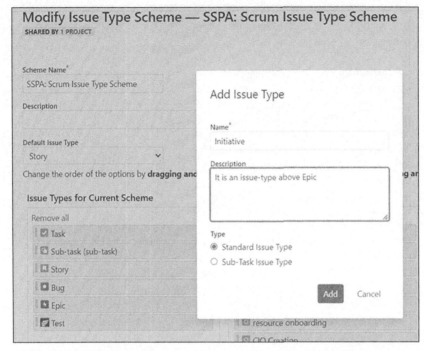

Figure 11.27: *Adding New Issue type to an Issue type Scheme*

- Navigate to `Plans` > `Settings` > `Hierarchy` configuration.
- It will take you to the Issue Hierarchy page in Jira.
- Select `Create level` and add a new level called `Initiative`.
- Select the Jira Issue as `Initiative` from the drop-down.
- Select `Save Changes`.

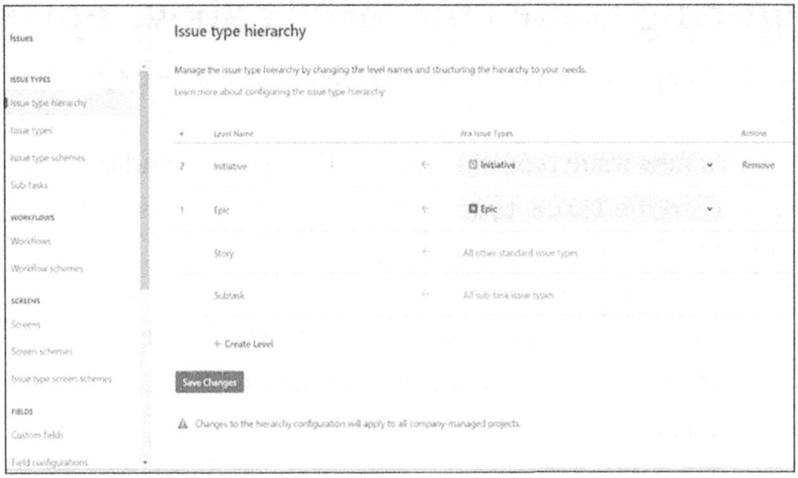

Figure 11.28: *Adding a new Issue Level in Hierarchy*

Navigate to **Timeline** view, select **Create issue,** and select **Initiative**. Similarly, you can add more levels to the issue hierarchy as per your organization's requirement.

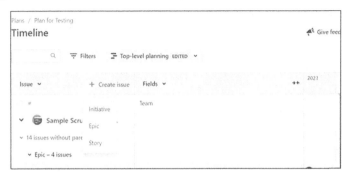

Figure 11.29: Creating Initiative from Timeline

Overview of Jira Product Discovery

Jira Product Discovery (JPD) is a tool designed specifically for product teams. Its purpose is to capture and prioritize ideas, foster collaboration between business and tech teams, and ensure alignment across all stakeholders. By utilizing JPD, product teams can work together, sharing a common vision and creating products that significantly impact both customers and the business.

With JPD, product teams can do the following:

- JPD helps teams work in a structured way by systematically gathering, organizing, and prioritizing ideas and insights.
- Integrated within Jira, JPD bridges the gap between business and tech teams, connecting product ideas to development work in Jira Software.
- Jira Product Discovery simplifies the process for product managers to capture and communicate the purpose behind their initiatives.

All Ideas View

In this system, an `idea` is considered as the fundamental unit of work. An idea can represent various aspects such as a user problem, an opportunity, or a potential solution. Each idea view includes fields to describe essential attributes such as goals, team, priority score, and impact.

- Moreover, JPD allows you to associate insights with an idea, such as notes from user interviews or support tickets.
- When an idea is ready for active development, it can be linked to delivery

tickets in Jira Software, streamlining the transition from concept to execution.

- People can create ideas in board view and list view, and they can also merge, archive, restore, and use templates for ideas.

Figure 11.30: *All Ideas View*

Impact Assessment View

Impact assessment allows you to assess the impact. In this view, you can set the goal and enter the value of the impact, which is the impact on the goal. If the impact is high, a score of five is assigned. You can also enter the names of customers for whom the idea is relevant. Insight is used to capture data explaining the importance of the idea and helps determine the priority of the idea itself.

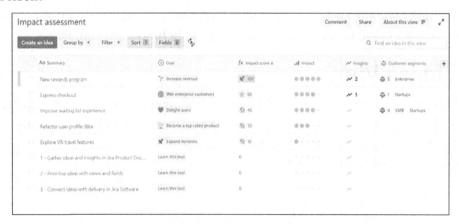

Figure 11.31: *Impact Assessment View*

Impact vs. Effort View

In the Impact vs. Effort view, `Impact` is on the Y-axis, and **Effort** is on the X-axis. You can view the impact versus effort in the form of a bubble chart and the impact score on the card on the right-hand side. For maximum impact with minimum effort, the score is considered as 100.

Figure 11.32: *Impact vs. Effort View*

Roadmap View

`Roadmap` view consists of four types of columns: `Now`, `Next`, `Later,` and `Won't do.` `New` column represents ideas with a high level of certainty that will be implemented soon. The `Next` column includes ideas that are expected to have an impact, but further exploration is required. The `Later` column contains long-term opportunities that are being tracked and will be implemented in the future. The `Won't do` column includes ideas that will not be implemented.

Figure 11.33: *Roadmap View*

Timeline View

It is the view where you can create monthly and quarterly Roadmaps. Time should be defined in ideas using a date field.

Figure 11.34: *Timeline View*

Delivery Status View

Here, you can see how the ideas are used. You may create a matching **epic** in Jira software for each product idea in Jira product discovery. The progress of delivering each idea is shown by the delivery progress. When you're ready to begin working on a specific idea with your team, just go to that idea, find the **Delivery** section, create an **epic,** and choose a project where you handle your product delivery.

Figure 11.35: *Delivery Status View*

Conclusion

We are now familiar with creating projects with sample data, creating a board based on multiple projects, or creating one based on a selected filter. We have also learned how to create an Advanced Roadmap, utilize all the features of Advanced Roadmap, and get an overview of Jira Product Discovery.

In the next chapter, we will learn about the Atlassian Marketplace and Plugins.

Points to Remember

- Advanced Roadmaps allow the integration of tasks and projects from boards and projects for planning purposes.

- It enables planning for multiple teams.

- You can plan for resource allocation by visualizing team workloads, identifying gaps, and making decisions.

- By considering progress across multiple projects, Advanced Roadmaps help in the accurate estimation of release dates, considering dependencies and other factors.

- People can track dependencies, manage tasks proactively, and ensure that tasks are completed on time.

- It allows people to plan based on the team's velocity and Capacity.

- Jira Product Discovery is a tool for planning and tracking ideas for Product Managers.

- Jira Product Discovery allows teams to organize and prioritize ideas.

- Product teams can work on ideas with the help of Jira Product Discovery and then align the ideas with the delivery of products.

- Jira Product Discovery has a separate Roadmap view and Timeline view.

References and Use Cases

1. Advanced Roadmap Hierarchy

https://community.atlassian.com/t5/Jira-Software-questions/Advanced -Roadmap-Hierarchy/qaq-p/2358694

2. How to make a specific issue type visible on Advanced Roadmaps without changing hierarchy?

https://community.atlassian.com/t5/Advanced-Roadmaps-questions/
how-to-make-a-specific-issuetype-visible-on-Advanced-Roadmaps/
qaq-p/2286898

3. How do we implement dual hierarchy in Advanced Roadmaps?

https://community.atlassian.com/t5/Advanced-Roadmaps-questions/How
-do-we-implement-dual-hierarchy-in-Advanced-Roadmaps/qaq-p/2344352

4. Advanced Roadmap Issue Hierarchy configuration - adding an issue type
    between Epic and Story

https://community.atlassian.com/t5/Advanced-Roadmaps-questions/
Advanced-Roadmap-Issue-Hierarchy-configuration-adding-an-issue/
qaq-p/2268111

5. Add Sprint to Plan on Advanced Roadmaps

https://community.atlassian.com/t5/Jira-Software-questions/Add-Sprint-to
-Plan-on-Advanced-Roadmaps/qaq-p/2363772

6. Enable capacity planning in Advanced Roadmaps

https://community.atlassian.com/t5/Advanced-Roadmaps-questions/Enable
-capacity-planning-in-Advanced-Roadmaps/qaq-p/2012131

7. Setting capacity in Advanced Roadmaps

https://community.atlassian.com/t5/Advanced-Roadmaps-questions/
Setting-capacity-in-Advanced-Roadmaps/qaq-p/2487781

8. Capacity planning availability

https://community.atlassian.com/t5/Jira-Software-questions/Capacity
-planning-avaliability/qaq-p/2446956

9. Unable to access Product Discovery after migration

https://community.atlassian.com/t5/Jira-Product-Discovery-questions/
Unable-to-access-Product-Discovery-after-migration/qaq-p/2179796

10. Why is Advanced Roadmaps miscalculating sprint capacity?

https://community.atlassian.com/t5/Advanced-Roadmaps-questions/Why
-is-Advanced-Roadmaps-miscalculating-sprint-capacity/qaq-p/1974521

CHAPTER 12

Atlassian Marketplace and Plugins

Introduction

The Atlassian Marketplace is like an online store for businesses and teams where they can find a wide range of apps and Plugins to make their Atlassian tools work better. It was launched in the year 2012. These apps are created either by Atlassian or other companies, providing you with a wide variety to select from and install. Marketplace offers apps and plugins for all of Atlassian's products, like- Jira, Confluence, Bitbucket, and Trello and has a large and growing community of developers. In this chapter, we will learn how to access the Atlassian marketplace, select Plugins, and details about some popular Plugins for administrators and teams.

Structure

In this chapter, we will cover the following topics:

- Atlassian Marketplace
- Selecting Applications from Atlassian Marketplace
- Understanding Key Terminology of the Applications
- Steps to Enable and Install Plugins
- Admin-tool Plugins for Jira Administrators
  - Script Runner for Jira
  - Jira Miscellaneous Workflow Extensions
  - JSU Automation Suite for Jira

- Popular Plugins
    - Custom Charts for Jira Reports and Time in Status
    - X-ray Test Management for Jira
    - Zephyr for Jira

Atlassian Marketplace

The Atlassian Marketplace is a platform where customers can explore and purchase Atlassian products and Plugins to extend the functionality of their Atlassian products. These Plugins can be developed by Atlassian or third-party developers. Other organizations that develop Plugin applications for Atlassian products can become partners and list their products on the Atlassian marketplace. The marketplace lets the customers pick and use what they need, making their work easier and more efficient. To access the Atlassian marketplace, go to **https://marketplace.atlassian.com/** on the browser.

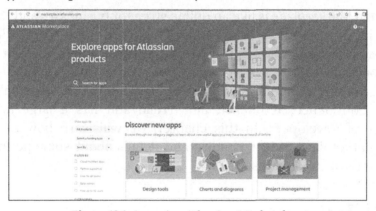

Figure 12.1: Accessing Atlassian Marketplace

Selecting Applications from Atlassian Marketplace

If you are new to the marketplace, the simplest way to search is to type the name in the search bar. However, there are other ways to search for applications within the marketplace. Customers can select from the `All Products` dropdown, then select the `Hosting types` dropdown, and `Sort` based on ratings and other criteria. The options are as follows:

1. **Products**: `Jira`, `Jira Service Management`, `Confluence`, `Bitbucket`, `Fisheye/Crucible`, `Bamboo`, and `Crowd`.

2. **Hosting type**: `Cloud`, `Server`, and `Data Center`.

3. **Sort by**: `Top rated`, `Top trending`, `Top selling`, and `Newest`.

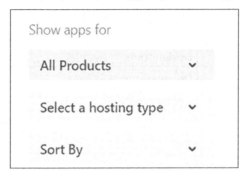

Figure 12.2: Options for selecting Plugins

Options to filter

1. `Cloud Fortified apps`: These are the apps that have advanced standards for security, support, and reliability.

2. `Partner supported`: These are the Plugins for which customers get guidance and training about the solutions from partners to match their actual requirements.

3. `Free for all teams`: These are free for an unlimited number of users.

4. `Beta version`: These are the Beta version apps for testing and getting feedback.

5. `Free up to 10 users`: These Plugins are free for up to 10 users.

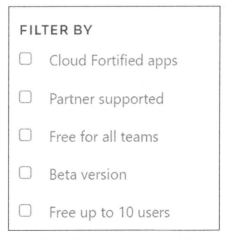

Figure 12.3: Filters to select an Application

Categories: The categories to select Plugins are listed in *Table 12.1:*

Integrations	Dashboard gadgets	Monitoring
Utilities	Document management	Reports
Project Management	Deployments	Repository connectors
Macros	Design tools	Repository hooks
Admin tools	Document management	Security
Blueprints	Documentation	Shared workflows
Build management	Email	Source code
CRM	IDE	Tasks
Charts and diagramming	IT and helpdesk	Testing and QA
Code quality	Language packs	Themes and styles
Code review	Messaging	Time tracking
Continuous Integration	Mobile	Workflow
Custom fields		

Table 12.1: *Various categories of Atlassian Plugins*

As a customer, applications can be selected based on various criteria such as Staff-pick, Number of installations, Reviews, Ratings, and fulfilling your actual requirement. Staff-pick means a selection of a few applications by Atlassian's Ecosystem team, which are helpful and good to start with.

Understanding Key Terminology of the Applications

Once you select the application or plugin, it displays all information about it in sequence as follows:

1. The name of the application.

2. The name of the application's marketplace partner.

3. Type of hosting - whether it is for Jira Cloud, Server, or Data Center.

4. Rating from the users.

5. Number of installations done.

6. It displays whether the app has been enrolled in a particular program, such as the Cloud Fortified program.

7. Various tags indicating if it is supported by the vendor, Atlassian product name, and other tags.

8. Overview of the application's main features and some more details.

9. Reviews from all the users.

10. Pricing – Customers can enter the number of users and check the pricing details based on the number of users. It also displays if it is free for 10 users. It has a cost calculator based on the number of users, and users get an option to select the billing cycle as monthly or annual.

11. Privacy and security - It includes information related to data storage and management, security, compliance, and any certification such as cloud fortified.

12. Support – All information related to app support, such as Contact, Documentation, Support resources, and Community.

13. Versions- It displays information about all the available versions.

14. Installation – Steps to try and install the application in your instance.

15. Information about whether the application is available for Cloud, Server, or Data Center.

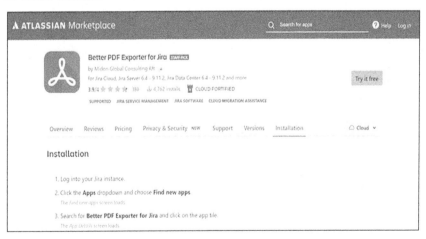

Figure 12.4: *Understanding Key Terminology of an Application*

Steps to Enable and Install Plugins

Permissions required: To Enable or Disable Plugins in Jira, you must be a Site Administrator.

If you are a Jira Administrator, click **...** under the **issue summary** on the **issue view**. Jira will prompt you to add apps. By clicking **Add apps**, Jira will display the page to **Find New Apps**. Jira administrators can manage applications from this page.

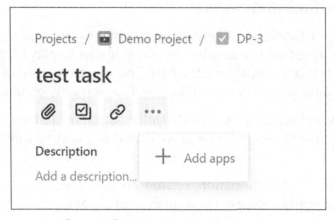

Figure 12.5: *Adding apps from the issue view*

Universal Plugin Manager

Universal Plugin Manager (UPM) is a tool to find, install, update, and unsubscribe all the Plugins for Jira software. The steps to add Plugins using UPM are as follows.

Here are the steps:

1. Navigate to ⚙ > **Apps**.

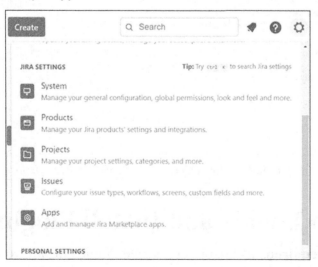

Figure 12.6: *Accessing UPM as a Jira Administrator*

2. On the **Find New Apps** page, Administrators can find new apps from the Atlassian marketplace.

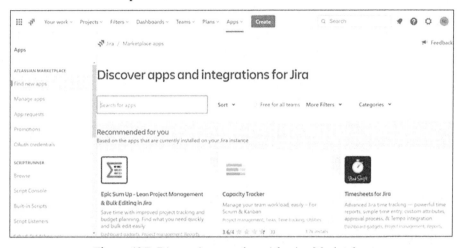

Figure 12.7: *Discovering apps from Atlassian Marketplace*

3. After selecting the app, click **Try it free** to start the free trial.

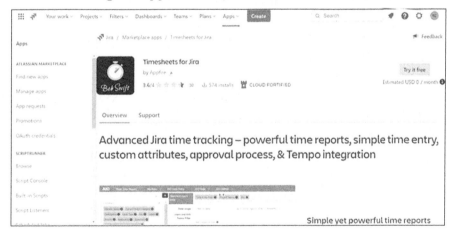

Figure 12.8: *Free trial option for an Application*

4. Click **Manage Apps**. You can install, update, enable, and disable applications from this page.

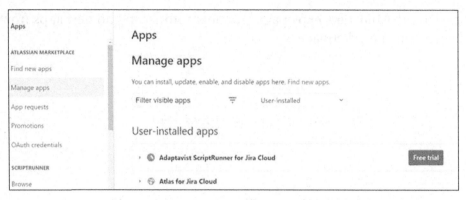

Figure 12.9: *Managing Applications from UPM*

The applications are of four types as follows:

- **User-installed**: These apps are bundled with Jira Cloud and are not included with the stand-alone version of the product. These can be disabled or enabled.

- **Action required**: These apps are unlicensed, expiring soon, or have available updates that will appear in this list, and you need to take action accordingly.

- **Paid via Atlassian**: These are purchased apps in the system, whether sold by Atlassian or a third-party vendor.

- **System Apps**: These applications come pre-installed with the standalone version of the product and are bundled with Jira Cloud. They are essential for your site's functionality and should only be disabled if specifically advised by Atlassian support.

To uninstall the app, navigate to the **App** and select `Uninstall` to cancel the app:

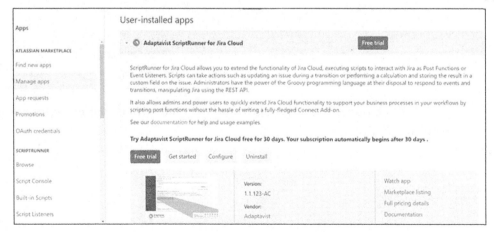

Figure 12.10: *Uninstalling the Application*

Admin-tool Plugins for Jira Administrators

In this section, we will provide an overview of applications specifically helpful for administrators. Navigate to **Admin-tools** from **Categories** on the Atlassian marketplace, where it displays all the apps useful for Jira Administrators.

Script Runner for Jira

- This app can be installed by following the installation process explained.
- This application offers additional security, reliability, and support.
- Users can try the free version, evaluate it, and then make a purchase.

Link to access and install Script Runner for Jira

https://marketplace.atlassian.com/apps/6820/scriptrunner-for -jira?hosting=cloud&tab=overview

Overview of features:

- This application allows you to deploy unlimited automations with remarkable accuracy, save time, and enhance team efficiency.
- Several features do not require coding knowledge. To begin utilizing the power of Script Runner, try using the ready templates provided.
- Tackle significant tasks, such as bulk issue updating, triggering actions in response to events like issue creation, scheduling routine tasks at any frequency, and enhancing search with specific JQL functions.
- Scheduled Jobs enable you to automate script running at regular intervals, saving your administrators time and reducing the risk of human error. You can specify when and how often a job should run.
- You can also use Script Runner for Jira Cloud's built-in scripts as an alternative to creating your own code, allowing you to automate manual, complex, and time-consuming tasks.
- Behaviors provide customizable options to modify the behavior of fields in Jira. For instance, you can create a behavior that hides a field for a specific user group until it becomes relevant for them to interact with that particular field.

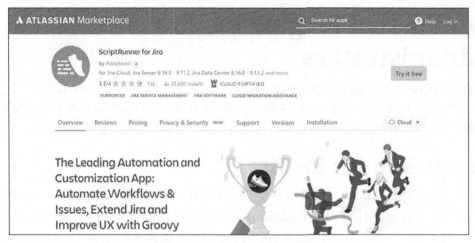

Figure 12.11: *Script Runner for Jira*

There are many other features in Script Runner for Jira that are helpful to Jira administrators, helping them save time and increase efficiency and productivity.

Jira Miscellaneous Workflow Extensions

- This app can be installed by following the installation process explained.
- This application offers additional security, reliability, and support.
- Users can try the free version, evaluate it, and then make a purchase.

Link to access and install Jira Miscellaneous Workflow Extensions

https://marketplace.atlassian.com/apps/292/jira-misc-workflow-extensions-jmwe?hosting=cloud&tab=overview

Overview of features:

- It is a flexible workflow automation application that combines no-code, point-and-click configurations with robust scripting capabilities.
- It allows you to create and customize workflows according to your preferences, utilizing an expanding collection of post functions, conditions, and validators that are beyond the native Jira features.
- Users without coding experience can easily modify workflows using Jira expressions with the help of on-the-fly syntax checking, inline help, and a script tester. Users can also craft their own conditions, validators, and post functions.

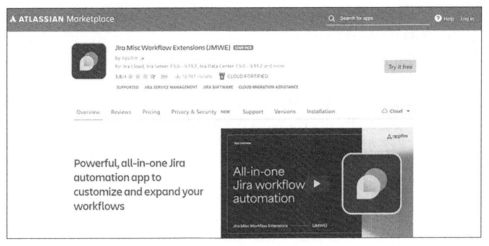

Figure 12.12: *Jira Misc Workflow Extensions*

Jira Miscellaneous Workflow Extensions offers many features beneficial to Jira administrators, enabling them to save time and enhance efficiency and productivity.

JSU Automation Suite for Jira workflow

- This app can be installed by following the installation process explained.
- This application offers additional security, reliability, and support.
- Users can try the free version, evaluate it, and then make a purchase.

Link to access and install JSU Automation Suite for Jira Workflow

https://marketplace.atlassian.com/apps/5048/jsu-automation-suite-for-jira-workflows?hosting=cloud&tab=overview

Overview of features:

- JSU offers an intuitive automation solution for Jira administrators who prefer to avoid coding and complexity, providing a no-code approach.
- Workflow configuration is consolidated into a simple and understandable **WHEN–IF–THEN** format, all managed in one central location.
- Edit workflows swiftly from the Agile project board, navigate seamlessly using global features, and gain a clear, at-a-glance overview of saved workflow rules for efficient maintenance.
- Popular use cases include:
  - Closing parent issue when all sub-tasks are closed.

o   Customizing workflows with JQL and preconditions.

o   Add a comment to an issue.

o   Set the Assignee field to *Unassigned* when the issue moves back to ToDo.

o   Pre-populate fields in linked issues.

o   Automatically share attachments with team members.

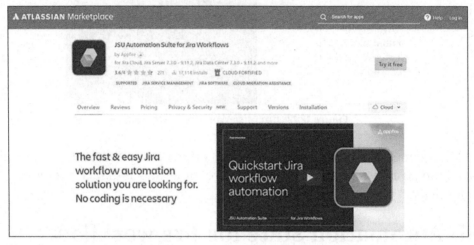

Figure 12.13: *Jira Automation Suite for Jira Workflows*

JSU Automation Suite for Jira offers other features beneficial to Jira administrators, enabling them to save time and enhance efficiency and productivity.

Popular Plugins

In this section, we will learn about an overview of a few popular Plugins to enhance report generation, statistical analysis, and test management.

Custom Charts for Jira Reports and Time in Status

This is an app that can be used with Jira software as a Plugin to create detailed reports.

- This app can be installed by following the installation process explained.
- This application offers additional security, reliability, and support.
- Users can try the free version, evaluate it, and then make a purchase.

Link to access and install Custom Charts for Jira Reports and Time in Status

https://marketplace.atlassian.com/apps/1220925/custom-charts-for-jira
-reports-and-time-in-status?hosting=cloud&tab=overview

Overview of features:

- The plugin has a feature to explore over 10 possible chart types in one or two dimensions, such as pie, bar, line, or table.

- Users can utilize shared dashboards in both Jira and Jira Service Management for collaborative monitoring.

- The tool provides support for various Third-Party Apps (such as Xray, Advanced Roadmaps, Mobile for Jira, and more), JSM Request Types, Organizations, and Channels.

- It is possible to create custom JQL, saved filters, and active search options to cater to the needs of advanced users.

- Users can evaluate the team's productivity and identify potential obstacles by analyzing the time they spend on their tasks.

- Teams can assess the team's efficiency and investigate potential obstacles by examining the duration they invest in their assignments.

- It allows a wide range of customizations, including custom ordering, merging and renaming values, showing/hiding segments, and more.

- It provides features to create comprehensive charts and reports for your Jira Dashboards, reporting on various metrics, including Time in Status.

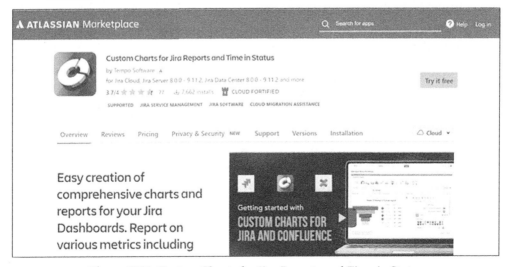

Figure 12.14: *Custom Charts for Jira Reports and Time in Status*

This plugin offers a diverse range of features that teams can leverage to create charts and reports for statistical analysis, as well as track important metrics.

X-ray Test Management for Jira

This is an app used to do Test Management with Jira software.

- This app can be installed by following the installation process explained.
- This application offers additional security, reliability, and support.
- Users can try the free version, evaluate it, and then make a purchase.

Link to access and install X-ray Test Management for Jira

https://marketplace.atlassian.com/apps/1211769/xray-test-management-for -jira?hosting=cloud&tab=overview

Overview of features:

- Users can efficiently manage both manual and automated tests as Jira issues.
- This application allows you to customize screens, fields, and workflows.
- It supports the entire STLC covering Planning, Design, Execution, and Reporting.
- It allows us to define tests in cucumber language and integrate them with test automation frameworks.
- It has a feature to arrange tests in folders and test sets for better organization.
- It allows the creation of test plans to monitor a specific set of tests, including both planned and unplanned test executions.
- It allows us to execute tests across various environments and consolidate the results.
- Users can utilize the Continuous Integration (CI) tool to report test results through the provided REST API.
- It allows us to examine the test coverage of requirements using interactive charts.
- It has a feature to analyze the status of test entities by Version, Test Plan, and Execution Environment.

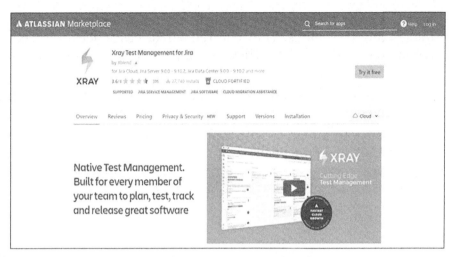

Figure 12.15: *Xray Test Management for Jira*

Xray Test Management for Jira is a feature-rich tool to plan, test, track, and release software.

Zephyr Scale-Test Management for Jira

This is an app used for Test Management with Jira software.

- This app can be installed by following the installation process explained.
- This application offers additional security, reliability, and support.
- Users can try the free version, evaluate it, and then make a purchase.

Link to access and install Zephyr Scale-Test Management for Jira

https://marketplace.atlassian.com/apps/1213259/zephyr-scale-test -management-for-jira?tab=overview&hosting=cloud

Overview of features:

- It allows monitoring requirements across test cases, test cycles, test plans, and execution outcomes. Users can access dynamic and comprehensive traceability along with test-case coverage statistics through integrated cross-project reports and gadgets.
- It enhances testing capabilities with Behavior-Driven Development (BDD), CI/CD, and automation integration using complimentary REST API, allowing seamless scalability.
- Users can share automated test execution results from tools like Jenkins, Bamboo, and others.

- It allows users to effectively organize extensive test case libraries using folders and test suites. They can reuse test cases across projects with parameters and test data. They can implement test cycles to track test executions systematically.

- It allows to maintain end-to-end traceability among requirements, test cases, and defects for comprehensive project management.

- It is possible to integrate with multiple automation tools like Selenium, JUnit, NUnit, and Frameworks.

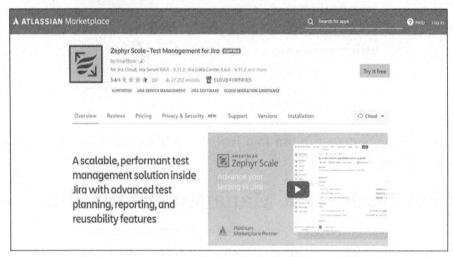

Figure 12.16: *Zephyr Scale-Test Management for Jira*

Zephyr Scale Test Management for Jira has many advanced features that can be explored in detail for test planning, reporting, and managing automation testing.

Conclusion

We have now become familiar with accessing the Atlassian Marketplace and selecting Plugins from the marketplace. We have also learned the criteria for selecting the Plugins and how to install, update, and uninstall them. Additionally, we have explored admin tools that can be useful and a few popular Plugins in other categories.

Implementing Jira in the real world requires evaluating the tool to ensure it aligns with your needs, planning, effective training, and consistent communication. Start by defining workflows customized for your teams and provide detailed training so that they understand all the features. Regularly update workflows and all other elements based on changing requirements. Utilize features such as reporting, analytics, and insights. If in doubt, Interact with the Atlassian community. Jira has evolved into a family of products, so explore new features and implement them to align with your project management and other requirements.

Points to Remember

- Only Jira Administrators can add or remove applications to Jira software from the Atlassian marketplace.
- Understand all the important terms mentioned on the page after selecting the application.
- Verify Plugin compatibility with your Atlassian product version.
- Check user reviews for reliability and satisfaction ratings.
- Read the documentation for installing the app and evaluating the features.
- Check the level of customer support provided by the vendor.
- Assess if the Plugin can be tailored to your specific needs.
- Ensure the Plugin complies with data security standards.
- Evaluate if the Plugin can scale with your organization's growth.
- Understand pricing based on number of users, licensing terms, and additional costs.
- There are various categories of Plugins, including tools for administrators, test management, code review, and many more. Explore the Atlassian marketplace site and make a purchase after evaluating.

References and Use Cases

1. What plugins should I try in Jira?

https://community.atlassian.com/t5/Welcome-Center-questions/What -plugins-should-I-try-in-Jira/qaq-p/2255234

2. Time of administration / Maintenance in operational condition

https://community.atlassian.com/t5/Jira-Software-questions/Time-of -administration-Maintenance-in-operational-condition/qaq-p/2408683

3. I only use the in-built Jira automation, but I want to learn how to use Script Runner.

https://community.atlassian.com/t5/Jira-questions/Scriptrunner/ qaq-p/2115830

4. How to Create Flexible and Custom Reports, Charts, and Graphs in Jira?

https://community.atlassian.com/t5/App-Central/How-to-Create-Flexible -and-Custom-Reports-Charts-and-Graphs-in/ba-p/1957785

5. Looking For Recommendations - Addon App Tool For Administrators

https://community.atlassian.com/t5/Jira-Software-questions/Looking-For -Recommendations-Addon-App-Tool-For-Administrators/qaq-p/1997455

6. Recommendations for apps - attaching text to tickets, user stories, etc. only visible by me.

https://community.atlassian.com/t5/Jira-Software-questions/ Recommendations-for-apps-attaching-text-to-tickets-user-stories/ qaq-p/2470833

7. I can't see the Custom Chart option anywhere in the dashboard. I'm actually trying to create an open vs closed chart

https://community.atlassian.com/t5/Jira-Service-Management/Custom -charts/qaq-p/2442709

8. How do I add a Custom Charts plug-in to my instance?

https://community.atlassian.com/t5/Jira-Software-questions/How-do-I -add-Custom-Charts-plug-in-to-my-instance/qaq-p/2127929

9. How to address rows in eazyBI?

https://community.atlassian.com/t5/Jira-Software-questions/How-to -address-rows-in-eazyBI/qaq-p/2322513

10. Recommended apps for Scrum dashboard

https://community.atlassian.com/t5/Jira-Software-questions/ Recommended-apps-for-Scrum-dashboard/qaq-p/2314992

Index

Made in the USA
Coppell, TX
08 September 2024

36941606R00223